Cornplanter

The Iroquois and Their Neighbors
Christopher Vecsey, *Series Editor*

Ki-on-twog-ky or Corn Plant, a Seneca Chief. Lithograph by J. T. Bowen, published by F. W. Greenough, Philadelphia, 1836. Courtesy of the Library of Congress Prints and Photographs Division.

Cornplanter

CHIEF WARRIOR OF THE ALLEGANY SENECAS

Thomas S. Abler

SYRACUSE UNIVERSITY PRESS

First Edition 2007
07 08 09 10 11 12   6 5 4 3 2

The paper used in this publication meets the minimum requirements
of American National Standard of Information Sciences—Permanence
of Paper of Printed Library Materials, ANSI Z39.48-1984∞™

For a listing of books published and distributed by Syracuse University Press,
visit our Web site at SyracuseUniversityPress.syr.edu.

ISBN-13: 978-0-8156-3114-9 (cl.)   ISBN-10: 0-8156-3114-6 (cl.)
ISBN-13: 978-0-8156-3138-5 (pbk.)   ISBN-10: 0-8156-3138-3 (pbk.)

Library of Congress Cataloging-in-Publication Data
Abler, Thomas S. (Thomas Struthers), 1941-
Cornplanter : chief warrior of the Allegany Senecas / Thomas S. Abler. — 1st ed.
p. cm. — (The Iroquois and their neighbors)
Includes bibliographical references and index.
ISBN 0-8156-3114-6 (hardcover : alk. paper)—ISBN 0-8156-3138-3 (pbk. : alk. paper)
1. Cornplanter, Seneca chief, 1732?-1836.   2. Seneca Indians—Kings and rulers—
Biography.   3   Seneca Indians—History.   4. Seneca Indians—Government relations.
5. Seneca Indians—Treaties.   6. United States—History—Revolution, 1775–1783.
7. Allegheny River Valley (Pa. and N.Y.)—History.   I. Title.
E99.S3C673 2007
973.04'9755460092—dc22
[B]   2006035221

For Trudi and Elizabeth

Thomas S. Abler is professor of anthropology at the University of Waterloo, in Ontario, Canada. He has actively researched topics in Iroquois history and culture since he was a doctoral student at the University of Toronto in the 1960s. With Elisabeth Tooker, he coauthored the article "Seneca" for volume 15 of the Smithsonian's *Handbook of North American Indians* (1978). He has also written *Hinterland Warriors and Military Dress: European Empires and Exotic Uniforms* (1999) and edited *Chainbreaker: The Revolutionary War Memoirs of Governor Blacksnake* (1989).

Contents

Illustrations

Preface

While serving as an editorial advisor to Syracuse University Press, the prolific and distinguished historian of the Iroquois Laurence Hauptman suggested that Syracuse publish a series of brief biographies of prominent eighteenth- and nineteenth-century Senecas. I was asked to do a volume on Cornplanter, a Chief Warrior of the Seneca population residing on the Allegheny River. Contracts were signed for three such biographies, but the only volume that came in on time was Christopher Densmore's splendid biography of the orator Red Jacket (1999). I had undertaken the task of doing a biography of Cornplanter with the optimistic intention of finishing the work in the year allotted. Some ten years later, the task is at last complete. Thus this work owes its birth to Hauptman and the editors of Syracuse University Press.

The Seneca Nation has been a prime focus of my research throughout my academic career. Although no research grant specifically supported the production of this book, earlier grants from the Phillips Fund of the American Philosophical Society, the New York State Museum and Science Service, the Canada Council, and the Social Sciences and Humanities Research Council of Canada, as well as sabbatical leaves from the University of Waterloo, have allowed me to pursue research that directly or indirectly influenced what I have written here.

I wish to acknowledge the importance of the labors of Francis Jennings and his colleagues at the D'Arcy McNickle Center for the

History of the American Indian at the Newbery Library in Chicago in compiling *Iroquois Indians: A Documentary History of the Six Nations and Their League* (1984). They have brought together published primary sources and documents from numerous archives in North America and Europe on fifty reels of microfilm, sparing a scholar interested in Iroquois diplomatic history long plane trips to distant archives, not to mention the expense of hotel stays and restaurant meals. I am grateful that the University of Waterloo Library was among the institutions that have chosen to purchase this remarkable resource.

Since my days as a neophyte doctoral student, I have benefited from the knowledge and advice of that community of Iroquoianists who convene each year (usually in Rensselaerville, New York) to exchange results of current research. In particular, I continually profited from conversations with William N. Fenton and Elisabeth Tooker, two senior scholars from the Iroquois Conference, both of whom died as I was writing the final chapter of this volume. The contributions of each to our knowledge of Iroquois history and culture have been enormous.

Two invitations to present material about Cornplanter and his contemporaries to audiences on the Allegany territory of the Seneca Nation allowed me to reestablish some old acquaintances and to meet many Senecas I had not previously known. The first was from the Seneca-Iroquois National Museum, which was celebrating its twenty-fifth anniversary in the summer of 2002. I gratefully acknowledge the hospitality I received from the museum's director at that time, Michelle (Midge) Dean Stock, her board, and her staff. Unfortunately, cancer has taken Midge from us; I believe she would have enjoyed this book had she lived to see it in print. The second invitation came in March 2005 from the Native American SUNY: Western Consortium based at the State University of New York at Fredonia. I presented a paper on that trip to a group on the Fredonia campus, which lies adjacent to the Cattaraugus territory of the Seneca Nation, and at the Seneca Nation Library on the Allegany territory. I am grateful to Wendy N. Huff, the coordinator of the Native American SUNY:Western Consortium, who arranged this visit, and to Jack Ericson of the SUNY's Reed Library, also at Fredonia, who provided transportation and endless conversation about the Seneca and Cornplanter heirs during my two-day visit.

My thanks to Anthony F. C. Wallace, Diane Rothenberg, and Mark Nicholas for providing me with yet unpublished work based on their research into Seneca ethnohistory. My thanks also to the readers of the initial draft of this manuscript for Syracuse University Press—Colin G. Calloway, Karim M. Tiro, and a third reader, who has chosen to remain anonymous. I hope I have satisfactorily responded to their suggestions for improvement.

Cornplanter

1

The Place of Cornplanter in History

He was known to the white world as the Cornplanter, alias John O'Bail. Under either or both names, he appears again and again in the historical record as the Seneca chief of paramount influence in the warfare and diplomacy of the American Revolution and its aftermath. The two names, "Cornplanter" and "John O'Bail," are frequently linked in a single phrase identifying him in contemporary documents or later publications outlining his life and achievements. This is perhaps appropriate, for the two names reflect his racially mixed ancestry. Cornplanter was a Seneca by birth—the Seneca are a matrilineal people and his mother was a Seneca of the Wolf Clan. Among the Seneca and other Iroquois, one belongs to the nation and clan of one's mother. His father, though, was a white fur trader from Albany (A. Parker 1927).[1]

---

1. No less a student than Lewis H. Morgan was confused about Cornplanter's ancestry, believing that Cornplanter and his half brother, Handsome Lake, shared the same Seneca father and had different mothers (Morgan 1851, 227). Morgan may have simply accepted Thatcher's statement (1836, 272) that Cornplanter had a white mother and a Seneca father. Morgan may also have been confused by Handsome Lake's having held, late in his life, a hereditary chieftainship normally associated with the Turtle Clan. Because clan membership is inherited from one's mother, if Handsome Lake had belonged to the Turtle Clan and Cornplanter to the Wolf Clan, they would have had different mothers. However, when

Neither name is completely accurate. Although English speakers frequently requested and were given "translations" of Indian names, the Seneca and other Iroquois often took names that meant nothing or did not translate easily into English. Sometimes, however, meaningful elements within a name would lead a speaker of the Indian language to provide a convoluted English "translation" of the name. "Cornplanter" is the usual English rendering of the chief's Seneca name. Although the Seneca name was commonly written "Gyantwahia," in linguist Wallace Chafe's phonemic orthography, it is "kayéthwahkeh" (Chafe 1963, 57; Abler and Tooker 1978, 516). Chafe tentatively—his question mark is telling—suggests it "literally" means "where it is planted (?)"; some names defy exact translation. The "O'Bail" derives from the name of Cornplanter's father. Although the Albany trader John Abeel had almost no contact with the son he sired, the father's name was retained for some reason, albeit usually transformed from the Dutch "Abeel" to the Irish-like "O'Bail." This even led a contemporary Protestant missionary (Alden 1827, 19n) to conclude that Cornplanter's father was a Roman Catholic priest. Alternative spellings ("Abiel," "O'Beale," "O'Ball") can also be found.

Chief Warrior

In war and in peace, Cornplanter provided leadership for the Seneca through several tumultuous decades. He had just assumed the position of Chief Warrior when, far to the east in Massachusetts, American colonists began their revolt against the British Crown, a revolt that would soon engulf North America from Quebec to Georgia in a desperate war.

The term "Chief Warrior" often appears in the documents of

Handsome Lake held the title normally associated with the Turtle Clan, it had been "borrowed" by the Wolf Clan, presumably because there was no suitable Turtle Clan member to fill the position. (On the borrowing of titles of one clan and matrilineage by a second clan and matrilineage, see Fenton 1950, 59–67; Shimony 1961, 58.)

the period, but with no clear definition. Although many writers equate it with *war chief,* the two terms are certainly different. The major duty of the Chief Warrior was to present the views and feelings of the warriors in council, in the same manner that the Speaker of the Women presented the views of the women to the council of chiefs.

Having at first counseled neutrality, Cornplanter proved a vigorous and able field commander when the Seneca were drawn into the American Revolution on the side of the Crown; he led Seneca warriors on numerous expeditions against rebel forts and settlements in the Mohawk Valley and elsewhere. He and his men were unable, however, to prevent a large portion of Seneca territory from being ravaged in 1779 during a major American invasion. The defeated British made no provision for their Native allies in the peace treaty they signed with the United States in 1783. Cornplanter and the Seneca found themselves sandwiched between an aggressive, expansionist United States to the east and the defiantly militant Indians of the Ohio country to the west. Britain, from its position in Canada and the posts it still held in the Great Lakes region, was another player in this complex drama.

The path that lay before Cornplanter and the other Seneca leaders was narrow, tortuous, and often hard to discern, but they were able to avert utter disaster at the very least, and perhaps even to maximize the benefits available to their people under the circumstances. The well-documented and, I hope, dispassionate presentation that follows will allow readers to judge for themselves the performance of Cornplanter and others in the Seneca leadership of the time.

Seneca Territories and the Cornplanter Grant

By the time Cornplanter retired to his personal land grant in Pennsylvania, a gift of the Pennsylvania legislature (Deardorff 1941), the vast majority of the Senecas, including many of his relations and descendants, had set down roots on the reservations his negotiations had established in New York State. In his lifetime, Cornplanter had seen Seneca power and territory shrink from a vast, politically independent area in western New York, northern Pennsylvania, and parts of Ohio to a few small reservations in western New York and his land grant in Pennsylvania on the upper Allegheny River. At the time of Cornplanter's death, the Seneca held just four reservations in New York—Buffalo Creek, Tonawanda, Cattaraugus, and Allegany.[2] Allegany, Cattaraugus, and Tonawanda remain in Seneca hands and are the homelands of most persons legally enrolled and recognized as Seneca, however many may reside away from these territories.[3]

Cornplanter and his generation experienced the turmoil and destruction of war and the need to alter their entire way of life in response to the extensive settlement of their former territories by non-Indians after the American Revolution. They had to decide whether they should adopt the teachings of Christian missionaries, and whether Seneca children should attend formal schools to acquire the language and literacy of their new neighbors. They had to learn new skills to survive within the transformed economic landscape these new neighbors had brought with them.

Cornplanter enjoyed a high reputation among the Americans with whom he dealt. Missionary Samuel Kirkland, whose evangelical activities were primarily among the Oneidas, considered Cornplanter "a particular friend" and "a person who exhibits uncommon genius [and who] possesses a very strong & distinguishing mind." In 1790, having pursued a quarter century of mission work among the Iroquois, Kirkland wrote in his journal: "I think I never enjoyed more agreeable society with any Indian than *Abeil*" (Pilkington 1980, 208).

2. The river is spelled "Allegheny," whereas the proper spelling for the reservation or territory is "Allegany."

3. The descendants of the few Senecas who migrated to Canada after the American Revolution still live there; those of the Senecas who once lived near Sandusky, Ohio, have been resettled in Oklahoma (Abler and Tooker 1978; Tooker 1978b; Sturtevant 1978; C. Johnston 1964, 52).

Cornplanter's Contemporaries

The historical record of Cornplanter and his generation is a rich one.[4] Many Senecas and other Iroquois of that generation are known to us through historical documents, which tell us not only their names, but also their views on important issues of the time; in some cases, they also let us glimpse individual personalities, abilities, and characters. Some were household names for many nineteenth-century Americans and Canadians.

Mohawk Chief Joseph Brant (Thayendanegea) was possibly the best known male among Iroquois contemporaries of Cornplanter. Featured while still a young man in the *London Magazine* article written by James Boswell (1776), Brant has been the subject of many biographies, telling and retelling the facts (and in many cases fictitious myths) of his career. Samuel Drake (1832) featured him in his frequently revised and reprinted *Indian Biography.* Like Cornplanter's, Brant's color portrait and biography appeared in Thomas McKenney and James Hall's three-volume opus (1836–44,

---

4. There have been a great number of biographies of Cornplanter, commencing even during his own lifetime. Both Drake's *Indian Biography* and Thatcher's *Indian Biography* appeared in numerous editions, commencing in the lifetime of Cornplanter and continuing long after his death. Various other biographies have appeared in journals, newspapers, and biographical dictionaries. To track them all down would be a daunting task. Moreover, although many contain interesting anecdotes and stories not incorporated in the text presented in this volume, many of these remain undocumented in the published sources or are demonstrably false. This literature must be approached with considerable caution. Among the more easily accessible published accounts of Cornplanter's life are Thomas L. McKenney and James Hall, *The Indian Tribes of North America, with Biographical Sketches and Anecdotes of the Principal Chiefs* (1836–44, 1:86–94); William Hall, "Garyanwahgah, The Cornplanter" (1879); Cyrus Thomas, "Cornplanter" (1907, 349–50); C. Hale Sipe, *The Indian Chiefs of Pennsylvania* (1926, 458–72); John Elmer Reed, "Chief Cornplanter" (1926); Henry King Siebeneck, "Cornplanter" (1928); Frederic A. Godcharles, "Chief Cornplanter" (1935); Paul A. W. Wallace, *Indians in Pennsylvania* (1961, 172); Joseph A. Francello, *Chief Cornplanter (Gy-ant-wa-kia) of the Senecas* (1998).

Joseph Brant (Thayendanegea) by Gilbert Stuart. Painted in London in 1786, this portrait was judged by one of Brant's daughters as the best likeness of her father (Kelsey 1984, 389). Courtesy of the New York State Historical Association, Cooperstown, New York.

2:117–37). Most notable, however, was the lengthy biography by William L. Stone (1838), which dispelled the myth of the "monster Brant" of American chauvinistic propaganda. Brant continues to be reexamined by biographers, most recently at length by Isabel Kelsay (1984).

Stone also produced a lengthy biography of the famous Seneca orator Red Jacket (Sagayewatha; Stone 1841); a much shorter one can be found in B. B. Thatcher's biographical compendium (Thatcher 1836, 2:270–303). Red Jacket's portrait (wearing the peace medal given him by George Washington) and biography appear in McKenney and Hall (1836–44, 1:1–13). His fame led to his name being used commercially, as in "Red Jacket Stomach Bitters" (Green 1988, 602–3). Most recently, the life of Red Jacket has been chronicled by Densmore (1999).[5]

Although both Brant and Red Jacket appeared with frequency in print in the nineteenth century, Cornplanter's own half brother, Handsome Lake, also had an enormous impact on the Iroquois, even though he received less publicity in the non-Indian world. His teachings continue to be preached in Iroquois communities where the traditional religion is practiced (see Sturtevant 1984; Tooker 1978b). The story of Handsome Lake's vision experiences and the principles for living he taught his followers are carefully preserved in oral tradition (A. Parker 1913).[6]

Mary Jemison was another contemporary of Cornplanter whose life was, and is, widely known. Of Irish parents, she was raised as a Seneca after her capture as a young girl in 1758. She lived the remainder of her life as a Seneca woman. Her story was recorded by James Seaver and first published in 1824, and continually reappears in print.[7]

5. Bibliographer Marilyn L. Haas (1994, 85–91) annotates twenty-one entries under her heading "Biographies . . . Red Jacket," eight of which were published in the nineteenth century. She indexes another fifty-one items in which Red Jacket figures as an important subject. Of fifteen works she indexes as printing translations of his speeches, eight were published in the nineteenth century.

6. The historical, cultural, and social implications of Handsome Lake and his movement are considered at length in Anthony Wallace's classic study *The Death and Rebirth of the Seneca* (1970).

7. Two reprints of the Seaver biography by major university presses have appeared recently (Seaver 1990; 1992). Counting the number of editions and reprintings of this work is a formidable task; it has been noted that thirty-five editions appeared before 1947 (Vail 1949, 26). Although often classed as a "captivity narrative," this work should be recognized for what it is, the life history of woman

Something of the reputation and stature these Iroquois commanded outside their own communities is conveyed by the monuments erected to three of them. In 1886, a bronze and granite monument was dedicated in Brantford, Ontario, in tribute to Joseph Brant (Kelsay 1984, 657). Red Jacket's remains lie under a large monument in Forest Lawn cemetery in Buffalo, New York, dedicated to him in 1884 (Buffalo Historical Society 1885). And a statue to honor Mary Jemison was erected in 1910 in Letchworth State Park, near her ancient home on Gardeau Flats in the Genesee Valley (Namias 1993, 161–65).

Well before these monuments were conceived and constructed, the Pennsylvania State legislature honored Cornplanter by erecting an eleven-foot-high column of Vermont marble at his grave on the Cornplanter Grant. Inscribed on various sides of the monument are

> Giantwahia, the Cornplanter
> JOHN O'Bail, alias CORNPLANTER, died at Cornplanter town, February 18, 1836, aged about 100 years.
> Chief of the Seneca tribe, and a principal Chief of the Six Nations, from the period of the Revolutionary war, to the time of his death. Distinguished for talents, courage, eloquence, sobriety and love of his tribe and race, to whose welfare he devoted his time, his energies and his means, during a long and eventful life.
> Erected by Authority of the Legislature of Pennsylvania, by Act January 25, 1866.

At the monument's dedication in October 1866, Colonel James Ross Snowden and Reverend W. A. Rankin spoke for Pennsylvania. John Luke of the Cattaraugus Reservation and Reverend Stephen S. Smith of Tonawanda also spoke, and Harrison Halftown interpreted. Cornplanter's grandson, Solomon O'Bail, "in the full regalia

---

who was culturally a Native North American (Abler 1989, 11; Walsh 1992). Readers have been cautioned about Seaver's "obvious editorializing" (Deraunian-Stodola and Levernier 1993, 74). Namias (1993, 151) notes that "the Jemison narrative also follows in the tradition of writing about ethnic women in which . . . it is difficult to find a clear sense of the ethnic woman's authorship."

of aboriginal royalty" addressed the assembled crowd in Seneca (Snowden 1867).

Although Cornplanter, Brant, Red Jacket, and Jemison were certainly the most widely known of the Iroquois of the time, many other individuals appear with frequency and considerable detail in the documentary record. Joseph Brant's sister, Mary (or Molly) Brant, who died in 1796, was probably as influential as her brother during her lifetime—perhaps more so (see Graymont 1979). Among the Seneca, Cornplanter's seniors included Guyasuta—often described as Cornplanter's uncle (mother's brother)—and Old Smoke (Abler 1979a, 1979b). Cornplanter himself was uncle to a young man originally known as "Nephew" and later as Governor Blacksnake (Abler 1989). Other prominent Senecas of the time included Big Tree, Farmer's Brother, New Arrow, Young King, Hudson, Jack Berry, Little Beard, Hiokatoo (Mary Jemison's husband), Little Billy, Peter Crouse, Twenty Canoes, Halftown, Captain Pollard, the Infant, and Red Eye. The documentary record describes at least some of the activities of a large portion of Cornplanter's supporters and rivals among the Seneca.

Cornplanter's path also crossed that of many prominent non-Indian politicians and soldiers of the American Revolution and the early years of the American republic. During the Revolution and in the frontier diplomacy afterward, he dealt with Loyalists and British Colonial officials such as Major John Butler, Guy Johnson, Sir John Johnson, Daniel Claus, John Graves Simcoe, Alexander McKee, Matthew Elliot, and Simon Girty. On the American side of the military and political divide, he dealt with Richard Butler, Anthony Wayne, Henry Knox, Timothy Pickering, and George Washington.

In his dealings, Cornplanter traveled over much of northeastern North America. He went to American seats of power—Fort Pitt (Pittsburgh), Fort Stanwix (Rome, New York), Philadelphia, New York City, and the new American capital, Washington, D.C. He visited British officials at Niagara and Detroit. The Iroquois hosted councils at Buffalo Creek (Buffalo, New York), and he carried messages to other Indian councils in the Ohio country.

Cornplanter was an active leader in most difficult times. His words to George Washington eloquently express the position his people occupied after the British defeat.

> When we . . . heard the invitation which you gave us to draw near the fire which you kindled, and talk concerning peace, we made haste towards it. You then told us we were in your hand, and that, by closing it, you could crush us to nothing, and you demanded from us a great country, as the price of that peace which you had offered us; . . . our chiefs had felt your power, and were unable to contend against you, and they therefore gave up that country. (*ASP: IA*, 1:140)

Cornplanter and contemporary Seneca leaders faced personal distress and external threat in the tense treaty negotiations. Cornplanter noted the suicidal threats of two of his fellow chiefs: "One chief has said he would ask you to put him out of pain. Another, who will not think of dying by the hand of his father or of his brother, has said he will retire to the Chateaugay, eat of the fatal root, and sleep with his fathers, in peace" (*ASP: IA*, 1:141). The second refers to a traditional method of committing suicide by eating the root of *Cicuta maculata* (wild parsnip), whose use over three centuries has been documented (Fenton 1941, 1986). "Two tubers," Henry Dearborn was told in 1838, "would kill the stoutest man, in half an hour. It brings on violent spasms & they appear delirious. They are convulsed, & the head & back drawn back as in cases of lock-jaw. . . . The death scene is horrible, so excruciating are the spasms" (Dearborn 1904, 111).

Cornplanter himself feared for his life. In a speech to George Washington, he proclaimed: "The great God, and not men, has preserved the Cornplanter from the hands of his own nation" (*ASP: IA*, 1:141).

Land Surrenders and Cornplanter's Reputation

Like his contemporary Joseph Brant and other leaders involved in the major land transactions that took place in the final decades of the eighteenth and the first decades of the nineteenth centuries, Cornplanter is viewed negatively by some current Haudenosaunee or Iroquois. I have heard him described as "an appeaser" rather than a great chief. Iroquois say that the skin of a chief should be seven thumbs thick (A. Wallace 1970, 30–31). Among those who dwell on the vastness of lands surrendered and the pittance received as compensation, criticism of Cornplanter and others of his generation persists to this day.

A more positive view of Cornplanter also exists, particularly among the vibrant group who identify themselves as Cornplanter heirs. That Pennsylvania granted Cornplanter a tract of land on the Allegheny River meant that his heirs continued to have ties to that land and to each other. Even when most of the heirs resided elsewhere, an annual picnic brought large numbers of them together each summer. And after Cornplanter Grant was flooded by the waters trapped by the Kinzua Dam, the picnic continued at Jimersontown on the Allegany territory of the Seneca Nation (Bilharz 1997).

Cornplanter's Portrait

In 1796, while in New York, Cornplanter had his portrait painted by Frederick Bartoli. The painting is in the New York Historical Society and is the basis of the print (see *frontispiece*) accompanying Cornplanter's biography in McKenney and Hall's work (1936–44, 1:174). Both have been frequently reproduced. His dress appears to be entirely of trade goods, yet demonstrates Seneca tastes. Silver arm wristbands, a silver gorget hung about his neck on a silver chain, and other silver ornaments (including a pendant suspended from his nose) reflect the popularity of trade silver among the Seneca and other Indians of the region (Fredrickson and Gibb 1980; Karklins 1992, 74–81). His body draped in a red blanket and he appears to be wearing a hunting shirt, a style of garment popular among both white and Indian males on the frontier (Windrow and Embleton 1973, 14–15, 27; Abler 1999, 138). George Catlin painted Red Jacket late in his life wearing such a garment. On his head, he wears the *gustoweh,* a type of headdress first described in detail in Lewis Henry Morgan's classic ethnography (1851, 226, 264). Its silver band and cluster of feathers at its apex is similar to later specimens preserved in museum collections. In his left hand he holds an unusual pipe tomahawk. Harold Peterson (1971, 34) states that it "seems to have been assembled from a spiked hatchet of exaggerated form and a clay pipe. From this picture it appears that the haft of the hatchet had been pierced to form a stem, and pipe bowl simply inserted in the end opposite the mouthpiece." Cornplanter's ears in the portrait reflect Native ideas of body modification for the sake of appearance (Einhorn and Abler 1998), but he also appears to be wearing a stock about his neck, a white fashion that caused its wearer considerable discomfort.

To some extent, the Bartoli portrait shows both how Indian and non-Indian worlds were linked and how they remained distinct in Cornplanter's time. Cornplanter–John O'Bail had a parent from each of these worlds, but the style of his life, like the style of his garments in his portrait by Bartoli, was shaped to conform to Seneca ideals and values. A leader among his people, Cornplanter guided them through the necessary reformulation of those ideals and values as the Seneca passed from the independent nation of his childhood to the reservation communities of his old age.

2

Before the American Revolution

Cornplanter's Parents and Kin

Information on Cornplanter's birth, childhood, and youth is tantalizing but frustrating in its incompleteness and contradictions. This chapter will present both the facts and the speculation about this period of his life, evaluating the latter and describing the cultural and historical milieu in which Cornplanter rose to his position of prominence during the American Revolution.

There is unanimity that Cornplanter's father was John Abeel, a third-generation North American. John Abeel's paternal great-grandfather, Christopher Janse Abeel, had been born in Amsterdam, Holland, but had migrated to North America, where he was employed as a master builder. His son, Johannes Abeel, was born in Albany in 1667 and twice served as mayor of that town before his death in 1711. He married Catherine Schuyler, and their son Christoffel (born 1696) married Margueritta Breese on 23 September 1720. The eldest of their seven children, Johannes (or John, Cornplanter's father), was born in Albany on 8 April 1722. Thus John Abeel's roots are both deep and joined to prominent Albany families (A. Parker 1927, 5–7).

Despite his ancestry, John Abeel was a trader with a somewhat unsavory reputation on the New York frontier. Indeed, in a letter to William Shirley, the acting commander of British forces in North America, Sir Willam Johnson (Parkman 1889, 1:233), referred to

Abeel as "that incorrigible Villian[sic]" (PSWJ, 9:398). In another letter, dated 7 December 1755, Johnson complained of "one John Abeels an Albany Trader who has for Some years past constantly carried great quantities of Rum to the Senecas Country Contrary to Law, & in open defiance of all authority. very much to the prejudice of the Service & the weakening of our Interest w^t s^d Nations" (PSWJ, 2:388). A correspondent to Johnson from the Seneca country complained in December 1755 that "they are drunk every day" because "Yaan Aabel . . . has received the battoes with rum" (PSWJ, 9:397–98). At Niagara, on 21 July 1761, Johnson again was troubled by Abeel's behavior. "About 9 o'clock, an Onondaga Indian came and complained to me of John Abeel's cheating him; on which I sent the Indian, with the orderly sergeant, and a few lines, to Abeel, and made him do justice to the Indian" (PSWJ, 13:229).

For a brief period, it seems that John Abeel's mother also became a thorn in the side of colonial officialdom. Contrary to the wishes of the Indian Department, several traders took children as hostages, as pledges for payment. Among these was a Seneca child held by a Mrs. Abeel from 1748 to 1750 on behalf of her son, presumably John Abeel (PSWJ, 1:207, 260–61). Johnson worried that such practices reinforced French claims that the English looked on the Seneca and their allies "as our Slaves, or Negroes" (PSWJ, 1:261). Although I have seen no document to that effect, the disappearance of the issue from surviving correspondence suggests that the Seneca child in Mrs. Abeel's household was returned to its parents.

At other times, Abeel was helpful to the British cause. In 1747, he received a musket for use on an Indian expedition against the French (PSWJ, 9:21). Some sources list "John Abeel" among the captives of the French at Quebec in May 1748, although others list "David Abeel" (John had both an uncle and a younger brother named David; PSWJ, 1:167, 241). In 1755, Johnson recommended that Abeel put his ability and influence to use in dealing with the Iroquois (PSWJ, 13:73). In the autumn of 1756, Johnson chose to order "Mr. Abeel to go through the Six Nations. To call them down to war" (PSWJ, 9:534). In November, Abeel was shot in the side by

Indians reported to have come from the French post of Niagara (the French denied any direct involvement in the affair; *PSWJ,* 9:557, 602). Later that year, Captain Jelles Fonda was told to use Abeel as an interpreter among the Seneca (*PSWJ,* 9:584). After bringing news from the Seneca country in January 1757 (including rumors of a French plot to murder English traders among the Seneca), Abeel and his Seneca companions were sent back by Johnson with gifts for prominent Seneca. Among the gifts was "a Bag of Cut Tobacco" for Old Smoke, "a Chief Man of the Senecas" (*PSWJ,* 9:585–88).

Most accounts suggest that Cornplanter was born in the Seneca village of Conawaugus (now Avon, New York) sometime in the 1740s. Careful examination of the evidence, however, suggests that this date is a decade too early. The relationship between Abeel and Cornplanter's mother is most often described as fleeting, but at least one source suggests that Abeel may have maintained the relationship for quite some time. In December 1763, Hendrick Frey conveyed a message from John Abeel's white wife to Sir William Johnson:

> Complaining of her mad husband, Signefying she fear'd her Life, and y[t] he harbours of Number of Sinneca Indians in his house, and instead of her, Keeps his old Bedfellow, haveing taken his wifes Bed and Gave it to the Squa, she tells me he has Disbandon'd all from the house that are of white couller and only Suffers a few Nigros to Stay, and that he takes Loaded arms Every night Into his Bead. (*PSWJ,* 13:321–22)

By 1763, Johnson himself had been living for several years with the Mohawk woman Mary (or Molly) Brant. They were raising three children (the eldest, Peter Johnson, had been born in 1759) and would have five more before Sir William's death in 1774 (J. Johnston 1971). Thus the interracial aspects of the Abeel affair would not have bothered Johnson, although the disruption of Abeel's formal marriage might have.

Whether or not the Seneca woman welcomed in John Abeel's

Albany home in 1763 was Cornplanter's mother, Abeel seems not to have maintained contact with his son. The lack of any relationship between them is made explicit in a letter Cornplanter sent to the Governor of Pennsylvania in 1822.

> As I grew up I began to pay some attention and play with the Indian boys in the neighborhood & they took notice of my skin being a different color from theirs and spoke about it; I inquired of my mother the cause & she told me that my father was a resedent of Albany—I still eat my victuals out of a bark dish—I grew up to be a young man and married me a wife—I had no kettle nor gun—I then knew where my father lived & went to see him & found he was a white man & spoke the English language—he gave me victuals when I was at his house, but when I stated to return home, he gave me no provisions to eat on the way—he gave me neither kettle nor gun neither did he tell me that the U. States were about to rebel against the Government of England. (Quoted in A. Parker 1927, 14)

Considerable misinformation has been published on Cornplanter's mother. She is named as "Queen Aliquippiso . . . a sort of head-leader among the Indians" (Williams 1883, 1). A genealogy of the Abeel family describes her as "an Indian princess, named Aliquipiso, of the Turtle Clan of the Seneca Tribe"(see A. Parker 1927, 7). Neither the name "Aliquippiso" or "Aliquipiso" nor the affiliation with the Turtle Clan appears correct for Cornplanter's mother. There was at that time a Seneca woman known as "Queen Alliquippa . . . the acknowledged chief of an Indian community in the vicinity of the Forks of the Ohio (Pittsburgh)" (P. Wallace 1961, 171). She was described in 1749 as an old woman favoring the British (Kent 1974, 258); she was said to have been given a matchcoat and a bottle of rum by George Washington in 1753 (Jacobs 1950, 53) and to have died the next year (P. Wallace 1961, 171). But I know of no convincing evidence linking Alliquippa with Cornplanter.

Although Cornplanter's mother was not the "queen" or

"princess" mentioned above, she did have important family connections.

The unceasing historical researches of Lyman C. Draper took
him to the Allegany Reservation, where he interviewed Governor
Blacksnake, Cornplanter's nephew, in February 1850. The Seneca
chief, then at least ninety years of age, told Draper that Cornplanter's mother was Gah-hon-no-neh, which was translated to
Draper as "She-who-goes-to-the-River" (DM, 4-S-68). She belonged to the Wolf Clan of the Seneca. Based on Blacksnake's testimony, Draper estimated 1743 as the year of Cornplanter's birth, but
other evidence supports a later birth date. Cornplanter had an older
half brother, known to history as Handsome Lake. Blacksnake reported that Handsome Lake's father died before Gah-hon-no-neh
and John Abeel became intimate. Handsome Lake was six years
older than Cornplanter (DM, 4-S-69).

The evidence of a later birth date for Cornplanter is convincing.
He is reported to have told visiting Quakers that "he was born
about the Time the Corn was a foot high 7 years before General
Johnson took fort Niagara" (Deardorff and Snyderman 1956, 600).[1]
Sir William Johnson captured Fort Niagara in 1759, giving Cornplanter a birth date of 1751 or 1752. A birth date of 1752 or 1753 is
also supported by Cornplanter's testimony in 1820 that he had been
seven years old when the British expelled the French from North
America (DM 16-F-227).[2]

On the other hand, there is the persistent assertion (see Williams

1. Merle Deardorff and George Snyderman (1956, 600) point out that John
Abeel "was most active among the western Seneca during the 1745-1755 period,
another argument in favor of the later date."

2. When I edited Blacksnake's memoirs (Abler 1989), I expressed no reservations about Draper's conclusion of Blacksnake's birth date. References to Blacksnake (the Nephew) from the 1790s, however, suggest a younger man than one
born in 1753. I have grown less and less convinced that the 1753 birth date for
Blacksnake is correct. Non-Indian authors have tended to ascribe a much greater
age than is warranted to elderly Indians they encountered who had been born
prior to written birth records. I think the age ascribed to Blacksnake by those
who met him in his last years is an example of such exaggeration.

1883; A. Parker 1927, 10–11) that Cornplanter had as an adolescent fought against the British at Major General Edward Braddock's defeat near the Monongahela River on 9 July 1755. The frontiersman Philip Tome wrote that he was told this by Cornplanter himself in 1817 (Tome 1854, 64–65). That Tome's assertion appears in a self-published book "replete with scenes of wild, stirring and thrilling interest" (Tome 1854, vi) does not, however, inspire the greatest confidence in its accuracy.

To understand the social position of Cornplanter's mother relative to her two famous sons and their subsequent careers, we need to undertake a brief excursion into Iroquois ethnography.

The Confederacy Council and Lineage Matrons

The Seneca were the westernmost nation of the Iroquois Confederacy (known variously as the Five Nations or the Six Nations). Other founding nations of the confederacy, moving from west to east, were the Cayuga, the Onondaga, the Oneida, and the Mohawk. The English designation "Five Nations" was used throughout the historical period and still appears in use on occasion. However, after the founding nations of the confederacy took the Tuscarora (a refugee group speaking a related language) under their protection early in the eighteenth century, the confederacy came to be known also by the alternate term "Six Nations."

The league was formed at some distant point in the past, prior to the European presence on the continent. Two men were keys in its foundation—Deganawida (because of a prohibition by many contemporary Iroquois on the use of his name now usually referred to in English as the Peacemaker) and Hiawatha—and many variants of an elaborate tradition record the struggles of these two to abolish war among the Five Nations so that all five could sit in the shade of the Tree of Peace (see Hale 1883; A. Parker 1916; P. Wallace 1946; Tooker 1978a; Woodbury 1992; Fenton 1998).

The Peacemaker planted the Tree of Peace at a council attended by fifty chiefs, which established a Confederacy (or League) Council of fifty positions. Each position was given the personal name of a founding chief, to be assumed by every subsequent chief occupying that position. Thus the names of the founders of the confederacy continue in use. The fifty positions are not equally divided among the Five Nations. The Seneca have eight positions; the Mohawk and Oneida nine each; the Onondaga fourteen; and the Cayuga ten.

Among the Iroquois, personal names are the property of the clan, which is both matrilineal and exogamous. Because spouses must belong to different clans and because clan membership is matrilineal, all individuals belong to the clan of their mother. One's personal name (or rather names because Iroquois drop their "baby" names and assume adult names when they mature) is "owned" by one's clan, and a senior woman in the clan is important in the naming of individuals in her clan.

It follows that the names of the confederacy chiefs are associated with clans. The larger clans are segmented into smaller groups, each descended from a different woman and each associated with a particular village, which might consist of as many as five hundred individuals and are known to anthropologists as *lineages.* Although each confederacy title is associated with a particular lineage of a particular clan, not all lineages have the right to appoint a confederacy chief. In lineages having confederacy titles, it falls to a senior woman—the lineage matron—to select the lineage male who will assume that lineage's vacant title on the Confederacy Council after consulting with other members of the lineage. This woman has both the right and the responsibility to remove an incompetent or corrupt chief and to replace him. It was common for a title to pass from one close relative of the matron to another, usually from her own brother to her son.

Handsome Lake's Title

Gah-hon-no-neh was a lineage matron, who most likely placed her elder son on the Confederacy Council. He held the position of *kanyotaiyo?,* in the orthography of Chafe (1963, 29). The name Handsome Lake is a translation of this council chief title, which is associated with the Turtle Clan (see Morgan 1851, 65; Chadwick

1897, 94; Fenton 1950, 66; Shimony 1961, 116). If a lineage had within its ranks no suitable candidate for a vacant position, it could "borrow" a member of another lineage (even another clan) or "lend" the title to the other lineage. Such temporary transfers of title often led to later disputes (see Shimony 1961, 104–17, for discussion of such disputes in the recent history of the Six Nations Reserve in Canada). As a member of the Wolf Clan, Cornplanter's half brother, Handsome Lake, held a borrowed title. Thus it seems that Gah-hon-no-neh, though not by birth entitled to award a position on the Confederacy Council to a matrilineal kinsman, was nevertheless given the opportunity to do so in her lifetime.

Relationship to Guyasuta

Other evidence suggests that, even though it did not by birth hold a confederacy title, the lineage of Gah-hon-no-neh was a still locally prominent family. Often described as Cornplanter's "uncle" (mother's brother), the Seneca leader Guyasuta (Abler 1979b), or "Gi-yo-so-do" as Lyman Draper called him, was a dominant political personality among the western Seneca and in the Ohio country in the years before the American Revolution. According to Draper's interview notes, Governor Blacksnake thought "*Gi-yo-so-do* was [not—which Draper has crossed out] a blood relative of Cornplanter's—[only—again crossed out by Draper] the same clan, *Wolf*" (DM, 4-S-68). Later, on the same page of Draper's notes from the interview,, Cornplanter is described as "nephew of *Gi-yo-so-do's*." Blacksnake mentioned a brother of Cornplanter's mother Gah-hon-no-neh, "*Jug-gue-a-sus,* or *Long Limb-of-a-Tree*—a distinguished chief, who fought in the Devil's Hole affair in 1763—who died before the Revolutionary War" (DM, 4-S-68). Because no mention is made of a sibling relationship between Guyasuta and Cornplanter's mother, it seems likely that Guyasuta was "uncle" to Cornplanter only in the extended sense of Seneca kinship.[3]

3. When we are told in documents that Guyasuta was Cornplanter's "uncle," it probably means Cornplanter considered Guyasuta his *hakhnoʔsĕh*. Lewis H.

Cornplanter's Sisters?

Governor Blacksnake, who identified Cornplanter as his own "uncle" (Abler 1989, 46), is himself identified as a "nephew" of Handsome Lake in the oral traditions of Handsome Lake's prophetic visions (A. Parker 1913, 23). If Blacksnake's mother was in fact a sister of Cornplanter and Handsome Lake, she was likely older than both her brothers. Lyman Draper concluded Blacksnake was born at Kendaia on Seneca Lake in 1753, which, if one accepts the birth date of 1743 that Draper gives for Cornplanter, would mean that Handsome Lake was approximately sixteen and Cornplanter ten when their nephew was born (DM, 4-S-14, 68–69). If the birth dates of Cornplanter and Handsome Lake were more recent than Draper believed, the brothers would have been even younger when their nephew was born. I suspect, however, that the age difference might well be correct, with Blacksnake having a birth date closer to 1760 than to 1753. Because Blacksnake reported that his and Red Jacket's mothers were "sisters" (DM, 4-S-74), Cornplanter might have had another older sister, although

---

Morgan discovered a Seneca would use the term *hakhnoʔsĕh* for mother's brother (but not for father's brother) and for a large number of other males, to include mother's mother's sister's son, mother's father's brother's son, mother's mother's brother's son, mother's father's sister's son, and even mother's mother's mother's sister's daughter's son. A common thread among those called "hakhnoʔsĕh" is that they are male relatives one generation senior to the speaker and related to the speaker through the speaker's mother. Males one generation senior to the speaker linked to the speaker through the speaker's father are *haʔnih,* to include the speaker's father. Consistent with this, a man refers to his own children, his brother's children, and the children of all male cousins as *he:awak* (son) or *khe:awak* (daughter). All children of a man's sisters and his female cousins are *heyĕ:wõ:tĕh* (nephew) or *kheyĕ:wõ:tĕh* (niece). This discussion of the intricacies of Seneca kinship terminology is based on fieldwork conducted by Morgan nearly a century after Cornplanter's birth (Morgan 1871, 293–382), and the meaning of kin terms may have shifted over time. Interested readers should also consult Floyd Lounsbury's elegant classic paper "The Structural Analysis of Kinship Semantics" (1964).

nowhere in the historical record is there a suggestion of a kinship link between Red Jacket and Cornplanter as close as that recognized between Blacksnake and Cornplanter. More likely, Red Jacket's mother was a parallel cousin of Cornplanter: in Seneca kinship, female parallel cousins (daughters of mother's sisters or of father's brothers) were also called by the same term as "sisters." Red Jacket was born about 1758, possibly in the town of Canadasaga.[4] His mother died about 1775.

Cornplanter also had a younger sister. The following death notice appeared in the mission newspaper on the Cattaraugus Reservation on 31 December 1846.

> On the 28th inst. Ga yăh'go gwus'găaah, a sister of the old chief, Corn Planter, and also of Handsome Lake, as he was called, the great prophet of the Pagans, who died at Onondaga Hollow many years ago. She is said to have been two years younger than Corn Planter, and of course according to the estimate of his age made at the time of his death, she must have been considerably more than 100 years old. (Mental Elevator, 14:120)

To summarize the historical record, Cornplanter's father was the notorious Albany trader John Abeel. Cornplanter was born near the middle of the eighteenth century to a Seneca woman, who was in later life a lineage matron in the Wolf Clan. Cornplanter was born and raised in the Seneca village of Conawaugus. His mother seems to have been related to the Seneca chief Guyasuta, also of the Wolf Clan. Guyasuta was possibly brother to Cornplanter's mother. Although Cornplanter had no full siblings, his mother bore at least two or three other children who lived to adulthood. The eldest of these probably was a female, who in turn was mother of the

4. See Christopher Densmore's *Red Jacket: Iroquois Diplomat and Orator* (1999, 4–7) for an excellent discussion of the place and date of Red Jacket's birth. Densmore's convincing argument that Red Jacket was born in 1758 supports the later birth date for Governor Blacksnake suggested above (closer to 1760 than to 1753). I do not see that Red Jacket could be significantly younger than Governor Blacksnake.

"nephew" later known as Governor Blacksnake. Also older than Cornplanter, by six years, was a half brother known in English as Handsome Lake, from the title he held on the Iroquois Confederacy Council. Finally, there was a younger sister who died on the Cattaraugus Reservation in 1846.

The World of Cornplanter's Childhood and Youth

The famed Iroquois Confederacy is often credited as being the dominant Native political force in northeastern North America before the American Revolution. Simple reference to a demographic summary of the Native populations of the Great Lakes and the Ohio country will show that the picture is more complex. If numbers alone counted, the Seneca would have been the dominant force in the Iroquois Confederacy, but the Iroquois themselves would have been relatively minor players on the political scene. Although disease and warfare doubtlessly had a demographic impact in the decades from Cornplanter's birth to the time of the American Revolution, the population estimates for 1768, given in table 1, provide some idea of the relative size of population of the Seneca and their neighbors.

The population figures found in table 1 should be taken with some caution. The population of four thousand found there for the Seneca is based on an estimate of one thousand "warriors" in 1768. Although estimates of Seneca strength throughout the seventeenth and eighteenth centuries hovered around this figure, ranging by two hundred above or below it, a 20 percent error is not unlikely.

In some ways, table 1 distorts reality in another fashion. Populations are given ethnic designations—Seneca, Cayuga, Delaware, Potawatomi, and so on—even though these populations were not ethnically homogeneous. Cornplanter's own ancestry is an example of this. A few other cases will reinforce this point. Among the leaders of the Oneida and Tuscarora during the American Revolution was Colonel Louis Cook (also known as Atiatoharongwen, Louis Atayataghronghta, or Colonel Joseph Lewis). The child of a black father and a Saint Francis Abenaki mother, Cook was raised at

TABLE

Native Populations, ca. 1768

Iroquois Confederacy		**9,280**
Seneca	4,000	
Cayuga	800	
Onondaga	1,040	
Oneida	1,200	
Mohawk	640	
Tuscarora	800	
Other Refugees	800	
Ottawa Valley—Montreal		**3,500**
Iroquois on the Saint Lawrence	1,500	
Lake of Two Mountains (Oka)	500	
Algonquin	1,500	
Between the Ohio and the Mississippi, south of the Ojibwa		**35,500**
Delaware and Munsee	3,500	
Wyandot	1,000	
Mahican	300	
Shawnee	1,800	
Mingo	600	
Ottawa	5,000	
Miami, Wea, Piakeshaw	4,000	
Kickapoo and Mascouten	2,000	
Potawatomi	3,000	
Mississauga-Ojibwa	7,000	
Winnebago	1,500	
Menomini	800	
Mesquakie (Fox)	800	
Sauk	2,000	
Illinois	2,200	

Sources: Tanner 1987, 66, map 15; Tooker 1978a, 421; Landy 1978, 520; Jefferson 1955, 103–7

Caughnawaga (Kahnawake) and lived among the Oneidas, Onondagas, and Mohawks of Saint Regis (Akwesasne) (Graymont 1983). In the Munsee town of Goschgoschink on the Allegheny River in 1769, missionary David Zeisberger noted "the presence . . . of Cherokee, Fox, Mahican, Shawnee, Mississauga, Nanticoke . . . even a 'baptized Jew from New England'!" (Deardroff 1946, 6–7). William Hunter (1956), who has documented the settlement among the Seneca of refugee Fox—Mesquakie or Squakie Hill Indians—also notes scattered Iroquois found in the Ohio country: "Iroquois residence in the Ohio country seems to have been characterized by family-size settlements and by Iroquois families scattered among other populations." He cites the example of Aliquippa's Town near the forks of the Ohio (Pittsburgh), which had four families as permanent residents in 1731 (Hunter 1978, 591). In her discussion of the ethnic diversity of the Glaize in Ohio in 1792, Helen Tanner notes the importance of "Coo-coo-chee, an independent and influential Mohawk woman [with] highly spiritual power and knowledge of herbal medicine." This woman with her husband and four children left her home among the Iroquois along the Saint Lawrence River to settle with the Shawnee and others in Ohio before the start of the American Revolution (Tanner 1978, 21).

Turning now to the linguistic complexity of the region, let us examine it in conjunction with the population figures presented in table 1. The Six Nations of the Iroquois Confederacy each spoke a separate language of the Iroquoian language family. Seneca is most closely related to Cayuga, but they remain different languages. The Mingo settlements in the Ohio country spoke one of the Six Nations Iroquois languages, whereas the Wyandot around Detroit spoke another Iroquoian language. Mohawk was the dominant Iroquois language spoken along the Saint Lawrence and by the Iroquois portion of the Lake of Two Mountains community; the Winnebago, west of Lake Michigan, spoke a Siouan language. The remainder of the groups listed in table 1 spoke languages of the Algonquian language family. A single language (with dialect differences) was spoken by the Algonquins, Ottawas, and Mississauga-Ojibwas listed in table 1, as well as by other Ojibwas living to the north and west of those listed there. Algonquin was also spoken by a portion of the Lake of Two Mountains community. Another language (with dialect differences) was spoken by the Mesquakie (Fox), Sauk, Kickapoo, and Mascouten; Miami-Illinois is a third language. Both Menomini and Potawatomi are distinct languages. Shawnee (with three dialects) is another. The six languages above are all classed as Central Algonquian languages, but are not closely related. Eastern Algonquian languages are more closely related to each other, and of these, Delaware, Munsee, and Mahican were spoken by peoples who migrated westward in the eighteenth century (on Iroquoian, see Lounsbury 1978; Mithun 1979; on Algonquian, see Goddard 1978a; 1978b; 1979). In addition to the languages mentioned above, there were a few other indigenous languages spoken by small pockets of refugees. A traveler in the region in the latter half of the eighteenth century would also have heard English, French, Dutch, German, and Spanish. The indigenous linguistic picture grew more complex south of the Ohio.

Although the Confederacy Council, its long origin myth describing the planting of the Tree of Peace, and its Condolence Ritual have been described in great detail by ethnographers in the nineteenth and twentieth centuries (Morgan 1851, 64–65; Hale 1883; A. Parker 1916; Fenton 1950; 1998; Shimony 1961), several other authors have emphasized the absence of documentary evidence in the seventeenth and eighteenth centuries that the council actually "governed" the Five Nations of the Iroquois. Indeed, the titles of the confederacy chiefs seldom appear in historical documents from those years, which, in contrast, recount instance after instance of individual nations, even individual villages, pursuing policies at odds with others in the confederacy. As historian Daniel Richter (1987, 15) notes: "If ethnohistorians had never heard of Morgan's League of the Iroquois, they might well conclude that the Five Nations were, like many neighboring peoples, organized in a loosely knit confederacy of nonstate, noncoercive village politics, in which any form of sovereign power in the Western sense—located at Onondaga [where the central council fire of the confederacy burned] or anywhere else—was unknown." Many ethnohistorians have espoused exactly this conclusion. George Hunt (1940, 160) is contemptuous of the importance of the confederacy. "The supposed unity of the League, or the unity of action that has been ascribed to it, may be dismissed, for such unity never existed. . . . Each tribe made war solely in its own interest, and the conspicuous feature of the League was its lack, not its possession, of political unity." William Fenton (1951, 52) has emphasized the importance of the local village, observing that "power remained in the hands of local chiefs," not with the Confederacy Council. Even Morgan (1851, 77) noted: "The government sat lightly upon the people, who, in effect, were governed but little." Allen Trelease also observed the inability of any central political officials to assert authority:

> Many writers have waxed eloquent over this "forest democracy," but it might as easily be termed anarchy. If the voice of the warriors (and the women) prevented absolute rule by the oligarchic body of sachems [the Confederacy Council], it also prevented the tribe from pursuing a resolute policy for any length of time. Tribal effectiveness was all too often diffused at the expense of factionalism or personal whim. (Trelease 1960, 22)

This is not to say that the Iroquois Confederacy was of no moment, however:

> The rich ritual surrounding the council was of far greater significance than the actual political unity it engendered. . . . However imperfect the relations between the constituent members of the Confederacy might be at some point in time . . . there has always been this powerful story of the founding of the Great Peace and the goal of returning to the unity of that glorious era. (Abler 1987a, 6)

Even Cornplanter's own nation, the Seneca, frequently split and followed contrary policies. The eastern Senecas, with villages around Seneca Lake, more often followed pro-English policies, whereas, as we will see, the Chenussios, who lived in the Genesee Valley and west toward Niagara and into the Ohio country, caused bitter problems for the British Indian Department and its northern superintendent, Sir William Johnson.

Seneca Settlement and Economy

The Seneca country included all of New York State west of a line between Cayuaga Lake and Seneca Lake as well as regions of Pennsylvania and Ohio. The Seneca lived for the most part in small hamlets of twenty or so single-family cabins. These might be of pole and elm-bark construction, although, in the latter half of the eighteenth century, log cabins and plank houses were found in increasing numbers on Seneca territory. Thus the twelve houses in the Seneca settlement of Honeoye were described in 1779 as "chiefly hewn logs," and in another hamlet houses were "well finished, chiefly of hewn plank" (Cook 1887, 160–61).

Central to the Seneca economy were three crops they had grown for centuries—corn, beans, and squash. To the Iroquois, these were known as "the Three Sisters" or "the Life-Supporters" (A. Parker 1910; Waugh 1916). Surrounding each settlement were large fields where these crops were cultivated. In the late eighteenth century, along with another indigenous domesticated crop, sunflowers, the Seneca also grew more recently acquired foods—peas, potatoes, turnips, carrots, watermelons, apples, and peaches.

When the Iroquois first encountered Europeans, the dog was the only domesticated animal in their settlements, although they raised captured bear cubs to be slaughtered at maturity for food. Pigs and chickens were early acquisitions—"some hogs and fowle" were destroyed by French invaders of the Seneca country in 1687 (NYCD, 3:432). Pork continues as an essential ingredient in Seneca " 'authentic' hulled corn soup" (Rothenberg 1992, 59). By the mid-eighteenth century, cattle and horses were also part of Seneca life; among fields of corn, beans, and squash were fields of hay to provide forage for livestock.

Many necessities in Seneca daily life were acquired from traders and merchants. Some, such as Cornplanter's father, John Abeel, brought their wares to the Seneca villages and towns. Others traded from established towns or forts such as Albany or Niagara. Brass kettles, steel tools, firearms, and woven textiles were all essential to Seneca life. Other trade items, such as silver jewelry and glass beads, were desired luxuries. For the English and the French, this trade was both profitable and an important part of their strategy to dominate North America and its peoples. Of the Iroquois, the Mohawks near Albany most closely and most actively followed a pro-English policy. The western Senecas (Chenussios), furthest removed from the English and trading with the French post at Niagara, were often hostile to English imperial expansion.

North American Conflicts during Cornplanter's Youth

Both England and France desired to control North America for economic and political advantage. Both sought the military aid of Indian nations in the border between the expanding empires. The final conflict in that struggle was acted out during the years of Cornplanter's youth.

In 1755, the British column commanded by Major General Edward Braddock was defeated by the French and their Native allies before reaching its goal of Fort Duquesne (now Pittsburgh). Although some have suggested that Cornplanter fought on the French side in this first major North American battle of the Seven Years War (Tome 1854, 64–56; Williams 1883; A. Parker 1927, 10–11), the best evidence for his birth date indicates he would have been no older than five at the time.

The tide turned against the French, and Fort Duquesne fell in 1758. During the next year, an English army penetrated the Seneca country to lay siege to the French fort at Niagara. Sir William Johnson used his diplomatic talents and influence to draw Seneca support away from France. Along with British regulars, Senecas including Old Smoke, an eastern Seneca of the Turtle Clan, intercepted and defeated a French force from the more western posts attempting to raise the seige. Under Johnson's command, the British took Niagara, and this, together with the British conquests of Quebec and Montreal, signaled the end of French power in North America.

The western Senecas quickly became disenchanted with the triumphant British garrisons. In 1761, Guyasuta and his fellow Seneca chief Tahaidoris circulated war belts—belts of wampum painted red—calling on the Seneca and nations to the west to rise up against the British. Sir William Johnson met with a large gathering of Indians from the Upper Lakes at Detroit that September and was able to keep the peace for a time. In late spring 1763, however, war broke out. Although the conflict is remembered as Pontiac's Rebellion, after the Ottawa chief who led the Ottawa, Potawatomi, and Wyandot besieging Detroit, the actions of Cornplanter's uncle, Guyasuta, were probably as important as those of Pontiac in fomenting the widespread hostilities (Peckham 1947, 106–7; Tanner 1987, 48–49).

The Seneca are given credit for destroying the forts at Venango, Le Boeuf, and Presqu'Isle in what is now northwestern Pennsylvania. Guyasuta was part of the force attacking the first of these (DM, 4-S-61). He may also have been in the action of Devil's Hole along the Niagara River in September 1763, when the Seneca ambushed a British convoy of wagons and packhorses traveling to Fort Niagara past the Falls. Two companies who rushed out from the fort at the sound of the fighting were also ambushed. In what has been termed "the worst drubbing of the war to British arms" (Peckham 1947, 226), the British lost five officers and sixty-seven soldiers.

A boy at the time of the battle at Devil's Hole, Governor Blacksnake told Lyman Draper that Old Smoke had led the Seneca in this battle (DM, 4-S-59, 65). This seems unlikely. A week before the battle, the Onondagas told Sir William Johnson that Old Smoke had gone to two rebellious western Seneca villages to pacify them. Johnson described Old Smoke as one "who has ever been our friend" (PSWJ, 10:830).

The spectacular successes achieved by the western Senecas and the nations of the Upper Great Lakes in 1763 did not drive the British from the region. In the summer of 1764, the British went on the offensive north of the Ohio. Short of arms and powder, the hostile Senecas approached Sir William Johnson in July seeking peace. Johnson demanded and received title for the Crown to a strip of land for the entire length of the Niagara River, the important "carrying place" from Lake Ontario to Lake Erie and the Upper Great Lakes (A. Wallace 1970, 116).

The conflict convinced British colonial officials of the need for an orderly frontier. They judged the cost of keeping Native peoples peaceful to be far less than that of waging war against them. The Royal Proclamation of 1763 drew a boundary between Indian lands and those open to non-Indian settlement and decreed that only the Crown could purchase lands from Indian nations.

The Indian Department felt the Iroquois Confederacy could play a key role in maintaining the peace. In the contest with France for imperial control of North America, it served Britain's interest to exaggerate the conquests and power of the Iroquois Confederacy, their allies (see Jones 1982). The British may even have believed their own rhetoric. Although Sir William Johnson was more realistic, his familial ties to the Mohawk through his consort, Molly Brant, and his base in the Mohawk Valley led him to use the Iroquois, whenever possible, to serve British imperial ends.

In October 1768, Sir William gathered some 3,400 Indians for a council at Fort Stanwix with the object of establishing a long boundary between lands open to colonial expansion and those to remain under Native control. The boundary agreed to in a treaty signed on 4 November 1768 became known as the "Fort Stanwix Treaty Line." It ran from just west of Fort Stanwix south to the Delaware River, west to and up the West Branch of the Susquehanna River, then west again to the Allegheny River north of Fort Pitt, and finally down the Allegheny and the Ohio to the mouth of the Tennessee River (see Tanner 1987, map 13). Although Native peoples who lived in the western portion of the region were present, such as the Shawnee and the Delaware, the treaty was signed by only five Indians, one for each of the founding nations of the Iroquois Confederacy. Guastrax signed for the Seneca (Beauchamp 1905, 210).

Dissatisfaction among the Shawnee and others with the Fort Stanwix Treaty Line and the inability of the colonies to control the actions of their frontier settlers caused tension to run high along this boundary. Sir William Johnson sent his old Seneca adversary Guyasuta as emissary to seek peace with the Indians in the Ohio country and to convince Iroquois who had settled there (the Mingo) to return to their homeland, a goal desired by both the British Indian Department and the New York Iroquois. Guyasuta succeeded in neither task. In 1774, after several Indians had been murdered by frontiersmen, the Shawnees and the Mingoes went to war. Described as a "brief orgy of irresponsibility, cruelty and despair" (A. Wallace 1970, 123), Lord Dunmore's War, named after the British colonial administrator who prosecuted it, inspired one of the most famous of all Indian speeches, that of Chief Logan (Jefferson 1955, 63).

Also in 1774, the British Indian Department lost its most able and influential figure. Sir William Johnson died while hosting a conference at his home in the Mohawk Valley, attempting to "brighten the covenant chain" that bound the Iroquois to the British Crown. Elsewhere, dissidents in the British colonies were fomenting unrest in the towns and cities of New England and the other colonies that, by April 1775, would result in open warfare with Loyalists.

Cornplanter was about to assume leadership of the Seneca, a role his elder kinsman Guyasuta had played for two decades and one he would share with others, most notably with Old Smoke. He would be swept into the turmoil of the American Revolution by circumstances and by a following he could not control.

3

The Seneca and the American Revolution

Initial Diplomacy

Cornplanter and his fellow Senecas were far from the initial battle scenes of the American Revolution. During the first two years of the war, however, they and the other Indian nations were subject to intense diplomatic pressures from both sides, who were well aware of the military potential of the large number of armed Indian warriors, many of them veterans of earlier conflicts, residing within striking distance of the frontier. For the first two years of the war, a principal goal of each side was to keep Indians out of the conflict. Thereafter, however, both sides demonstrated a willingness to employ Indian warriors, with the rebellious Americans being in the judgment of some the first to do so (see Wise 1970; Sosin 1965).

Long in the hands of Sir William Johnson, the post of northern superintendent of the British Indian Department fell to his son-in-law, Colonel Guy Johnson, upon Sir William's death in 1774. The outbreak of war between Britain and the revolutionaries divided the Mohawk Valley population and drove the loyal members of the British Indian Department and many of their supporters to flee the valley to either Fort Niagara or Montreal.

The rebellious Continental Congress chose to divide its Indian Service into three departments: Southern, Middle, and Northern.

The headquarters of the Middle and Northern Departments were in Fort Pitt and Albany, respectively. Thus the Seneca, with their connections both to the Six Nations Confederacy with its council fire at Onondaga and to the Ohio country, were courted by officials representing the Continental Congress in both locales.

Historical factors pulled the Seneca and other Native peoples in opposite directions—toward the British Crown and toward the American revolutionaries. On the one hand, the Iroquois Confederacy had historical ties through the covenant chain to the Crown. Familial ties to the Johnson family through Molly Brant bound the Mohawk firmly to the Crown. The loyal staff of the Indian Department assembled under the leadership of Sir William Johnson included many who spoke one or more of the Iroquois languages and who had considerable understanding of Iroquois culture. The western Senecas had been tied to Fort Niagara since its construction by the French in the 1720s. There they had their easiest access to trade and there they obtained employment as porters at the "carrying place" or portage past Niagara Falls. And, unlike Fort Pitt, Fort Niagara remained firmly in British hands throughout the war.

On the other hand, the western Senecas had never had as firm a grasp of the covenant chain as their eastern brethren. Indeed, under French influence, they had been actively hostile to the British. At the western door of the Iroquois Confederacy, the Seneca looked to the Ohio country and had settled on the Allegheny River, the major tributary to the Ohio River (the Seneca called the entire length of the Allegheny and Ohio Rivers "Ꝑohi·yo?"—whence the English name "Ohio" [Chafe 1967, 59]). Although the British continued to control most of the fortifications in that region, Fort Pitt (or Pittsburgh) at the forks of the Ohio, on the location once dominated by the French Fort Duquense, was now in the hands of the Continental Congress and rebellious elements from Pennsylvania.

On the one hand, being at least nominal members of the Church of England helped pull the Mohawk into the British fold. On the other, having been converted, at least to some extent, to Presbyterians by the New England missionary Samuel Kirkland inclined the Oneida, the Mohawk's western neighbors, toward the rebels. New England was a hotbed of revolutionary fever (in the languages of the Six Nations, the Iroquois still use the word "Bostonians" to refer to Americans).[1] Kirkland was able to convince the Oneida to take the side of the rebellious Americans. Farther to the west, the Onondaga, Cayuga, and Seneca remained outside the sphere of missionary influence and were not drawn by religious affiliation to one side or the other in the war.

Two other issues influenced the entry of Native peoples into the war: trade (and other economic support) and land. The British being economically much more powerful had more trade goods and also had the means to provide the presents so necessary for frontier diplomacy. In addition, it was necessary to support with arms and goods warriors and their families while in the field. In this area, then, the royal forces enjoyed considerable advantage over the rebelling colonials.

With respect to land issues, the Crown also enjoyed an advantage. The Native population rightly perceived that the Crown would, if not protect them from the land hunger of the colonies, at least ensure that land transactions were orderly and that land was purchased rather than taken from them. For all its faults in Native eyes, the 1768 Fort Stanwix Treaty Line did establish a boundary behind which the Native nations could maintain their freedom and independence.

Some of the advantages the Crown enjoyed were countered in the initial year of the war by two circumstances. First, Guy Johnson and Joseph Brant both left North America for England in July 1775. Johnson went because his family was losing its control in the Indian Department. His brother-in-law, Daniel Claus, had been replaced and the appointment of Johnson himself was not firm.

1. Because there is no "B" in Iroquoian languages, "Bostonians" becomes "wahstohro:non" in Mohawk (Maracle 1990, 319) and in Cayuga "Gwahs·doh·oh·geh·ó:nõ" (Froman et al. 2002, 9, 607). The suffixed final syllables, which Lewis Morgan wrote simply as "o-no," "convey the idea of 'people' " (Morgan 1851, 51).

Joseph Brant went because of Mohawk problems with land purchases in their Mohawk Valley homeland. For the first year of the war, the British Indian Department was without its head and lacking the support of its most loyal ally, save possibly Joseph's sister Molly, among the Mohawk. Daniel Claus, much more able than Guy Johnson, was also with the group who sailed from Montreal to Britain.

Later in 1775, an American army under the command of General George Montgomery, with Benedict Arnold among its leading officers, invaded Canada. Although defeated at Quebec City in December, the force was able to cut British communications up the Saint Lawrence to the Great Lakes and to prevent supplies from reaching British forces and the Indian Department at Fort Niagara, Detroit, and other upper posts. Even had the British wanted to send Indians into the field against the rebelling colonies, with the Saint Lawrence blocked, they could not have supported them.

Well aware of the costs of participating in colonial wars, many Native leaders argued passionately for neutrality. Many Native peoples, however, most notably the Shawnee and the Cherokee, viewed the outbreak of the American conflict as a welcome opportunity to right grievances, to halt the illegal settlement of unceded Indian lands, without endangering trade and the supply of arms and gunpowder. Indeed, they could now obtain supplies from one side to attack the other. They could take action against settlements viewed as loyal to the Continental Congress or other rebellious governments without threatening trade with the posts controlled by British forces in the interior. Even though such independent actions were not in the Crown's interest, the British found they could not control their Indian allies.

The Councils at Fort Pitt

The first council with extensive Seneca participation after the outbreak of war gathered at Fort Pitt in the fall of 1775. Guyasuta was there, and it is likely that Cornplanter was there also. The principal reasons for gathering were matters outstanding from Lord

Dunmore's War of the previous year. The Seneca lent support to the American demand that the Delaware, Shawnee, Ottawa, Wyandot, and Mingo return "our flesh and blood and all our Negroes and Horses" who had been captured and taken to Ohio villages and towns during those hostilities. The revolution being waged far to the east was deemed a less important issue (Thwaites and Kellogg 1908, 70–124).

A Seneca delegation attended another council at Fort Pitt in the summer of 1776. Meetings with Indians were held there throughout that summer, and Guyasuta attended one in July (Thwaites and Kellogg 1908, 171). Testimony of Cornplanter's nephew indicates that he, Cornplanter, and Red Jacket were all at Fort Pitt that summer to hear a call "to great a Number of our Red Brethren the Six Nations, and others to not Join Either Party" (Abler 1989, 48). Appointed to speak for the Seneca delegation, Red Jacket replied that they had "clean ears" to hear the message presented, which they would take back to the Seneca country for the people to decide. The Seneca found themselves called to a third council, this one a major gathering called by Philip Schuyler, an Indian commissioner for the Continental Congress's Northern Department.

The Council at German Flats

The thirteen American colonies had declared their independence from Britain in July 1776. In their Declaration of Independence, the rebellious colonials complained that Britain had sent "merciless Indian Savages" against their settlements. In point of fact, Indians had played little part in the war up to that time. Indeed, when the Cherokee had used the war as an excuse to attack squatters on their lands in the south, the British, with no substantial military presence, had tried to delay any Cherokee action until it could be coordinated with their own. In the north, the Mohawks of Caughnawaga (now Kanahwake) and a few from New York fought against the American army invading Canada and again at the battle of the Cedars on 20 May 1776, when the Americans retreated from Canada.

It was to reassert the wisdom of a neutral course that led Philip Schuyler to convene a large council on 6 August 1776. Because of an outbreak of smallpox, the council met at German Flats in the Mohawk Valley rather than in Albany, with some twelve hundred Indians—men, women, and children—in attendance. The egalitarian nature of Native politics demanded that decisions be reached in open council with the greatest possible consensus.

The protocol of Iroquois councils demanded that Schuyler "condole" the visiting Indians for the recent death of their chiefs. This ritual was meant to clear the grieving mind of the other side so that decisions in the council would be unimpaired. Schuyler refused to do this, for the dead chief had been killed fighting the Americans at the Cedars.

In a speech to the council (Lossing 1872–73, 2:107–12), Schuyler complained of the Six Nations' participation in the actions around Montreal in the past year. He also complained that the Mohawk had protected Sir John Johnson, son of Sir William Johnson. They had allowed Sir John to gather his highland Scots retainers and other Loyalists and to safely escape to Canada to fight on the side of the Crown. He reminded them that the previous year the Mohawk chief Abraham had promised "not to take any part, but as it is a Family Quarrel to sit still and see you fight it out." He declared, "We wish for your Friendship not out of Fear but out of Love, and that a good Understanding may prevail between the white Inhabitants of this great Island [North America] and the Six Nations until the Sun shall grow dim with age." As was always done in councils, Schuyler punctuated his address with gifts of strings and belts of wampum. He concluded: "This Belt on which our Wishes are described, and which denotes what we hope will take place, that is, a firm Union between the Six Nations and the thirteen united States of America.—This Belt we say confirms our Words, *The Large Belt*."

Unfortunately, few surviving wampum belts can be confidently associated with the negotiation of particular treaties or with particular councils. Although not usually associated with the 1776 council at German Flats, the Washington covenant belt certainly fits the description of the large belt Schuyler presented there. Containing some ten thousand shell beads, it is the longest Iroquois wampum belt extant, being some six feet long and some five inches (fifteen wampum beads) wide. If the usual interpretation is correct, that the house and the central two figures depicted on the belt represent the Iroquois Confederacy and its doorkeepers, and that the thirteen other figures with whom they are holding hands represent the thirteen states, the Washington covenant belt illustrates well the union called for in Schuyler's speech (see Abler 1989, 41).

Schuyler was disingenuous when he argued that the Americans had not attempted to enlist Indians into the war. As early as the 1775 seige of Boston, they had engaged the Stockbridge Indians (Mahicans) to fight on their side (Graymont 1972, 79–80).[2] The assembled Iroquois, however, reaffirmed their commitment to neutrality and promised to restrain their young men (Graymont 1972, 106–8).

His Majesty's Allies

Entering the War

The American Revolution was in its third year when Cornplanter and the Seneca finally overcame their reluctance and joined the conflict. It is a clear mistake, as S. F. Wise (1970, 183) has pointed out, to assume "that the Indians were instruments to be 'loosed.' " It took considerable persuasion to sway the Seneca to take up arms in the King's cause, once the British deemed such action militarily desirable. In late March 1777, Lord George Germain instructed Guy Carleton to recruit Indians for offensive actions in New York and elsewhere (Sosin 1965, 120).

By this time, Guy Johnson and his associates had returned to

2. The Mahican had been neighbors of the Mohawks near Albany. They had moved to Stockbridge, Massachusetts. Alternate spellings of the name include "Mohican" and "Mohegan."

North America and were available for service. Joseph Brant had returned to New York City in time to witness the Battle of Long Island in July 1776. From there, he and Gilbert Tice of the Indian Department went overland to Iroquoia (the homeland of the Iroquois—upstate New York from the Mohawk Valley to Niagara). Daniel Claus traveled up the Saint Lawrence to Montreal.

Best evidence suggests a minor council took place at Oswego in the spring of 1777 (see Abler 1989, 65–69). Cornplanter, Guyasuta, Old Smoke, and Red Jacket were all present. So were Cornplanter's half brother, Handsome Lake (still a common warrior at the time, he did not bear this title until after the end of the war) and Cornplanter's nephew, Governor Blacksnake, who recorded his memory of the event.

The Senecas and other Iroquois present were asked to help punish the King's disobedient American children. They were told of the wealth of the King and the numbers of his armies and the poverty of the Continental Congress and its supporters. Cattle were slaughtered to feed the multitude and, in Blacksnake's words, a "flood of Rum" (Abler 1989, 71) greeted the Indians on arrival. After hearing the British official's initial address, the Iroquois met among themselves to debate. According to Blacksnake's memoirs, Joseph Brant and Cornplanter took opposite sides in the debate over whether to accept the British call for action. Brant argued that, if they failed to take action, if they slept, they would suffer at the hands of one party or the other—"we should be liable to cut our throat by the Red coat man or By american if we by stile" (Abler 1989, 74).

Blacksnake told historian Lyman Draper that Old Smoke, in his seventh decade, spoke against going to war, as did Guyasuta and Handsome Lake (DM, 4-S-17). In his memoirs, Blacksnake focused on the conflict between Cornplanter and Brant. Cornplanter told the assembled Iroquois: "War is war Death is Death a fight is a hard business" (Abler 1989, 75). He urged that the Iroquois not enter the conflict now, that they continue to wait and see.

When he replied to Cornplanter, Brant addressed him as "Nephew." Although using a kinship term was appropriate (both were members of the Wolf Clan), by calling Cornplanter "Nephew" instead of "Brother," even though he was no more than ten years his senior, Brant was putting Cornplanter in a subordinate position. He is also said to have called Cornplanter "a very coward man it is not hardly worth while to take Notice what you have said to our people you have showed you cowardness &c" (Abler 1989, 75).

When the council reconvened and they met again with the British, the ability of the King to provide economic support was emphasized by the British spokesman: "We therefore Say come go long with the father and he will give you all you wants and your children and woman that they Shall not suffered, Such clothing and Provisions . . . we will furnish you all your wants take it up the Hatched and Sharp adges [swords] and paint against the Enemy" (Abler 1989, 76). Such economic arguments were especially effective on a frontier, where normal trade and activities were disrupted by war. The British also called attention to the old alliance between the Six Nations and the Crown. In council, they brought out the "ancient Belt of wampum, one of twenty Rows was called the old covenant between the Indians Nations and the whites" (Abler 1989, 77).

Blacksnake reports that the Indians, both warriors and women, were divided on the wisdom of joining the war. He implies (it is not always easy to be certain of the meaning of his text) that the economic arguments won over the women, who then put pressure on their husbands and brothers and nephews.

Mary Jemison's memories of this council support those of Blacksnake. She reports chiefs were swayed from a neutral position by arguments emphasizing the wealth and power of the King. The British claimed "rum . . . as plenty as the water in Lake Ontario" and that their allies "should never want for money or goods." At the council, the British gave to each man "a suit of clothes, a brass kettle, a gun and tomahawk, a scalping knife, a quantity of powder and lead, [and] a piece of gold." She reported some of these brass kettles were still in use in Seneca homes in the 1820s (Seaver 1990, 50–51).

Old Smoke may have been the first Seneca to agree to the

British proposal—Blacksnake suggests he was a focus of their efforts. Eventually, the war belt presented by the British was accepted by each of the Six Nations. Brant committed the Mohawk; Old Smoke and Guyasuta accepted for the Seneca; Fish Carrier took the belt for the Cayuga; Lying Nose for the Onondaga; Rail Carrier for the Oneida; and Dragging Spear for the Tuscarora (DM, 4-S-19). The Six Nations did not go united into the war, however. Few Oneidas and Tuscaroras were at this conference and most would fight against the Crown rather than for it.

Fort Stanwix and the Battle of Oriskany

The headwaters of the Mohawk River were linked through a short portage to Woods Creek, Oneida Lake, Oswego River, and the entire Great Lakes–Saint Lawrence drainage. It was at this strategic portage that the British had built Fort Stanwix, the scene of William Johnson's treaty negotiation in 1768. In poor repair, the fort was occupied, garrisoned, and strengthened by revolutionary troops, under whose occupation it was briefly renamed "Fort Schuyler." Most historians, however, have simply called it Fort Stanwix, the name it bore both before and after the war.

British strategy in the summer of 1777 included a plan to cut off New England from the colonies (or "states," as they had declared themselves) farther south by occupying the Hudson Valley. A large army under General John Burgoyne marched south from Montreal while troops under the command of Lieutenant Colonel (brevet Brigadier) Barry Saint Leger marched from the west to join them. Saint Leger's force included Sir John Johnson's Loyalist corps—the Royal Regiment of New York—as well as regulars of the Eighth and Thirty-fourth Foot and a company of German jaegers (riflemen). John Butler commanded a body of men from the Indian Department. As Mary Jemison remembers, men of the Six Nations were asked to "sit down, smoke their pipes, and look on" (Seaver 1990, 152; on Saint Leger's command, see Stone 1838, 1:218–20; Graymont 1972, 129). The number of Indians with Saint Leger was equal to or greater than the British and Loyalist contingent. By far the largest portion of the Indians were Senecas. Fort Stanwix blocked Saint Leger's march to the east.

Blacksnake names his uncle Cornplanter and Old Smoke as the two Seneca leaders throughout the war. Cornplanter was then in his prime and, like his Mohawk counterpart Joseph Brant, of the disposition to lead a vigorous life campaigning. Old Smoke was a veteran of decades of frontier diplomacy and warfare. Despite his seventy-some years, he was constantly in the field (DM, 4-S-48) and indeed commanded the first Senecas to draw blood during the Revolutionary War.

Having set out from Fort Stanwix on 25 June 1777 to hunt passenger pigeons, a Captain Gregg and Corporal Madison were shot and scalped by Old Smoke's party, although Gregg would survive his wounds (Stone 1838, 1:226–27; DM, 4-S-22). Throughout July, Indians surrounded the fort, killing or capturing those bold enough to venture outside its walls. On 2 August, the first troops of Saint Leger's main force arrived. On 3 August, Captain Gilbert Tice of the Indian Department entered the fort under a flag of truce, but his demand for surrender was rejected (Lowenthal 1983, 26). By 5 August, Saint Leger had his meager "train" of siege artillery—two six-pounders, two three-pounders, and four coehorn mortars—in place.

The Mohawk Valley militia was quick to respond to the attack on Fort Stanwix. Some 800 men under General Nicholas Herkimer set out to raise the seige. Molly Brant yet remained in her Mohawk Valley home, and she sent word of Herkimer's advance (Graymont 1972, 129–31).

Saint Leger delegated the task of meeting this threat to his Indian allies, the light company of the Royal Regiment of New York, and Butler's company of Indian Department officers. Sir John Johnson was in nominal command, but it was really an Indian battle with Indian leadership.

An oft-repeated American myth holds that the frontiersman was superior to the British regular in fighting Indians because he understood and adopted the tactics of the foe. Herkimer's frontier militia, however, showed neither appreciation of Indian tactics nor knowledge of prudent military technique against any sort of enemy. It marched in a single, rather disorganized body, with no troops dispatched as an advance or rear guard or to guard its flanks. As the militiamen struggled on a narrow causeway, over marshy ground in a ravine at Oriskany, just six miles from the fort, the Indians and Loyalists opened fire. Pursued by Brant's Mohawks, the rear of the column immediately fled, suffering heavy casualties. Although the main body held its ground, it, too, suffered heavy losses. Herkimer himself was mortally wounded in the fighting. The frontiersmen retreated back to their homes the next day.

Although there is no account of Cornplanter's actions in this bloody battle, casualty figures for the Indian–Loyalist side suggest that the Senecas were in the heaviest fighting of the day. As is most often the case, figures on battlefield losses do not agree. Daniel Claus of the Indian Department noted: "We lost Capt Hare and Wilson of the Indians, Captn Lieut McDonald of Sir John's Regt 2 or 3 privates and 32 Indians, among which were several Seneka chiefs killed. Captn Watts, Lieut Singleton of Sir John's regt and 33 Indians wounded" (Claus in NYCD, 8:721). Blacksnake reported that thirty-five Senecas, including five chiefs, were killed in the battle (DM, 4-S-24-25); Mary Jemison put the figure at thirty-six or more (Seaver 1990, 53).

Herkimer's force lost possibly ten times as many fighters as the Indians and Loyalists. Claus said they left five hundred dead on the field (NYCD, 8:721). Others (see A. Wallace 1970, 130) have suggested that less half that number may have been killed, but the losses relative to the numbers engaged (perhaps eight hundred Mohawk Valley militia and five hundred to eight hundred Iroquois and Loyalists) make Oriskany one of the bloodiest battles of the war.

While the Senecas were engaged in a desperate fire fight (and occasional hand-to-hand combat) with Herkimer's men, part of the Fort Stanwix garrison under Colonel Marinus Willett plundered their camp, taking away "as much Baggage as the soldiers could carry" (Lowenthal 1983, 31). Although the sortie provided little relief for Herkimer's desperately engaged men, it left the Indians with "nothing to cover themselves at night, or against the weather, and nothing in our Camp to supply them till I got to Oswego" (Claus in NYCD, 8:721). It also struck a severe blow to the morale of the Senecas on the expedition. They found that the raiding troops had carried off precious medicine bundles, whose Little Water Medicine had the power to cure wounds and restore health (Fenton 2002, 22).

Old Smoke, Joseph Brant, Daniel Claus, and Sir John Johnson all wanted to follow up the Oriskany victory by attacking the rebels in the Mohawk Valley. Saint Leger refused to do this, wishing to capture Fort Stanwix first and feeling he needed all available men to accomplish this objective (Graymont 1972, 136). He did not have sufficient artillery, however, and many Indians simply went home. On 23 August, Saint Leger decided he had to withdraw.

The Battle of Wyoming

Cornplanter and Old Smoke headed the Seneca contingent of a force of Loyalists and Indians that invaded the Wyoming Valley in eastern Pennsylvania in midsummer 1778. Major John Butler led 110 troops from his recently raised Loyalist corps, Butler's Rangers, while 464 Indians, mostly Senecas, made up the bulk of the force (Cartwright 1876, 30-31, DM, 4-S-27). Brant and his Mohawks were not there.

The valley was well settled and fortified with a series of stockades or forts, to which the population fled when the Indian-Loyalist invaders were sighted. The first two forts they approached—Wintermoot's Fort and Jenkin's Fort, surrendered.

Next came Forty Fort. Cornplanter and a party of Senecas crept up to a nearby hilltop, from which he was able to count the fort's large garrison (DM, 4-S-29). Thus the Indians and Rangers were well prepared when Colonel Zebulon Butler and Colonel Nathan Dennison led four hundred militiamen out to attack the invaders on 3 July 1778. The American Revolution was fought with smooth-bore muskets of limited range (a maximum of one hundred yards). The raw militia fired three volleys before coming in range of the veteran force of Indians and Rangers, who then returned fire. When the Indians outflanked them, the militiamen panicked, turned, and ran back toward Forty Fort. Defenseless against the pursuing invaders, the routed militiamen suffered losses estimated at three hundred. Among the Indians killed were five Senecas, two Cayugas, and one Onondaga (DM, 4-S-28).

It is not unusual to see the Battle of Wyoming described as a "massacre" (as in Kelsay 1984, 218). Those who died there, however, were under arms and had marched out to give battle. Throughout the history of warfare, troops who panic and run have suffered losses comparable to those at Wyoming. A fairer description of the battle would be a one-sided victory resulting from the steadiness, courage, and tactics of a larger veteran force of Indians and Rangers over a smaller untried force of frontiersmen.

Forty Fort and five other Wyoming Valley stockades surrendered on July 4. All eight forts were destroyed, as were an estimated one thousand houses. Despite myths that have grown up around the Battle of Wyoming, there is no evidence that prisoners or civilians were harmed (Graymont 1972, 167–72; Swiggett 1933, 127–33).

The Battle of Wyalusing

Militiamen from northern Pennsylvania, including some released after capture at Wyoming on the condition they refrain from fighting for the remainder of the war, took the offensive in September. Under the command of Colonel Thomas Hartley, approximately 250 troops advanced northward up the Susquehanna River; Hartley later wrote of the journey, "the Difficulties in Crossing the Alps . . . could not have been greater than those our men experienced" (*PA*, 7:5). The targets of his expedition—about which he would later write—were the Delaware and mixed Delaware–Iroquois towns on the upper Susquehanna.

The Pennsylvania troops were under observation by Indian scouts from the time they left Fort Muncey. The Delaware sent runners to the Seneca villages to request aid to repel the invading

Pennsylvanians from the south. Brant and his Mohawks were at Fort Niagara, too far away to give help. Cornplanter, Old Smoke, and other Seneca chiefs met together and decided to go fight the invaders.

The Delaware evacuated the towns of Sheshequin and Tioga. Hartley's men burned these and captured "fifty or sixty Head of Horned Cattle and some Horses" (*PA*, 6:773). With this and other booty, they decided to retreat. On September 28, they reached Wyalusing. The next morning, the Pennsylvanians were attacked by the pursuing Delawares and Senecas. Hartley claimed victory in the skirmish, but he lost four killed and ten wounded and continued his retreat. The Indians followed the Pennsylvanians to Wyoming, where another three soldiers were ambushed, killed, and scalped (Abler 1989, 101–2, 137–39).

The Battle of Cherry Valley

Cornplanter and his Senecas were in the field one more time in 1778. Red Jacket, who throughout the Revolutionary War showed little enthusiasm for battle, announced after the expedition had reached Tioga that the season was too late to make war (it was early November) and returned home (DM, 4-S-31). Perhaps because of the lateness of the season, the aged Old Smoke was also absent. This left Cornplanter as the leading Seneca among the 320 Indians. The Indian-Loyalist-British expedition also included 150 Rangers commanded by Captain Walter Butler, son of Major John Butler, and 50 British regulars from the Eighth Foot. Joseph Brant was along, but nearly left the force because of conflict with the young Butler. The goal of the force was the exposed settlement of Cherry Valley just south of the Mohawk drainage.

As the force advanced toward the settlement, Cornplanter, Brant, and some forty other Indians captured four men from Cherry Valley, among them Adam Hunter, an acquaintance of Walter Butler who also had Loyalist sympathies. Hunter provided the ranger captain with detailed information on the garrison (Graymont 1972, 186; DM, 4-S-31).

On 6 November, a friendly Oneida Indian had warned the inhabitants of Cherry Valley of the approaching enemy. Despite this warning, however, the local commander, Colonel Icabod Alden, refused to allow the settlers to take refuge in the fort. Moreover, he and his fellow officers remained in their quarters at the Wells House within the settlement, away from the fort and its garrison.

Knowing from Hunter where the enemy officers were, Butler and the Indian leaders planned their attack. Captain John McDonell was to surround the Wells House, cutting the officers off from their troops. Although the approaching Loyalists and Indians encountered two men from the valley out cutting wood, disrupting the plan of attack, Little Beard and the Senecas under his command were able to reach Wells House. They killed everyone they found there, whether military or civilian. In the brief fight that followed, other civilians were also killed—some thirty in all. Sixteen officers and soldiers of the garrison, caught outside the walls of the fort, were also killed. Some seventy persons were taken prisoner and all buildings in the valley, except for the fort, were burned. Cornplanter and his Senecas returned home for the winter.

The Capture of Fort Freeland

With the able-bodied men from Seneca and Cayuga settlements gone to war during the late summer and fall of 1777 and throughout the summer and fall of 1778, and with the Mohawks and their Loyalist neighbors displaced from their homes and farms in the Mohawk Valley, harvests were not sufficient to feed all who gathered in and around Fort Niagara. One solution was to raid the frontier settlements of the enemy for livestock, which could then be driven back to the Indian towns and the British posts to provide meat for the hungry residents.

In July 1779, Cornplanter and Captain John McDonell of Butler's Rangers led an expedition into the Susquehanna Valley for this purpose. With Cornplanter were 120 Senecas and Cayugas, including his half brother, Handsome Lake, and his nephew, Governor Blacksnake, Mary Jemison's husband, Hiokatoo, Little Beard,

Farmer's Brother, and Jack Berry (DM, 4-S-33). McDonell commanded a company of fifty Rangers.

Fort Freeland and its garrison of thirty surrendered, along with the fifty women and children sheltered within its walls. Captain Hawkins Boon, with eighty men, marched to attack the raiders, but they were repulsed with some losses by the Rangers and Indians. Boon himself was killed. In all, the Indian–Loyalist expedition killed sixteen of the enemy and took thirty prisoners back to Fort Niagara. One Indian was killed. Their first act upon reaching the settlement at Fort Freeland was to slaughter sheep found in a pen for food. The raiders then "burnt thirty miles of a close-settled country, which inhabitants had abandoned" (Cartwright 1876, 37; see also DM, 4-S-33-34; *PA,* 7:597; Graymont 1972, 202). They seized some 120 head of cattle and herded them back to the Indian country and Fort Niagara. Approximately half were distributed in the Cayuga and Seneca towns the expedition passed through on its return to the British fort (Graymont 1972, 203).

Newtown and the Sullivan Campaign

The impact that the raids of the Senecas, Cayugas, Mohawks, and their Loyalist and British allies had on the American war effort can be gauged by the resources General George Washington and his staff committed to invade the Seneca and Cayuga territory in the summer of 1779. The Continental Congress appropriated the sum of 32,743 pounds to support the invasion (NYSH 1929, 9). Indeed, so large a portion of his army was deployed that Washington feared his remaining forces might have been left dangerously undermanned (NYSH 1929, 122). A total of three thousand soldiers and an artillery train of four six-pounders, four three-pounders, two howitzers, and a coehorn mortar were placed under the overall command of General John Sullivan, with General James Clinton as second in command.

Sullivan spent late June and all of July at Wyoming organizing his troops for the expedition. With fifteen hundred men, he marched up the Susquehanna, burning the Delaware town of Chemung on

13 August and the town of Owegea on 19 August. Here he joined forces with General Clinton, who had brought another fifteen hundred troops from New York and who had destroyed Tuscarora towns on the way.

Although the British at Fort Niagara were well aware of the American intentions, they did little to protect the Indian country. Major John Butler did spend the summer there, at Old Smoke's town of Canadasaga. However, he had with him only two hundred Rangers and British regulars. These troops and about six hundred Indians were at Catherine's Town, at the southern end of Seneca Lake when Sullivan approached on 26 August. Butler and Brant proposed that the outnumbered Indians and Loyalists retreat, harassing Sullivan's army as they did so. Most of the Indians, however, wished to stop the invaders. "The Delawares had pointed out a Place where they said the Enemy ought to be opposed," Butler reported, "& the Senecas & others in consequence of this were obstinately determined to meet them in a Body, and I of course was obliged to comply" (NYSH 1929, 136).

The Delaware leader was Hoch-ha-dunk. Leading the Seneca were Old Smoke, obliged to ride a horse because of his age, and Cornplanter. Other Senecas present were Handsome Lake, Blacksnake, Farmer's Brother, Little Beard, Jack Berry, and Red Jacket (DM, 4-S-35).

The site chosen to oppose Sullivan was across the main route to the town of Newtown. By the time the Indian-Loyalist defenders chopped down trees to build a breastwork on 28 August, Sullivan's troops were close enough to hear their axes.

Sullivan did not attack until the next afternoon. When shells from his two howitzers and coehorn mortar burst behind the Indians, they thought they were being surrounded. Cornplanter and Old Smoke pulled part of the Indian line back, which allowed Poor's Brigade to outflank them on the left. The Indians and Rangers were then forced to retreat, although casualties on both sides were light. Butler estimated he lost ten killed and twelve

wounded, while only four of Sullivan's men were killed in the battle (NYSH 1929, 137; Graymont 1972, 213).

After the feeble attempt to stop Sullivan's overwhelming force at
Newtown, the Cayuga and Seneca evacuated their towns and villages in the path of the advancing Americans. Cornplanter attempted to rally resistance near the town of Canandaigua, but could
divert few men from the task of moving their women and children
to safety before the vast American army (on atrocities committed
by Sullivan's men, see Abler 1989, 112–13). In the only damage the
Seneca inflicted on Sullivan's army, they killed sixteen members of
a scouting party led by Lieutenant Thomas Boyd of Morgan's Virginia Rifles near Genesee Castle. Among these were Boyd himself,
the Oneida Honyose (who was executed after being taken prisoner), and a captured American who died at the stake (Seaver 1990,
55–57). There is no evidence that Cornplanter took part in the
fight. Blacksnake was there and witnessed the execution of Honyose (Abler 1989, 140–41).

Marching only as far as Genesee Castle, Sullivan's army left
Seneca towns to the west, including Conawaugus, where Cornplanter resided, untouched. On its way, however, it had burned 40
other villages and towns—Delaware, Cayuga, and Seneca. Many of
the houses destroyed were substantial log cabins with chimneys
and glass windows. At Genesee Castle, the Americans burned some
130 houses, and 50 more at Canadasaga. They destroyed all the
crops they could find in the fields—"Corn, Beans, peas, Squashes
Potatoes, Inions, turnips, Cabage, Cowcumbers, watermillions,
Carrots, parsnips &c.," as well as "mush milions" (Cook 1887, 90).
They slaughtered cattle, hogs, and poultry, burned the hay being
raised or stored for fodder, and cut down the extensive apple and
peach orchards surrounding the Seneca and Cayuga towns. What-
ever they could not carry away as plunder, they burned.

Sullivan's was not the only offensive against the Six Nations in
1779. Even though most of the Onondagas had remained neutral,
troops from Fort Stanwix attacked them in late April 1779. Burning

three of their villages, a force of some 560 men under Colonel Goose Van Schaick killed 12 Onondagas and captured 33 others. The Onondaga later complained that their women had been raped, contrary to the Indian practice of warfare (see Abler 1992). On 24 April, Van Schaick's troops returned to Fort Stanwix "with much spoil and little glory" (Beauchamp 1905, 239).

In August 1779, Continental troops under Colonel Daniel Brodhead marched up the Allegheny River from Pittsburgh to divert Senecas who might otherwise have attacked Sullivan (Cook 1887, 306). Brodhead's men destroyed 165 houses in 11 towns and more than 500 acres of crops along the Allegheny River and French Creek. Among the towns destroyed was Burnt House—destined to figure prominently later in Cornplanter's life.

Canajoharie, John Abeel, and the Schoharie Valley

The first response of the Seneca and Cayuga to the destruction wrought by the invasions of Sullivan and Brodhead was to flee to the protection of Fort Niagara. In late September 1779, there were some five thousand Indian refugees in the neighborhood of the fort (Graymont 1972, 220). Governor Blacksnake told Lyman Draper that these refugees occupied some eight miles of land north of the fort, "presenting the appearance of one continued Indian village from Fort Niagara to Lewiston" (DM, 4–S–40).

The Indian Department and the British military lacked resources to feed the refugees, whom they encouraged to return to settlements left untouched by the invading Americans or to feed themselves by hunting through the winter. By November, some two thousand of the refugees had left the vicinity of Fort Niagara (Graymont 1972, 222). Cornplanter, his kinsmen, and others whose homes and fields had been spared by the American troops fared far better than those who tried to live on wild resources through a winter that Mary Jemison would remember as "the most severe that I have witnessed. . . . The snow fell about five feet deep, and remained so for a long time, and the weather was extremely cold, so much so indeed, that almost all the game upon which the Indians depended for subsistence, perished. . . . Many of our people barely escaped with their lives, and some actually died of hunger and freezing" (Seaver 1990, 60).

Cornplanter was at his untouched home village of Conawaugus in February 1780 when he learned by runner that emissaries carrying a message from Philip Schuyler, an Indian commissioner for the Continental Congress, had arrived in Fort Niagara. The four emissaries, two important Oneida chiefs, Good Peter and Skenandon, and two Mohawks who had remained neutral or friendly to their rebellious neighbors, Little Abraham and White Hans, brought with them a letter to Guy Johnson, the British Indian commissioner, proposing an exchange of prisoners. They also convened a council of the Six Nations and presented wampum belts calling for those hostile to the new American States to withdraw from the war. Old Smoke spoke for the Seneca, and Aaron Hill for the Mohawk. They refused to accept the wampum belts. Guy Johnson jailed the four emissaries at Fort Niagara, and Little Abraham died while in the jail. The other three were released in the spring when they agreed to take up arms for the Crown (Graymont 1972, 225–28; Abler 1989, 144–45).

Although the massive commitment of funds and men in Sullivan's and Brodhead's expeditions caused considerable distress to a large portion of the Seneca and Cayuga Nations, relatively few warriors were killed by the Americans. Neither was the will of these nations to wage war broken. Guy Johnson estimated the number of fighting men of the Iroquois allied to the Crown at twelve hundred; by July 1780, two-thirds of these were in the field on expeditions against the rebel settlements to the east (NYCD, 8:797).

Cornplanter and Old Smoke led a large Seneca contingent in an Indian force at Canajoharie on the Mohawk River on 2 August 1780. Other Senecas who were there included Governor Blacksnake, Red Jacket, Farmer's Brother, Little Beard, Handsome Lake, Jack Berry, and Hiokatoo (DM, 4-S-43). Most of the population took refuge in Fort Plain. The Indians went about burning the abandoned buildings and rounding up any residents who had not fled to the fort.

Cornplanter recognized one old man among the prisoners. It was his father, John Abeel. The Senecas had already put Abeel's house to the torch. After expressing his regret for this, Cornplanter offered his father two choices. Abeel could return with him to the Seneca country, where Cornplanter would support him, or he could remain with his white relatives in the Mohawk Valley. Abeel chose not to go with his Seneca son. Governor Blacksnake notes that the decision to release Abeel was not solely Cornplanter's. "At a council of leaders, it was agreed to let old O'Bail & most of the other prisoners go free—which was accordingly done, as a compliment to Cornplanter" (DM, 4-S-44–45).

After the destruction of Canajoharie and the nearby settlement of Norman's Kill, the bulk of the Indian force under Brant and Old Smoke withdrew westward. Cornplanter led a small party in the hope of additional booty, specifically horses.[3] Southeast of Canajoharie, the Senecas found the horses they were seeking, but were forced into a brief but bloody skirmish to capture them. The Senecas killed eight and took two prisoners, and secured several fine mounts and colts (DM, 4-S-45–46). Horses had assumed a position of some importance among the Seneca and their neighbors. In addition to their usefulness as draft animals, especially in the gathering of firewood, horses were also important in transporting men and supplies on the military expeditions undertaken by the Indians against the frontier settlements. Riders on horseback following well-worn trails through the forests and meadows in the Indian country were a common sight.

In the fall, Cornplanter led his Senecas as part of a major effort coordinated by the British military to inflict a massive blow on the inhabitants of the Mohawk Valley. Sir John Johnson marshaled his

---

3. On horses and horse theft on the Cherokee frontier, see William McLoughlin's *Cherokee Renascence in the New Republic* (1986, 55–56).

forces at Lachine, outside Montreal, and traveled up the Saint Lawrence to Oswego and from there to the Indian town of Tioga. Johnson brought with him three companies of the Royal Regiment of New York, two hundred of Butler's Rangers, and one company each of British regulars and German riflemen. At Tioga, they rendezvoused with Major John Butler and still more of his Rangers and the contingent of Indians, including Cornplanter, Old Smoke, and their Senecas. This large force had with it a brass three-pounder cannon known as a "grasshopper" and pulled by a single horse as well as two mortars (Swiggett 1933, 233; Stone 1838, 2:105–6).

Military preparations for this large army did not, unfortunately, include gathering sufficient provisions to feed it. Before even reaching its destination, the expedition was forced to kill and eat its horses, including the one used to carry the aged Old Smoke on the arduous journey. When the enemy was at last attacked, Cornplanter and seven other Senecas, including both Handsome Lake and Governor Blacksnake, broke into a house to find its residents had fled, leaving their breakfast on the table. The Indians, who had not eaten for two days, halted their war making while they filled their stomachs. Immediately thereafter, they took prisoner those who had taken refuge in a fort but had neglected to lock its gate (DM, 4-S-48–52).

Johnson's army, which entered the Schoharie Valley on the morning of 16 October, marched northward down the river, ignoring or bypassing forts that refused to surrender but burning all buildings outside the walls of these forts. On 17 October, they were on the Mohawk River itself, burning the countryside around Fort Hunter. A portion of the army crossed to the north bank of the river that evening. It moved to the west the next day, burning along both banks of the river. Both Caughnawaga and Stone Arabia were put to the torch.

The rebels then stirred themselves to retaliate against the invaders. From Fort Paris, Colonel John Brown led a small sally, but he and some forty of his men were quickly driven back and killed (Kelsay 1984, 297). A militia force under General Robert Van Rens-

selaer had marched from Albany and Schenectady to attack Johnson. The armies clashed at Klock's Field on the night of 19 October,
but there was no clear victor. Both withdrew the next day (Stone
1838, 2:116–25).

Moving south from Montreal, Johnson's men had beached their
boats on the shore of Onondaga Lake when, on 23 October, troops
from Fort Stanwix marched out to destroy them. The Americans
were captured by Indians under the command of Cornplanter and
Joseph Brant, who took three officers and fifty-three soldiers prisoner (Stone 1838, 2:124; DM, 4-S-56).

Johnson's expedition into the Schoharie and Mohawk Valleys, a
granary for the Continental Congress's cause, wrought destruction
comparable to that of Sullivan's army in the Indian country the previous year. Johnson's army destroyed some 150,000 bushels of grain
and burned two hundred houses. New York's Governor George
Clinton was moved to report that the frontier of his state was now
at Schenectady (Graymont 1972, 238–39).

There is no evidence that Cornplanter took any further part in
the war, which effectively ended on 19 October 1781 with the surrender of General Charles Cornwallis to Continental and French
troops at Yorktown, Virginia. The British Indian Department at Fort
Niagara discouraged any further offensive action while peace negotiations were under way across the Atlantic.

Judging from the losses they suffered and those they inflicted
upon the enemy, the Seneca and the other Iroquois nations allied
with the Crown were victorious. It is true that Sullivan and Brodhead had burned a large number of Indian towns and destroyed a
large quantity of crops, but comparable losses were inflicted both
before and after 1779 on the rebellious settlers in the Mohawk Valley and in northern Pennsylvania. Because of the nature of the war,
one can not be precise about casualties, but it would seem fair to estimate that the Iroquois allied to the Crown killed five to ten times
the number they themselves lost in combat. The Americans could
not with any justification claim to have defeated Cornplanter and
his fellow Senecas.

The destruction suffered in the war shifted the center of the Seneca population to the west. Many of the towns and villages destroyed by Sullivan were reoccupied, although not by all their former residents. In 1780, the established communities of Tonawanda and Cattaraugus received an influx of settlers, and pioneering Seneca began to build homes on Buffalo Creek. Cornplanter himself lived at Tonawanda for two years. In 1782, he, his half brother, Handsome Lake, and his nephew, Governor Blacksnake, moved from Tonawanda to the Allegheny River, living at Jenuchshadego or Burnt House, which had been destroyed by Brodhead's troops in 1779 (DM, 4-S-78–79). This was the home of Cornplanter's second wife (which may have reflected the Iroquois practice of matrilocality after marriage). Henry O'Bail, the son he fathered by his first wife, did not, however, remain with his mother's relatives, as one would expect in a matrilineal society. Rather, he went with his father, Cornplanter, to the Allegheny River.

The British Surrender

Quebec Governor and Commander in Chief Frederick Haldimand and the officials of the Indian Department learned with distress the preliminary terms of the peace London had negotiated with the new American republic. The boundary dividing British North America from the United States ran through Lakes Ontario, Erie, Huron, and Superior. Title to land south of these lakes had never been surrendered by the Native peoples living there. Haldimand and his subordinates were faced with the delicate task of informing His Majesty's allies that they and their heritage had been ignored by His Majesty's government in its peace talks with the Americans.

The Indians themselves faced an even more difficult task. Given their abandonment by the Crown, what should they now do? In the ensuing decade, Cornplanter led his Senecas down a path not favored by many other Indian leaders. Chapter 4 will consider the complexities he faced as a Chief Warrior of the Seneca in pursuing that path.

4

Making Peace

The Treaty of Paris and Its Ramifications

The preliminary articles of peace between the British and the rebellious Americans reached on 30 November 1782 and the formal Treaty of Paris, signed in September of the following year, divided North America east of the Mississippi and north of Florida between the new United States of America and Britain. The boundary agreed upon ran through Lakes Superior, Huron, Erie, and Ontario. Britain retained its interest in North America (and the fur trade) north of this line; in theory, Britain surrendered all interests south of the line. The relationship between the Native peoples south of the line, most of whom had shed blood during the American Revolution as allies to Britain, and the victorious American republic was not mentioned in the treaty. When the conditions of peace were debated in Parliament in London, only two members of the House of Lords, and only one at any length—Lord Walsingham—spoke out against the abandoning of His Majesty's Indian allies (Graymont 1972, 260–62; Mintz 1999, 173).

British colonial officials in North America were not as callous or cynical as their political superiors in London. Indeed, they could not afford to be, for they deemed it possible that the well-armed Indian veterans of the American Revolution might turn on their former allies if and when they learned the extent of the betrayal by the London government. As time progressed, and under the leadership of Governor Frederick Haldimand, they employed three stratagems to diffuse any hostility toward the British and Loyalists. First, they attempted to assure their former allies that the Americans would observe the old Fort Stanwix Treaty line negotiated by Sir William Johnson in 1768, and recognize Indian title to lands west of that line. When the British Indian Agent Alexander McKee addressed the great gathering of thirty-six Indian nations at Sandusky, Ohio, in September 1783, he told them that the peace agreement with the Americans could not "deprive you of an extent of country, of which the right of Soil belongs to, and is in yourselves as Sole Proprieters, as far as the boundary Line agreed upon . . . in the year 1768, at Fort Stanwix" (Michigan Historical Collections, 20:177). The second was to maintain a British presence in the posts in the territory west of that line. The Treaty of Paris called for Britain to turn these posts over to the Americans, but British officials in North America found diplomatic excuses to delay a transfer of power. By doing so, they preserved Britain's trade ties to its former allies in the upper Indian country and gave Britain some influence over the behavior of these peoples. The third stratagem was to procure lands on the British side of the new border for those of Britain's former allies who wished to remove to Canada.

It also should be noted that the American states were at times in conflict with each other with respect to their policy toward Native peoples on their frontiers. The side that emerged as victors in the American Revolution was only loosely governed by the Congress of the Confederation (which succeeded the Continental Congress in March 1781) and individual state governments were jealous of rights and prerogatives. The Articles of Confederation gave Congress the responsibility of "regulating the trade and managing all affairs with the Indians, not members of any of the States, provided that the legislative right of any State within its own limits be not infringed or violated" (Manley 1932, 23), but some states embarked on their own Indian diplomacy, anxious that their own interests be served, rather than those of the Congress.

The royal charters that had established both Massachusetts and

New York gave their respective state governments some basis in Euro-American law to assert that the Seneca Nation resided within their "limits," even though the Seneca also claimed and used a good part of western Pennsylvania. It also could be asserted with justification, however, that the Seneca and other nations of the Iroquois Confederacy clearly were not "members" of any of the newly independent states and hence were the responsibility of Congress.

Initially, New York State took a haughty and aggressive stance toward the Six Nations. In June 1783, New York appointed Peter Schuyler, Abraham Cuyler, and Henry Glen as Indian commissioners with the intention of obtaining title to Oneida and Tuscarora lands (New York viewed these two nations as allies in the recent war) and of removing the Oneida and Tuscarora westward into the Seneca country. New York, or elements within the state, spread suggestions that it intended to expel the other nations of the Iroquois Confederacy beyond its borders into Canada.

Cornplanter reported the arrogant attitude of the Americans to a Six Nations council on 2 July 1783. According to his Oneida sources, Major General Philip Schuyler (former Indian commissioner for the Continental Congress and uncle to Peter Schuyler) had delivered a speech stating "as we are the Conquerors we claim that the lands and property of all the white people as well as the Indians who have left and fought against us" (Calloway 1994, 284). In fact, General Schuyler had delivered no such speech. To the contrary, he favored making peace with the Six Nations rather than risking hostilities by laying claim to their territories. Indeed, when New York State legislators proposed that the Iroquois be driven from the state, the experienced general argued that such a policy would lead to a costly Indian war. He argued further that there were not only economic but also military benefits in keeping the Iroquois on the American side of the border, that doing so would deny the British in Canada Iroquois manpower in the event hostilities should break out between the Crown and the new republic at some point in the future (Manley 1932, 28–32).

As a response to the new political situation, thirty-six Indian nations—among which the Wyandot, Shawnee, Ottawa, Pottawatomi, Ojibwa, Mingo, Cherokee, Creek, and the Six Nations—held a grand council at Sandusky in September 1783. The Mohawk war chief Joseph Brant (also a captain in the British Indian Department) said it was the position of the Six Nations that the lands north and west of the Ohio River (the 1768 Fort Stanwix Treaty Line) remain in Indian hands, and that the Six Nations would stand with the western nations in demanding the Americans deal with all of them collectively rather individually (Michigan Historical Collections, 20:179–80; Smith 1946, 63).

Treaty Negotiations at Fort Stanwix

This was not to be. Congress, New York, and Pennsylvania all were moving toward negotiating peace and land surrenders with the Six Nations. Because the Six Nations had demonstrated their ability to inflict massive destruction on the New York and Pennsylvania frontiers during the Revolutionary War, it was in the general interest to remove the Iroquois from among the list of possible belligerents. On 15 October 1783, Congress officially resolved to arrange peace with the Indians on its northern frontier. Commissioners to carry out this policy were not appointed until the following spring, however, and not until late summer 1784 did a quorum of commissioners gather to pursue their appointed task. The Indians had expressed a desire to meet at Fort Niagara, but the United States commissioners preferred a locale nearer to Albany. The British, who still garrisoned Fort Niagara, had been cautious about allowing communication between representatives of the Congress or the states and the indigenous population. Also, Governor George Clinton of New York, who viewed relations with the Six Nations as the responsibility of New York rather than of the Congress, had already called on the Six Nations to appear at Fort Stanwix. Peter Ryckman carried Clinton's call for a peace council to the Six Nations on 6 June 1784. In a reply signed by Joseph Brant, the Indians agreed to a meeting at Fort Stanwix, which they felt was more convenient than anywhere closer to Albany. They asked Clinton to inform Congress because they wished "to see proper persons from the different States present, and we expect to make one Peace with the whole" (Manley 1932, 58). In his letter of 11 August 1784 to Henry Glen, one of New York State's Indian commissioners, Joseph Brant said that he was coming only with "War Chiefs," who were "not impowered to conclude a final Peace with the United States," but he indicated that "Ten Principal Chiefs of the several six Nations" would come if they were to meet someone who could conclude a peace treaty with the United States (Manley 1932, 60). Later that month, in a letter to a British officer, Brant noted his delegation was suitable for dealing with one state, New York, but not the United States (Manley 1932, 61).

The Negotiations with New York

Governor Clinton himself journeyed to Fort Stanwix to meet with Joseph Brant and the chiefs of the Six Nations who accompanied him. Cornplanter was among the war chiefs who came with Brant to meet with the New York officials. Matters could not begin until the arrival of the Oneida and the Tuscarora, who did not appear until 3 September. The first day of the public council, 4 September 1784, was used by Clinton to reassure these last two nations that New York made no claims on their lands, but desired to establish boundaries. The Oneida and Tuscarora replied that the eastern boundary of their lands had been established in 1768.

Clinton again addressed the council on 5 September, this time speaking to those of the Six Nations who had sided with the Crown in the late war. He pointed out that New York had the power to deal with Indians within its borders and that New York had traditionally dealt diplomatically with the Iroquois. The Iroquois delegation retired to prepare their reply.

The reply of the formerly hostile Iroquois was delayed by rain until 7 September, when the council continued despite the absence of Governor Clinton, who had fallen ill. Cornplanter opened the council by asking the New York delegation if they were ready to hear the reply. Joseph Brant then spoke. He summarized the proceedings thus far and expressed the "Difficulty in our

Minds" caused by the competing claims of the Indian departments of New York and the Congress. Brant repeated the confusion felt by the Iroquois and pointed out that the western nations (Indians of the Ohio country) had refused to attend any council held east of Niagara.

After a two-day recess, the council met for its final session, in which the New York delegation again asserted its authority and received a reply from Brant that the Six Nations would deal with New York only after a general peace had been concluded with representatives of the Congress (Fenton 1998, 611–12; Manley 1932, 71–72; Hough 1861, 49–55). Brant then returned to Fort Niagara, apparently thinking nothing substantial was going to happen at Fort Stanwix, and having business with the Canadian governor, Sir Frederick Haldimand, regarding lands for his followers on the British side of the new border. Clinton left with the New York delegation, but instructed Major Peter Schuyler (also a New York Indian commissioner and the nephew of Major General Philip Schuyler) and Peter Ryckman to remain and observe the proceedings between the Indians and the Indian commissioners representing the Congress (Manley 1932, 72–75).

The Treaty with the Congressional Commissioners

The three United States commissioners, Oliver Wolcott, Arthur Lee, and Richard Butler, finally arrived at Fort Stanwix on Saturday, 2 October. Also present was the Marquis de Lafayette, the young French nobleman who had served as a volunteer on General George Washington's staff during the Revolution.

The next day, the council was formally opened by Commissioner Wolcott, who introduced both Lafayette and M. Marbois, secretary to the French Legation. To Cornplanter fell the task of responding, which he did in a speech described by Griffith Evans, the storekeeper for the congressional delegation, as "short and to the subject." Cornplanter impressed Evans as "a Seneca chief of great confidence and a man by all accounts of great abilities naturally" (Fenton 1998, 613; see also Manley 1932, 76–81; Kent 1974, 84).

Cornplanter emphasized the peaceful feelings of the Indian delegation. "We know . . . that birds often fly about with evil chirpings,
and that ill winds blow from every quarter to trouble and distract
the minds of persons when engaged in affairs of as import a nature
as the present, but we trust that our ears be shut so as to reject all
their evil words." With a string of wampum, Cornplanter opened
the ears of the congressional commissioners to receive the words of
the Indian delegation (Jennings et al. 1984, reel 42: 1793 22 Apr).

Then spoke Lafayette, whom the Oneida, fighting as American
allies during the war, had adopted and given the name "Kayewla."
Though not all three U.S. commissioners were enthusiastic about
the idea, it was felt that an address by Lafayette might produce an
effect favorable to the American negotiators (Fenton 1998, 614).
Lafayette upbraided those Iroquois who had fought on the Loyalist
side and instructed the Indians to accept the terms being offered by
the congressional delegation. The oft-repeated assertion that Cornplanter's Seneca kinsman Red Jacket replied to this speech appears
to be unfounded (Densmore 1999, 16–17). Lafayette was answered
by an aged Oneida chief, Grasshopper, and Onegenta, a Mohawk
from Caughnawaga or Kahnawake (Kent 1974, 41). Having made
his appearance, the celebrated Lafayette and his entourage left Fort
Stanwix to continue their tour of North America. Their departure
was followed by an interlude of several days during which the
United States commissioners, using the New Jersey and Pennsylvania troops under their command (New York had declined the request to provide a military escort), attempted to prevent the New
York representatives, Peter Schuyler and Peter Ryckman, as well as
the merchants who had been attracted to the gathering, from inter-
acting with the Indians and countering the influence of the congressional representatives. Although serious treaty negotiation did
not commence until 12 October (Manley 1932, 82–86; Fenton
1998, 616–17), on 8 October Cornplanter delivered a speech to the
congressional commissioners described by the missionary Samuel
Kirkland as comparable to those of Cicero "for force, eloquence
and accuracy" (Kent 1974, 85).

Meanwhile, the Mohawk chief Captain Aaron Hill arrived with a few more Iroquois as well as with some Delawares and Shawnees who had come along to observe. When the treaty negotiations opened on 12 October, Hill spoke first. He explained that few Iroquois and even fewer Iroquois leaders had attended the council because they viewed it as preliminary to a major council to be held in the future. Even more than this unfulfilled expectation, their scant attendance throughout the council would underlay later unhappiness with the Fort Stanwix treaty of 1784 among the Seneca and other Iroquois.[1] Hill also promised that, although he had brought no prisoners from the late war with him, that they would be soon collected and sent to the American settlements. Commissioner Lee then replied that the Iroquois had been conquered in the late war and that Congress expected them as a defeated people to cede land to the United States. This was not the tone to which the Iroquois had become accustomed in nearly two centuries of negotiating with Europeans who had been anxious to forge or maintain alliances with the Iroquois Confederacy. An observer reported the harsh tone of the speech "made the Indians stare." Lee asked the Indians to propose a boundary line between their lands and those of the United States. The Iroquois delegates were told to retire, reach a decision, and reply when ready (Manley 1932, 87; Fenton 1998, 617).

Perhaps in an attempt to further divide the Six Nations, the commissioners then focused on Cornplanter, commenting favorably on his written commission to speak for six Seneca towns and indicating their willingness to deal with a person of his reputation, "a person of his wisdom and good name" (Kent 1974, 87; Fenton 1998, 617; Jennings et al. 1984, reel 42: 1793 22 Apr).

On Sunday, 17 October, the Six Nations began their reply. News had come from the Seneca country informing Cornplanter that a

1. Dorothy Jones (1982, 29) has observed that "policy decisions among the Iroquois had to rest on a broad consensus . . . the more individual Iroquois who were present and involved in negotiations, the greater the likelihood of reaching an agreement that would be binding on the League."

daughter had died.[2] The ritual of condolence was performed to re-lieve the Seneca chief of his grief and to clear his mind to partici-pate in the council (Jennings et al. 1984, reel 42: 1793 22 Apr).

The Mohawk Aaron Hill spoke for the Iroquois on that day. In a long speech, he presented several strings of wampum and a wampum belt to the congressional commissioners. This was the tra-ditional manner in which the words of an Indian diplomat were conveyed to those sitting on the other side of the council fire. He emphasized in his message that the Six Nations preferred to deal with the Congress rather than with the individual states. He claimed he spoke for many peoples—"We are the only persons ad-equate to treat of, and conclude a peace, not only on the part of the Six Nations, but also on that of the Ottawas, Chippiwas, Hurons, Potowatamas, Messasagas, Miamis, Delawares, Shawanees, Chero-kees, Chicasas, Choctas, and Creeks, and establish peace in the name of them all." The issue of the boundary line would be addressed the next day. Evans, the storekeeper for the congressional delegation, described Hill's address as that of "an impolitic statesman" (Fenton 1998, 617–18; Manley 1932, 87–88).

On Monday morning, Cornplanter took over as spokesman for the Six Nations. The storekeeper viewed Cornplanter's address, in contrast to Hill's, as "long and artful," even though Cornplanter's major point was the intention of the Seneca to maintain the 1768 boundary line. Like Hill, Cornplanter also emphasized that the In-dian delegation consisted of warriors, not the sachems or peace chiefs—"I who stand before you am a warrior." On the completion of Cornplanter's speech, the council again adjourned, and the after-noon was taken up with a lacrosse game between the Oneidas and the Mohawks of Caughnawaga (Kahnawake) (Fenton 1998, 618).

The congressional commissioners delivered their ultimatum two days later, on Wednesday, 20 October. They asserted that they were there only to treat with the Six Nations, so that the interests of the

2. William Fenton (1998, 617) says it was a son of Cornplanter who had died.

western nations were not relevant. Moreover, they added with more bluster than adherence to the truth, the Six Nations were "a subdued people . . . overcome in a war" (Jennings et al. 1984, reel 42: 1793 22 Apr). As such, they were to supply hostages to be kept until the captives taken in the late war were returned. Although the Oneida and Tuscarora were to be secure in their lands, the Six Nations had to surrender all title to lands west of a line four miles east of the carrying path around Niagara Falls to the mouth of Buffalo Creek south to the Pennsylvania border, as well as to a land six miles square around the fort at Oswego. Cornplanter thanked the commissioners for speaking like men, having "declared your minds to us fully, and without disguise." The Indians retired to reply the next day.

Cornplanter and three other Senecas met the congressional commissioners privately in the morning of 21 October. Cornplanter objected to the surrender of western lands without consulting the Ohio nations. Richard Butler, the congressional commissioner from Pennsylvania with some experience in dealing with the Seneca, replied that, in the past, the Six Nations had always looked after their own affairs without having to consult others. The four Senecas gave in to the American demands. They agreed that the Oneida Good Peter would speak for them (Kent 1974, 98–100).

When the public council opened on the afternoon of 21 October, Hill again spoke first, stating the Iroquois favored peace, but remained a free and independent people. He was followed by Good Peter, who told the commissioners that the Six Nations agreed with the American proposals (Fenton 1998, 620). The brief treaty was signed by the three U.S. commissioners, Cornplanter, who signed last with his mark as "Seneka Abeal: Kayenthoghke," and eleven other Iroquois delegates—two Mohawks, two Onondagas, two Senecas (these six from the elder brothers' moiety of the Iroquois Confederacy), two Oneidas, a single Cayuga, and two Tuscaroras. The Mohawk Aaron Hill, who, along with twelve others, had signed the treaty as witness (Kappler 1904–41, 2:5–6), also served as one of the six hostages the Iroquois surrendered to guarantee that the captives in their midst would be returned.[3]

The Treaty with Pennsylvania

Unlike New York, Pennsylvania chose to cooperate with Congress. It also sent three commissioners to treat with the Six Nations at Fort Stanwix, but these enjoyed amicable relations with their congressional counterparts and in fact signed the congressional treaty as witnesses. They acceded to the express wishes of the Iroquois delegates, that, as representatives of one state, they negotiate only after an agreement had been reached with the representatives of the Congress.

Pennsylvania's commissioner, Samuel J. Atlee, addressed the public council on 22 October, emphasizing the long history of land purchases by Pennsylvania from the Delaware and the Six Nations and the desire of Pennsylvania to purchase more, although "these lands being remote and consequently less valuable than those our fathers have heretofore purchased, you [Six Nations] ought not to expect so great a consideration for them." Cornplanter replied to "our brothers of Pennsylvania" for the Six Nations. The council then adjourned.

When talks resumed on the morning of 23 October, Cornplanter made two requests of the Pennsylvania commissioners. The first was that the Iroquois be allowed to hunt, as before, on unimproved lands in the purchase area.[4] The second was that, "as lands af-

3. The other hostages included at least two men who had signed the treaty—the Onondaga Oheadarighton and the Seneca Tayagonendagighti—and three who apparently had not; at least, the names of Thathnonthale, Thonaute, and Sionouhaloani do not appear to resemble those of any of the signatories to the treaty, even allowing for errors in orthography and transcription (Kappler 1904-41:2:6; Jennings et al. 1984, reel 42: 1793 22 Apr).

4. Daniel Richter (1999, 147–48) argues that Cornplanter was duped on the issue of hunting rights; the Seneca thought they were getting rights to hunt in perpetuity, whereas Pennsylvania only allowed them to hunt until the lands were "improved." In general, Richter sees the role of Pennsylvania as far less open and

ford a lasting and rising profit, and as the Pennsylvanians have always been generous," the Iroquois receive "something next year as a farther consideration." The Pennsylvania commissioners agreed to both requests (Kent 1974, 104–6).

Thus Iroquois interests in lands in Pennsylvania north and west of the 1768 treaty line (except for the Erie triangle—see below) were surrendered in return for an immediate payment in goods valued at $4,000 and an additional payment in goods valued at $1,000 to be delivered at Tioga in a year's time (Manley 1932, 95; Kent 1974, 114). The agreement was signed by three Senecas, two Mohawks, three Oneidas, two Onondagas, two Tuscaroras, and a Cayuga—but not by Cornplanter (Richter 1999, 142).

Although both Henry Manley (1932, 95) and William Fenton (1998, 620) have asserted that it was for this purchase that Cornplanter received his grant of land on the Allegheny River in Pennsylvania, this was not the case. As we will see—and as Merle Deardorff (1941) has documented—the Pennsylvania grant of land to the Seneca chief came later in the history of negotiations between the Seneca and Pennsylvania authorities. The "two good Rifles of neat workmanship" promised Cornplanter and Hill by the Pennsylvania delegates arrived six months late, and damaged in transit at that (Richter 1999, 145–47).

Aftermath of the Fort Stanwix Treaty of 1784

Cornplanter had entered the negotiations at Fort Stanwix as one of the leading war chiefs of the Seneca. The Loyalist officer Colonel John Butler included Cornplanter in a group of five chiefs whom he considered "the most Intelligent, as well as being the most attached to our Interest" (Kent 1974, 113). However, in the negotiations at Fort Stanwix, he ingratiated himself to the Americans as

---

honest than does Donald Kent (1974), who, it must be noted, was writing as an expert witness on the government side against the claim being put forward by the Seneca before the United States Indians Claims Commission for lands in Pennsylvania.

someone who would bend to the forces of realpolitik, a performance not well received at home. That the Six Nations gave in to every American demand at Fort Stanwix revealed the union of Indian nations proclaimed at Sandusky the year before for what it really was—an empty fiction.

Upon hearing their terms, the Mohawk Joseph Brant canceled a trip to England and roundly condemned the Fort Stanwix treaty. Although Brant was certainly the most visible leader of the Iroquois during the Revolution, that he had ties to the family of Sir William Johnson through his sister, Molly, and was both literate and bilingual may have led some to overstate his importance. For all his earlier support of the 1768 treaty line and all his later condemnation of the Fort Stanwix treaties, Brant's more immediate concern in 1784 was the removal of his followers—principally Mohawk, Cayuga, and Onondaga—to lands under British sovereignty north of Lake Erie on the Grand River in Canada (C. Johnston 1964, xl, 52). This removal greatly limited the interest and ability of his considerable following to support the Ohio nations in their defense of the 1768 treaty line.

The news of the Fort Stanwix Treaty was not favorably received by the Seneca and other nations in the Niagara region. Many of the Onondagas, Cayugas, and Senecas who had fled to the protection of the British fortress at Niagara after the American invasions of their country in 1779 had settled at Buffalo Creek or farther to the west. The Onondaga even rekindled the council fire of the Iroquois Confederacy at Buffalo Creek. The Fort Stanwix agreement, though it established peace, also surrendered lands from Buffalo Creek westward. The general population rejected it. Cornplanter's nephew, Governor Blacksnake, recalled a half century later that the council took two days to have the treaty explained to them. After deliberating on the third day, they rejected the treaty and decided "to keep continue war" because they were "not willing to give up their Rights of the Soil" (Abler 1989, 170). Negotiation was still deemed possible; it fell to Cornplanter and other Iroquois leaders to rewrite the treaty in a form more palatable to their followers.

Hostility among the Seneca toward the treaty was such that, in July 1785, Cornplanter, Guyasuta, All Face, and some thirty other Senecas arrived at Fort Pitt, explaining to the United States commander, Colonel Josiah Harmar, that they were "being drove from their nation by their subjects, for selling the land to the United States." Cornplanter in particular was a target, since he "was a chief man at Fort Stanwix." He confessed confusion at being told by the Americans that the British had ceded their lands to the United States and by the British that they had not done so and that lands would remain in Indian hands unless Indians chose to sell them to the United States (Kent 1974, 136–37, 168–70). What Britain had done in the Treaty of Paris was to cede to the United States the interests it had under European law in lands south of Canada, ignoring the Indian title to the lands. It then proceeded to urge the Indians to defend their title without, however, offering them any significant military support to do so. This clearly placed the Indians in a very difficult situation.

The Allegany Senecas were of two minds about their relationship with Pennsylvania. Although unhappy with the land agreements Pennsylvania had imposed on them, Cornplanter and others appreciated that the Allegheny River provided a natural trade route to Fort Pitt (Pittsburgh), the most logical post from which they could obtain trade goods. Thus it was in the Allegany Senecas' interest to maintain a peaceful relationship with Pennsylvania despite the stresses placed on that relationship by the actions of both the Pennsylvania government and an unruly segment of the frontier population of Pennsylvania and nearby Virginia and Kentucky (see Richter 1999).

Cornplanter was still under attack when the British convened a council at Fort Schlosser on the Niagara River in March 1786. The Cayuga chief Fish Carrier told the council that those who sold lands at Fort Stanwix lacked the authority to do so (Kent 1974, 173).

The exact time that Cornplanter moved to the Allegheny River valley is not clear. Although it may have been in the final years of the American Revolution, it is just as likely to have been in response to criticism of his role in the Fort Stanwix treaty of 1784. Moving in response to political conflict and factionalism is common in an egalitarian society such as that of the Seneca Nation and may well have motivated Cornplanter and his followers to move to the Allegheny. In any case, from about 1784 on, his residence was his wife's village of Burnt House (Jenuchshadego, or, in Chafe's phonemic Seneca orthography, Tyonohsate·keh—see A. Wallace 1970, 185; Deardorff 1941; Chafe 1963).

Journey to the Halls of Congress

Cornplanter decided to mend political fences by journeying to New York City to deal directly with Congress. He first went to Fort Pitt, where he hoped to contact the Indian commissioners for the Congress. Arriving on 17 March 1786, he learned that the Indian commissioners had left to report to Congress. So that he might contact them, Cornplanter asked the acting commander of Fort Pitt, Major John P. Wyllys, for a passport to provide safe passage through the tense frontier (Overton 1980, 20). Cornplanter's wife and sons, who had traveled with him that far, remained at Fort Pitt while Cornplanter and five other Seneca men journeyed on. Daniel Richter (1999, 148–49) notes that Cornplanter feared for his own safety at home and that there was a real possibility of war between the Seneca and non-Indian inhabitants of the Pennsylvania frontier. According to his nephew, Blacksnake, Cornplanter's companions were Blacksnake himself and "*Kog-ga-do-wa* of Tonawanda—*Che-wah-ya—To-doin-jo-wa,* or Split World, & *Jo-nah-hah,* of Cattaraugus" (DM, 4-S-22).

It was in Carlisle on 29 March that Cornplanter and his party caught up with Richard Butler, a congressional commissioner from Pennsylvania, whom Cornplanter had gotten to know at Fort Stanwix. Cornplanter expressed his lack of understanding of the treaties between the Americans and the Ohio Indians negotiated at Fort McIntosh in January 1785 and even of the one between the British and Americans at the close of the Revolution. His anger with the British was such that he even suggested attacking the growing Loyalist settlements opposite Fort Niagara (Overton 1980, 21). After a short time, Cornplanter's party set out for Philadelphia, accompanied by Butler, who had agreed to serve as interpreter.

In Philadelphia, Cornplanter was welcomed by the Sons of Saint Tammany, a fraternal club of Philadelphia's elite that took its name from a noted Delaware chief, and had its "Wigwam" on the banks of the Schuykill River. After receiving a thirteen-gun salute, Cornplanter addressed an assembly said to have numbered two thousand (Deardorff 1941, 9). An opponent of the club published a letter, supposedly from Cornplanter, in the periodical *Watson's Annals*. The letter claimed that the annual gathering of the Sons of Saint Tammany, whose aim was "to destroy the force of the Christian religion," had ended "in drunkenness and disorder"(Deloria 1998, 45–46).

Cornplanter's party set out by coach on 21 April for New York City, where Congress was meeting (Overton 1980, 22). En route, the coach overturned and the silver gorget Cornplanter always wore gashed his forehead above his left eye (Jennings et al. 1984, reel 38, April 25, 1786; Abrams 1965, 62; Sublett 1965, 88). The injury left him permanently disfigured, leading his nephew to remark: "If you ever Seen him when he was life his Brow was lop Down Nearly covered over his eye" (Abler 1989, 176).

In New York City on 2 May 1786, Cornplanter addressed the Congress. Again, he asked that the terms of the Treaty of Paris be confirmed; he declared that, as "the old Inhabitants of this Island" (North America), his people desired the help of the Americans in avoiding disturbances. He hoped the Americans would care for his people, for "it is a great while since we have had any body to take care of us." He also asked that Richard Butler be appointed Indian commissioner.

In reply, David Ramsay, chairman of the Congress, showed Cornplanter the Treaty of Paris with the King's signature and its definition of the boundary between Canada and the United States. Ramsay also stated that the United States considered the treaties thus far negotiated with the Six Nations and other Indian nations as binding. He did, however, assure the visiting Senecas that United States citizens would not be allowed to intrude upon or molest Indians within the bounds of territories reserved for Indians in those treaties. The Six Nations were asked to use their influence to bring peace with the western Indians. On 2 June, Cornplanter in turn replied that he would work for peace and asked that Richard Butler kindle a council fire at Fort Pitt (Kent 1974, 173–75). Each member of Cornplanter's party was given a silver medal, silver armbands, a laced hat, a blanket (two for Cornplanter), a coat, a pair of shirts, a breechcloth, and two pairs of leggings as well as vermilion, green, or purple linen, and silk handkerchiefs (Overton 1980, 22–23).[5]

The Council at Buffalo Creek

It is not clear exactly what occurred during the council at Buffalo Creek in the summer in 1786. Having been to England and returned, Joseph Brant had hoped for a council that would be united against American expansion. The British and their friends attempted to prevent Cornplanter, freshly returned from meeting with Congress in New York City, from participating. When it became clear they could not, the British refused to send a representative to the council, feeling it would be dominated by those favoring the "Bostonians" (the name the Iroquois used for Americans). A report by Cornplanter's brother to the American authorities at Pittsburgh suggests that Cornplanter was able to win over all but the Mohawk to his pro-American stance. The ancient Seneca chief Old Smoke, however, reported to the British officials that, though the Six Nations favored peace, they rejected Cornplanter and his message, that Cornplanter had "assumed a character he has no right to" (Kent 1974, 177–79). Brant wrote Loyalist John Butler that, when news of Cornplanter's role at the Buffalo Creek council reached the

---

5. Albert Overton (1980, 24) asserts that Cornplanter sat for the famous portrait by Frederick Bartoli on this journey to New York City. Others (see Abler 1987b) have dated the portrait a decade later.

western nations, they became fearful of having no support from the British or the Iroquois (Kent 1974, 183).

A number of Senecas talked with Commissioner Richard Butler at Fort Pitt in February 1787. Present were Cornplanter, Guyasuta, All Face, the Black Chief, and Captain Girty, along with two Mohawks and an Onondaga chief. After reporting the intelligence Black Chief and All Face had gained among the Ohio Indians, Cornplanter used the meeting to press for a general council to settle the issues left unresolved by the Treaty of Fort Stanwix and the equally unsatisfactory Treaty of Fort McIntosh signed in January 1785 with the Wyandot, Delaware, Chippewa, and Ottawa (Kent 1974, 186).

Despite the unhappiness of the Iroquois, Cornplanter maintained his commitment to a peaceful course. Indeed, according to a report received by the American commander of Fort Franklin, at the junction of the Allegheny River and French Creek, when the British convened another council at Fort Erie in the autumn of 1787, Cornplanter and his followers refused to accept British presents of arms and ammunition (Guthman 1975, 59–60).

Massachusetts, New York, and Seneca Lands

Far from the Seneca country, negotiations were taking place that would have a great impact on Seneca land transactions for more than a century, negotiations that remain a factor in the relationship between the Seneca Nation, the United States government, and the State of New York. Both New York and Massachusetts traced their corporate identity back to their founding by royal charters in the seventeenth century, and these charters—that of Charles I to the Massachusetts Bay Colony and that of Charles II to his brother, the Duke of York—gave each colony claim to what is now upstate New York. In Hartford, Connecticut, in 1786, ten commissioners (four from Massachusetts and six from New York) resolved the states' competing claims by allowing New York "government, sovereignty, and jurisdiction" over the region but allowing "Massachusetts, its grantees and assigns" the "preemption right"—that is, the right to purchase lands from the aboriginal inhabitants—to lands in New York west of longitude 77° west (New York State Assembly 1889, 16–17; Abrams 1976, 43). Massachusetts promptly sold this right to the land speculators Oliver Phelps and Nathaniel Gorham for $1,000,000 in Massachusetts currency (Sumner 1891, 253). This sole right to purchase these lands was transferable, and one land company after another purchased the right from its predecessor; over the years, the Seneca Nation has dealt with a series of land companies anxious to acquire what remained of their diminishing domain.

Although Phelps and Gorham moved quickly to make their fortune on Seneca lands, some enterprising New Yorkers had moved first. Two companies, one based in New York City headed by John Livingston and including Major Peter Schuyler, who had represented New York interests at Fort Stanwix in 1784, and a second held at least partially by Loyalists in Canada (Ketchum 1865, 2:45), obtained 999-year leases on all Iroquois lands west of the 1768 Fort Stanwix Treaty Line. This was an attempt to circumvent the law preventing private citizens from purchasing Indian lands (Phelps and Gorham could purchase lands, although they, too, were private citizens, because they had obtained that right from Massachusetts). Among the signatories agreeing to the lease was Cornplanter, although it is alleged "the leases had been procured by bribery and corrupt means" (New York State Assembly 1889, 17). Both New York and Massachusetts opposed the lease, and the transaction was nullified in February 1788 (Abrams 1976, 43).

Phelps and Gorham had purchased the "preemption right" in April 1788. Within three months, they had purchased some 2,600,000 acres of Seneca lands, east of the Genesee River. For this, the Seneca received $5,000 and an annual payment of an additional $500 (New York Assembly 1889, 18; Abrams 1976, 44). Hoping to hold the treaty council at Canadasaga, a large number of Indians and others gathered there in early June. On 19 June, however, messengers arrived saying that the treaty council must be held at Buffalo Creek. Those assembled made the journey to the west. Fish Carrier, the Cayuga chief, opened the council on 26 June. Both Joseph Brant and Colonel John Butler, the British Indian agent, were in attendance.The missionary Samuel Kirkland was also there, and he noted the degree of economic support, in the form of plows and harnesses, that the residents of Buffalo Creek had received from the British Indian Department. Kirkland established contact with a large number of chiefs of the Six Nations in attendance, including Cornplanter, with whom he talked on 30 June. Kirkland's journal records information he gathered on the population of the Six Nations remaining in the United States (he estimates that these numbered no more than 4,350) but provides little detail on the treaty negotiations, which were concluded with the sale of land to Phelps on 9 July 1788 (Samuel Kirkland Papers, Journal from May to 12 August 1788). Cornplanter, who signed this agreement, later claimed that they had been cheated, having been told they would receive twice the amount that they actually were paid by Phelps ($5,000 and $500 per year—see below). Cornplanter also stated it was on the advice of Kirkland that the Seneca had made the land sale (Jennings et al. 1984, reel 45: 1810 16 Sept [II]).

The Fort Harmar Treaties

In January 1789, the Americans convened a large council at Fort Harmar, their post at the junction of the Muskingum and Ohio Rivers (present-day Marietta, Ohio). Heading the American negotiators was General Arthur Saint Clair, governor of the Northwest Territories.The Wyandot complained of Brant's hindering communications and of Cornplanter's behavior. Cornplanter in his reply (Brant was absent) defended his own peace efforts and distanced himself from Brant's anti-American actions (Kent 1974, 207–9). "I well remember we made a strong and firm peace [at Fort Stanwix]; and no one can say that I have pulled a hair out of the head of our brothers, the Thirteen Fires, since" (Jennings et al. 1984, reel 42: 1793 22 Apr (II)). Saint Clair refused to reconsider the treaties of Fort Stanwix and Fort McIntosh. He also sought to foment "a jealousy that subsisted between" the Indian nations present (Guthman 1975, 162). His attempt to divide the Indians was successful: after a month of council sessions, two treaties were signed, one with the Six Nations (except for the Mohawk) and the other with the assembled members of the Wyandot, Delaware, Chippewa, Ottawa, Potawatomi, and Sauk. Among the Senecas signing the first treaty were Cornplanter, Guyasuta, Big Tree, New Arrow, Halftown, and Twenty Canoes (Kent 1974, 211–12; Kappler 1904–41, 2:23–24). Both Cornplanter and Saint Clair addressed the council after the treaties were signed (Jennings et al. 1984, reel 42: 1793 22 Apr (II)).

As a reward for his cooperation, the Ohio Company of Associates gave Cornplanter title to 640 acres (one mile square) near Marietta, Ohio. Tradition among the Cornplanter heirs is that the deed was stolen from Cornplanter on the way back to his home on the Allegheny. In October 1940, one of the heirs drew a map of Marietta indicating the location of the lands for Merle Deardorff, but efforts of the heirs to reclaim title have proven fruitless (Deardorff 1941, 8).

Richard Butler was also present at Fort Harmar to represent Pennsylvania, which had business to transact. Knowledge of the western country was such that when the Fort Stanwix treaty with the Six Nations was signed, Pennsylvania thought that running its boundary with New York along latitude 42° north directly to the west would intersect with Lake Erie, giving Pennsylvania possession of a substantial portion of the Erie shore, including Presqu'Isle (present-day Erie). When surveying the Pennsylvania–New York border proved this not to be the case, Pennsylvania was forced to negotiate for lands between the western border of New York and the southern shore of Lake Erie at latitude 42° north, a piece of land known as the "Erie Triangle" because of its shape. At the time of this purchase, the Pennsylvanians believed that Lake Chautauqua lay to the west of the New York boundary, thus thought they were paying for more land than they obtained in this purchase. The Seneca were also mistaken about the location of the Pennsylvania–New York border; in negotiations with Pennsylvania, they reserved for themselves lands from Lake Chautauqua and Conewango Creek *east* to the New York border, lands that vanished when a survey showed them to lie, not in Pennsylvania, but in New York. When the error was discovered, Pennsylvania was unwilling to provide a reservation within their actual purchase of the Erie Triangle (see Kent 1974, 217–19; Richter 1999, 153–54). Following these negotiations, Richard Butler wrote to the Pennsylvania Supreme Executive Council suggesting that the state give Cornplanter a grant of a thousand acres or more for his services (Deardorff 1941, 8).

In addition to Pennsylvania's failure to secure lands the Seneca requested around their villages (because the lands lay in New York State), Pennsylvania failed to deliver the payment promised to the Seneca for its purchase of the Erie Triangle. To get the promised payment, some 170 Senecas traveled the hazardous route to Pittsburgh in January, being robbed three times by frontiersmen along the way, only to be given moth-eaten blankets (Richter 1999, 154–55).

Sometime after the signing of the Treaty of Fort Harmar with the Six Nations, some of the Senecas attempted to depose Cornplanter as a chief. Defended by Big Tree, among others, Cornplanter was able to withstand these attacks on his position and status. Nevertheless, the cession of the Erie triangle remained a contentious issue among the Seneca for another four years, and nearly led to open hostilities with the United States (A. Wallace 1970, 166).

Journey to Philadelphia

The seat of the United States government, now under its new Constitution with George Washington as its first president, had been established in Philadelphia. Cornplanter traveled there in the fall of 1790 to present a number of Seneca grievances to both the Pennsylvania and federal governments. With Cornplanter on the trip were Halftown, Big Tree, Guyasuta, the Nephew (Governor Blacksnake), and one other, possibly New Arrow or Captain Strong (Abler 1989, 160; Richter 1999, 155). Joseph Nicholson went as interpreter. The group arrived in Philadelphia on 22 October 1790.

Even as Cornplanter and his associates made their way to Philadelphia, President Washington's representative, Timothy Pickering, traveled to Tioga to meet with Seneca chiefs in an attempt to calm troubles on the frontier. Among the issues was the murder of two Seneca men that spring at Pine Creek. Pickering met with leaders from Buffalo Creek, including Farmer's Brother and Red Jacket. A rising young orator, Red Jacket made a particularly strong and favorable impression on Pickering with a long speech on 23 November. In it, Red Jacket recounted the hospitality given the first Europeans to come to "this island [North America]" and the manner in which that hospitality was answered (Densmore 1999, 31–33).

In Philadelphia, Cornplanter first met with the Pennsylvania Council on 23 October; he outlined Seneca unhappiness in a long speech six days later. The council replied the next day with presents, and the delegates might have left for home, had not Big Tree been attacked and shot in the leg (A. Wallace 1970, 174). The injury led the delegation to remain in Philadelphia in order to confer with George Washington himself. Cornplanter also took the opportunity afforded by the meeting with the Pennsylvania government to inquire about the lands that the state had promised him. He indicated he would prefer lands on the Allegheny River rather than in the Erie Triangle, but was told that the state was changing its constitution, so he would have to wait until the new government was formed in December (Deardorff 1941, 9–10).

The missionary Samuel Kirkland received a letter on 29 November requesting him to journey from his mission among the Oneidas to meet with the Seneca delegation in Philadelphia. The letter may have come from the federal government, as Kirkland was later paid $26 plus expenses by the War Department for his time in Philadelphia. When he arrived in Philadelphia, Kirkland was welcomed in a speech by Cornplanter, who had first met Kirkland in

1784, most likely at the Fort Stanwix treaty negotiations. Corn-planter confided to Kirkland the goals of the delegation, which Kirkland recorded in his journal.

> To represent & state the abuses which the Seneka nation had suf-fered from the White people, several of their nation having been murdered in the back parts of Pennsylvania; to obtain an explana-tion & adjustment of the boundaries of their territory as agreed upon by the Commissers of Congress & those of the State of Pennsylvania soon after the *peace* 1784; a proposal to be made to Congress for assistance & means to promote agriculture & gradu-ally introduce the arts of civilized life among the Seneka Nation; lastly the situation of the Indians at the westward & the real grounds of their uneasiness, &c. (Pilkington 1980, 208)

The many complaints of the Seneca were laid out in a lengthy message directed to "Destroytown," the Seneca name for the Amer-ican president, the text of which was dated 1 December 1790 and signed by Cornplanter, Halftown, and Big Tree (under the name "Great-Tree"). The text itself suggests that Cornplanter was the principal author. Addressing Washington as "Father," Cornplanter argued that the Six Nations were powerless to resist the demands of the Americans at Fort Stanwix, who acted "as if our want of strength had destroyed our rights" (*ASP: IA,* 1:140). He went on to complain of deceptions in the lease demanded by John Livingston and that Phelps, when he purchased Seneca lands, had promised $10,000 "in hand" plus an additional $1,000 each year but, in fact, had paid $2,500 initially and only $500 as the annual payment. A basis of all these transactions was "that the king had ceded the lands to the Thirteen Fires" (*ASP: IA,* 1:141). This is not true, Corn-planter argued, since "the land we live on, our fathers received from God, and they transmitted it to us, for our children and we cannot part with it" (*ASP: IA,* 1:142).

Cornplanter forcefully indicated the distress and hopelessness among his people. One chief hoped to die at the hands of the Americans; another announced he would die by his own hand in the traditional Iroquois way, eating wild parsnip (*ASP: IA,* 1:141; Fenton 1941, 1986).

So intense was the Seneca reaction to the treaties negotiated thus far that those who had signed them, including Cornplanter, were in danger of assassination. He told Washington that only God had spared his life (*ASP: IA,* 1:141).

Shortly after the signing of the Fort Stanwix Treaty, Cornplanter reported, two Senecas charged with murder had been given up to the American authorities. Instead of being tried, however, they had been lynched. In contrast, "innocent men of our nation are killed one after another, and of our best families; but none of your people who have committed the murder have been punished" (*ASP: IA,* 1:142).

In his reply, dated 29 December 1790, Washington promised to protect the Seneca lands as defined by the Treaty of Fort Stanwix with the United States. He assured the chiefs that now, as opposed to the past, only the federal government could treat with the Indians and Seneca lands could only be purchased under the authority of the American government. That government would "never consent to your being defrauded, but it will protect you in all your just rights." Washington pointed out the Livingston lease was illegal, but said that the government had no evidence of fraud on the part of Phelps. However, the Seneca could pursue the issue in the federal courts. Assistance was promised to help the Seneca establish farms and rewards were promised to help bring those who had murdered Senecas to justice (*ASP: IA,* 1:142–43).

In a response to Washington dated 10 January 1791, Cornplanter, Halftown, and Big Tree argued that the Treaty of Fort Stanwix had been negotiated "while you were too angry at us, and, therefore, unreasonable and unjust" (*ASP: IA,* 1:143). They asked for the return of lands to the west of the boundary drawn at Fort Stanwix, as that is the land where Halftown and his people reside. They indicated pleasure that the courts were open to them to pursue their claims of fraud and welcomed the assistance of the government is developing plow agriculture and the building of saw mills (*ASP: IA*, 1:144).

Washington, addressing the Seneca as "Brothers," replied on 19 January 1791. He pointed out that the Fort Stanwix Treaty land cession had been confirmed in a treaty signed by Cornplanter, Halftown, and Big Tree at Fort Harmar two years earlier. He expressed pleasure that the Seneca were going to attempt to persuade the Ohio Indians to treat for peace and again promised economic assistance (*ASP: IA*, 1:144).

In their parting address to the president, dated 7 February 1791, the three Seneca chiefs asked that Joseph Nicholson be appointed interpreter and that they be allowed to send nine Seneca boys to be educated by the government (*ASP: IA*, 1:144). Henry Knox, the secretary of war (and responsible for Indian affairs), answered that the federal government would send one or two men to teach the Seneca agricultural skills and that a schoolmaster would also be sent among them, this being viewed as a better means to educate the Seneca than sending Seneca children east to school (*ASP: IA*, 1:145).

In the meantime, on 3 February 1791, the Pennsylvania legislature approved the gift of three tracts of land within its borders to Cornplanter: 600 acres containing Burnt House (Jennesadaga), the home village of Cornplanter's wife and his current residence, on the Allegheny; 600 acres containing the Delaware village of Hickory Town; and 300 acres containing an oil spring on Oil Creek. These tracts were not surveyed until July 1795 (Deardorff 1941, 10–11), when Cornplanter's grant on the Allegheny was found to be "six hundred and sixty acres, 45 perches and allowance of six per cent for roads" (Congdon 1967, 34–35). Big Tree was given title to an island in the Allegheny River on which he had a home, and Cornplanter, Halftown, and Big Tree were entrusted with $800 for the whole Seneca Nation (Richter 1999, 157). As a parting gift, the Seneca delegation received an additional sum of 65 pounds from Pennsylvania. This gift proved of no benefit, however. As Cornplanter's party ascended the Allegheny north of Pittsburgh, Virginia militiamen robbed them of the goods they had purchased with it in Philadelphia (Richter 1999, 158–59).

In the final decade of the eighteenth century, the Seneca were certainly far from happy about the agreements their chiefs, under the leadership of Cornplanter, had signed at Fort Stanwix and Fort Harmar. But they also knew the costs of war. They well remembered that in 1779 a massive American force had invaded their country and destroyed many of their villages. Although the Americans certainly did not want war with the Seneca either, they were much more concerned with the troubles they were experiencing in the Ohio country. Chapter 5 will review their efforts to employ the Seneca and others of the Six Nations as ambassadors of peace to the Ohio nations. Cornplanter played a leading, even though unsuccessful, role in the pursuit of this dangerous task.

5

Ambassadors to the Ohio Indians

War in the Ohio Country

The Ohio Indians and the Iroquois "Empire"

The relationship between the Six Nations and the Indians of Ohio and the upper Great Lakes will probably never be completely understood. We must be cautious in interpreting Iroquois claims to authority over the Ohio Valley and upper Great Lakes nations, claims that were to the advantage of both the Iroquois Confederacy and British colonial officials, however valid they might seem (see Jones 1982; Jennings 1984). The relationship was a fluid one, with Iroquois influence over the western nations waxing and waning from time to time.

It is perhaps significant that another member of the Seneca Wolf Clan, Guyasuta, played a leading role in the politics of the Ohio Indians. Although he may not have been Cornplanter's maternal uncle, Guyasuta certainly was uncle to Cornplanter in the classificatory sense of Seneca kinship terminology.[1] Guyasuta has been credited with fomenting the general uprising of Indians in the upper Great Lakes after the expulsion of the French from the region (often called "Pontiac's Rebellion," after the Ottawa leader who also played a leading role in the conflict). Following this, however, he went on to

---

1. See chapter 2, note 3.

serve as Sir William Johnson's deputy in dealing with Indians in Ohio. Although well on in years, he played a minor role in the American Revolution and was a signatory of the 1789 Treaty of Fort Harmar between the United States and the Six Nations. Until his death in 1794, Guyasuta continued to travel throughout the region, but with lessened influence. When he appeared at Pittsburgh in September 1792, American General Anthony Wayne suggested "the principal Object of his Visit, was evidently a supply of Clothing for himself—which the Governor, gratified him in" (Knopf 1975, 98). By this time, it would appear that Cornplanter had stepped into the role formerly played by his "uncle," as was customary among the Seneca.

Formation of a Grand Confederacy

The Ohio country and the relationship of its inhabitants to the Senecas in New York were far different in the post-Revolutionary period than they had been before the Treaty of Paris in 1783 and the Treaty of Fort Stanwix with the United States in 1784. The Ohio nations were determined to maintain the Ohio River as a permanent boundary between the European invaders of the North American continent and its indigenous population, a boundary that had been established by the 1768 Treaty of Fort Stanwix with the British. These nations, the Algonquian-speaking Miami and Shawnee and other speakers of Algonquian languages such as the refugee Delawares, as well as the Iroquoian-speaking Wyandot (descendants of the Huron driven from Ontario in the so-called beaver wars of the seventeenth century) and Mingo (Iroquois, migrating to the Ohio country from New York and acting independently of their brethren in New York) had not seen their homes and fields destroyed by invading Americans, as had the Senecas, Cayugas, and Onondagas of New York. Given that the British continued to occupy trading posts within their territory, and continued to supply them with the necessary arms and ammunition to resist the American invaders, the Ohio nations had greater reason than Cornplanter and his Senecas to hope that armed resistance to the Americans would yield positive results.

Under the leadership of Joseph Brant, the Six Nations had at first joined in the general expression of solidarity among His Majesty's former Indian allies following the Treaty of Paris. A great council was held at Sandusky, Ohio, said to have been attended by thirty-six Indian nations, including the Six Nations, the Ohio and Michigan nations (Shawnee, Wyandot, Ottawa, Delaware, Potawatomi, Ojibwa, Mingo, and others), and great southern nations such as the Cherokee and Creek. Although issues occasioned by the 1783 peace between the Americans and the British, such as the return of prisoners, were discussed, the talks focused on the boundary between the United States and the Indians to the west. Even though the British had surrendered interest in lands south of the Great Lakes and east of the Mississippi, the Indian nations who had never surrendered title to those lands expressed unanimity that the 1768 Fort Stanwix Treaty Line, reserving lands north and west of the Ohio River to the indigenous population, be maintained. As noted in the previous chapter, Alexander McKee of the British Indian department supported this stance. This unity expressed at Sandusky in September 1783 has been described as a "grand confederacy"—"not crushed until the success of Wayne in 1794" (Smith 1946, 63). Such a view overstates the ability of the Indian nations to maintain unity among themselves.

The Americans quickly moved to dismember the Sandusky "confederacy." Their first success was the 1784 Treaty of Fort Stanwix with the Six Nations, discussed in chapter 4. At Fort McIntosh in January 1785, they were able to dictate a similar treaty of delegates of the Wyandot, Delaware, Chippewa, and Ottawa nations. Both of these treaties were confirmed by two treaties signed at Fort Harmar in January 1789. There was great dissatisfaction among the Indians about the terms of these treaties, and the Seneca and others of the Six Nations expressed that dissatisfaction in delegations sent to see Congress and the president. When the Ohio nations expressed their refusal to give up their lands through armed resistance, however, the Americans attempted to reach a military solution to the land issue in Ohio.

Military Resistance in Ohio

No other Native North American nations inflicted greater losses on American military forces than the Ohio nations did resisting the invasion of their lands. In late October 1790, Josiah Harmar led an army some fifteen hundred strong north of the Ohio, where they burned several towns. After losing more than two hundred men in four days, however, Harmar was forced to withdraw. It was at this point that the Americans, while not ruling out a military solution, began to explore their ties with the Six Nations in an attempt to reach a diplomatic solution to their Ohio problem.

Their first diplomatic initiative came to naught. Traveling on a secret mission, Colonel Thomas Procter (who had commanded the artillery on General John Sullivan's expedition to destroy Seneca towns in 1779) approached Cornplanter and other Senecas in the summer of 1791, asking them to accompany him to the west to bring a message of peace to the Ohio nations. Cornplanter declined; he had political problems of his own at home. Procter was stopped at Fort Niagara by the British commander and allowed to go no farther (*ASP: IA,* 2:145–65).

The United States resumed its pursuit of a military solution. General Arthur Saint Clair led his men to arguably the worst defeat suffered by the United States Army at the hands of indigenous people. On 4 November 1791, at least 630 of his men were killed in fighting on a branch of the Wabash River near the present Indiana-Ohio border, including Major General Richard Butler, who had served as commissioner of Indian affairs for both Congress and Pennsylvania and who had accompanied Cornplanter to New York in 1786 (Coe 1968, 307; *ASP: IA,* 1:36–38).

The Americans were forced to rebuild their army in the region, a task entrusted to the capable veteran of the American Revolution General Anthony Wayne. In the meantime, another attempt was made, this time by President George Washington, Secretary of War Henry Knox, and Indian Commissioner Timothy Pickering, to enlist the Seneca in general and Cornplanter in particular to bring the Ohio Indians to a negotiated peace settlement.

The Seneca as Ambassadors of Peace

The Delegation to Philadelphia in 1792

In an effort to persuade the Seneca and others of the Six Nations to take the cause of peace to the Ohio Indians, a large Indian delegation was invited to meet with President Washington, Secretary Knox, and Commissioner Pickering in Philadelphia in the spring of 1792. Fifty arrived on 13 March 1792, and were addressed by Washington ten days later. Cornplanter was not among them, but the delegation included Red Jacket, who probably then received his famous large silver medal (Densmore 1999, 37–39).

The American artist John Trumbull painted portraits of the Oneida chief Good Peter, the Seneca chief The Infant, and a third Indian, perhaps Cornplanter's nephew, Governor Blacksnake (see Cooper 1982, 130–33, 144–45; Abler 1987b). The delegates received a white wampum belt, a symbol of peace, from President Washington and a map from Pickering to convey to the Ohio Indians the boundaries of the lands currently claimed by the United States, lands that had been sold to the United States in treaties since the end of the Revolution. The delegates returned to Buffalo Creek in June; when they left for the Ohio country in September, "they were accompanied by the firm friend of the United States, the Cornplanter" (*ASP: IA,* 1:229–33). Cornplanter and New Arrow were also in the pay of General Wayne to provide him intelligence on the nations and numbers of Native fighters who might be fielded against American forces should the peace talks fail (Sword 1985, 225). New Arrow was the head man or chief of a Seneca village just nine miles up the Allegheny River from Cornplanter's village on what was to become the Allegany Reservation (Kent and Deardorff 1960, 294, 301).

Red Jacket, after an 1826 portrait by Robert Walter Weir. Frontispiece to the biography of the Seneca orator by William L. Stone (1841). Red Jacket wears the very large peace medal presented to him in 1792 by George Washington. Courtesy of the Dana Porter Arts Library, University of Waterloo, Waterloo, Ontario.

The Council at the Glaize

In September 1792, Senecas and others of the Six Nations journeyed into Ohio in force; General Wayne was told they numbered

500, their large number dictated by fear of violence from the Ohio nations. Wayne was told that Cornplanter, reacting to a report that messengers from the Six Nations to the Ohio Indians had been murdered, was "very uneasy, & said that if any of his people were killed, he wou'd immediately go to War with the Hostile Indians" (Knopf 1975, 98). Guyasuta told Wayne that Cornplanter's life was in danger among the Ohio Indians; in a letter to Secretary Knox, Wayne himself said "I feel uneasy for the safe return of the Cornplanter" (Kent 1974, 222; Knopf 1975, 119)

The Six Nations met with the Ohio nations at the Glaize, where the Maumee River joins the Auglaize, from 30 September to 8 October. The British Indian agent Simon Girty warned an arriving Six Nations delegation that, rather than being offered peace, they instead would be offered a tomahawk. A Shawnee chief, Messquakenoe, noted that, although the Six Nations had agreed four years before to a common defense of the lands north of the Ohio, "we have never seen you since that time" (Sword 1985, 225–26). Alluding to their military successes, the Shawnee chief told the Seneca that the American president knew well the paths into their country ran deep with blood, and on these paths it was impossible for peace messengers to travel. This he contrasted with the paths the Americans could take into the territory of the Six Nations; these paths were "smooth and easy" (*ASP: IA*, 1:323–34).

Despite the hostility between the Senecas and the Ohio Indians, Cornplanter's nephew, Governor Blacksnake, managed to meet a girl at the council, probably Shawnee but possibly Osage, whom he found extremely attractive. Her father invited the Senecas to dance in his mat-covered lodge, where Blacksnake learned that she was not married. When the young man turned to his uncle for advice, however, Cornplanter told him to drop the matter. A half century later, Blacksnake recalled the episode with sorrow and regret (Abler 1989, 194–95).

Given the hostility they encountered, Blacksnake recalled that the Seneca fled quickly home, not pausing before French Creek except at night to fry up some venison and to sleep (Abler 1989, 199).

Cornplanter and Anthony Wayne

On 15 March 1793, Cornplanter, New Arrow, Big Tree, and Guya-suta with three warriors and the interpreter Nicholas Rosecrantz arrived at General Wayne's encampment of Legion Ville, downriver from Pittsburgh (Knopf 1975, 203). Suspicious of Cornplanter, Wayne had less than two weeks before written to Secretary Knox that "I shall not be honored with his presence until I meet him in a hostile manner in the field" (Knopf 1975, 196). Cornplanter urged Wayne not to move until the possibilities of negotiating a treaty had been exhausted, but Wayne viewed this as a stratagem to keep him in place until the rivers were too low to serve his army for transport. The American general answered "that the only means to secure peace—was to be well prepared for war" (Knopf 1975, 230). Wayne also reported a "tost" given by Cornplanter: "My mind & heart is upon that river (pointing to the Ohio) may that Water ever continue to run, & remain *the boundary of a lasting peace,* between the Americans & the Indians on its opposite shores" (Knopf 1975, 206). Thus it appears that Cornplanter was making some effort, in his role as intermediary, to influence the actions and policy of the Americans to be of some advantage to the hostile Ohio nations. Cornplanter and New Arrow left to attend another council with the Ohio nations at the rapids of the stream known to Wayne as "Miami of the Lakes" and now known as the "Maumee" (Knopf 1975, 303). Although Cornplanter had told Wayne that members of the Six Nations did not accept payment for "doing good," the American commander provided the two Seneca chiefs and their party with mares for transport and with other gifts (Knopf 1975, 206).

Three American commissioners—Benjamin Lincoln, Beverly Randolph, and Timothy Pickering—journeyed to the west in the summer of 1793 in the hope of negotiating a peace with the western nations at Sandusky. They traveled to the British post at Fort Erie and up Lake Erie to the mouth of the Detroit River. From there, at the house of the British Indian agent Matthew Elliott, they exchanged messages by runners with a "private" Indian council being held at the Maumee Rapids. Among those present at the Maumee Rapids council was a delegation of the Six Nations, including Cornplanter, Farmer's Brother, Joseph Brant, Fish Carrier (a Cayuga chief), and Great Sky of the Onondaga (Jennings et al. 1984, reel 42: 1793 30 July–16 Aug). A total of 500 Indians from the Six Nations were present: 110 of them Senecas, led by Cornplanter; 130 Mohawks from the Six Nations' lands on the Grand River in Canada; and 260 Oneidas, Onondagas, Cayugas, and Senecas loyal to chiefs other than Cornplanter (Jennings et al. 1984, reel 43: [1795(?)] (II)). The chiefs of the Six Nations as well as the Mahican chief, Captain Hendrick Aupaumut, argued the cause of peace and suggested that prudence dictated that the assembled nations accept the concessions (including additional payment for lands taken north of the Ohio) and demands of the American commissioners, and grant to the Americans lands north of the Ohio that had been occupied by settlers.

The mood of the vast majority of those present, however, was not to compromise on the Ohio line. In a message signed with the marks of sixteen nations and confederacies (but not including any of the Six Nations residing outside Ohio), sent by runners from the Maumee Rapids to Detroit and dated 13 August 1793, the Indians demanded the removal of settlers from north of the Ohio. Instead of paying Indians for the lands, the Ohio Indians argued, the Americans should instead use the funds to pay the settlers to move back south of the Ohio. "We know that these settlers are poor . . . they would most readily accept it." As for themselves, the Ohio Indians said, "we can retreat no further, because the country behind [to the west] hardly affords food for its present inhabitants. And we have therefore resolved to leave our bones in this small space, to which we are now confined" (Cruikshank 1923–31, 2:19–20). The American commissioners returned home, leaving the Ohio theater to the military operations of General Wayne.

Those from the Six Nations who participated in peace missions to Ohio were rewarded at a later date by the United States. An undated and unsigned document reveals that each of the five hundred attending the council was to receive a blanket, calico for a shirt, and stroud for a breechcloth and leggings. Their families were also to receive blankets and cloth for clothing; some two hundred "Poor Widows, Orphans, & Old men, the relieving of whom is peculiarly grateful to the Indians[,]" were to receive similar gifts. Chiefs were to be given black silk handkerchiefs, scarlet cloth for leggings, Irish linen, and vermilion. Thread, needles, and scissors were to be given for making shirts, petticoats, and leggings. Also to be presented were powder, lead, one thousand gun flints, fifty kettles, and two hundred knives (Jennings et al. 1984, reel 43: [1795(?)] (II)).

The memory of the perils faced by Cornplanter and his companions in these peace negotiations with the western Indians has endured among his descendants. Perhaps in reference to Seneca participation in this final peace effort, George Abrams (1976, 46; see also A. Wallace 1970, 164–65) reports a widely told Seneca story. Insulted and held as prisoners in the Ohio country, the Seneca delegates were finally allowed to go home. Their food had been poisoned, however, and several died on the return journey to their villages on the Allegheny River. This story, reportedly told by Solomon O'Bail, Cornplanter's grandson, to his daughter, Emily Tallchief (see A. Parker 1913, 136–39), was confirmed to General Wayne by the Seneca chief Big Tree, who reported that New Arrow was among those who died and that Cornplanter "was also near dying" (Cruikshank 1923–31, 2:195–96).

Big Tree

Chief of a Seneca town on the Genesee River who frequently pursued an independent course, Big Tree accompanied Cornplanter on many of the diplomatic missions. Despite general Seneca support of the British-Loyalist cause during the Revolution, Big Tree chose to remain neutral, reputedly because of a personal friendship with George Washington. While in Legion Ville (the American army camp) with Cornplanter and New Arrow in March 1793, he told Anthony Wayne that, when he learned that General Butler—"a very dear friend—the friend of my Heart"—had been killed in the defeat of Saint Clair, he considered suicide by eating of the "fatal root." Instead, he reported, the Great Spirit instructed him to avenge the death of his friend by killing three of the hostile Ohio Indians. He had killed one Delaware and asked Wayne whether he might join the Americans to complete his task.

In early January 1794, Big Tree appeared again in Wayne's encampment, announcing that the "Nephew" (Governor Blacksnake) was ready to serve against the Ohio Indians whenever Wayne requested it and that he (Big Tree) could bring in forty warriors to fight beside the Americans (Knopf 1975, 304). Blacksnake recalled that he and his men had a brief exchange of fire with a group of Delawares, whom he described as "anemy [sic] to us" in which three Delawares were killed (Abler 1989, 202). The action described by Blacksnake would seem to have taken place at about the time that Big Tree was informing Wayne of the willingness of the "Nephew" to fight alongside the Americans.

When Delawares arrived at General Wayne's camp under a flag of truce, Big Tree, who claimed they were spies, had to be restrained from executing them with his sword. He gave them an ultimatum to give up their prisoners within thirty days. After they left, however, Big Tree sank into a depression. Despite every effort by Wayne and his men to humor him and make him comfortable, and despite being presented with the complete uniform of officer in Wayne's Legion, Big Tree turned his knife upon himself and died at 3 P.M. on 23 January 1794, owing, in Wayne's words, to "a disturbed imagination which has been very conspicuous at certain intervals for a considerable length of time!" (Knopf 1975, 302–5). "The United States have lost a true & faithful friend," Wayne wrote Secretary Knox. Instructing interpreter Nicholas Rosecrantz to go to the Seneca to perform a ritual of condolence (Knopf 1975, 302–5; see Fenton 1986, 453–54), Wayne sent presents to Big Tree's wife and daughter, as well as "a Suit of mourning to his two brothers & a Rifle to each." He ordered the commander of the garrison at Fort Franklin to build a house and provide for Big Tree's family (Cruikshank 1923–31, 2:196).

The Councils at Buffalo Creek

In October 1793 and in February and June 1794, councils were held at Buffalo Creek. Cornplanter, Joseph Brant, and Farmer's Brother were the dominant chiefs in the public portions of these councils (Densmore 1999, 41), which expressed Seneca frustration and hostility, and in which both British Indian Department officials and the United States Indian Agent Israel Chapin played active roles.

At the June 1794 council, Cornplanter warned Chapin: "It is not because we are afraid of dying that we have been so long trying to bring about a peace. We now call upon you for an answer, as Congress and their commissioners have oftentimes deceived us; and if these difficulties are not removed, the consequences will be bad" (Campisi and Starna 1995, 478). Cornplanter returned to his Allegheny home with ample presents from the British. There he confronted a surveyor by striking the war post and reciting his war exploits (A. Wallace 1970, 166–67). Continued negotiations led to a recasting of the relationship between the Seneca Nation and the United States, confirmed that fall in the Treaty of Canandaigua.

6

The Treaties of Canandaigua and Big Tree

Growing Seneca Hostility

When Cornplanter signed treaties and agreements with the United States and others immediately after the Revolution, his pro-American stance drew support from many Senecas who were weary of fighting and who had suffered enormous losses as a result of Sullivan's invasion of their country in 1779. The Seneca were also relatively removed from American settlements, so they did not feel any immediate pressure on their lands when they met the delegations from New York, Pennsylvania, and the Congress at Fort Stanwix in 1784. Since the occupation of their former territories was not immediate, many Senecas probably did not realize the extensive nature of the concessions made by Cornplanter and his fellow chiefs. In the decade following the signing of the Treaty of Fort Stanwix, however, land-hungry Americans rapidly pushed westward. As surveyors appeared near their villages, it became readily apparent to the Senecas what Cornplanter and the other chiefs had been forced to give away in the treaties signed at Fort Stanwix and Fort Harmar.

Those who penetrated the Indian country to survey lands were of two varieties. There were official surveyors who worked for governments or land companies who enjoyed government sanction and who surveyed and staked out lands in regions that, in the view of the federal or state governments, had been transferred from Indian ownership. There were also individuals who illegally surveyed and staked out claims in the expectation that courts in the future would award them title to lands on which they had made "improvements." Such "improvements" were made, for example, "by girdling a few trees, and driving four forked sticks in the ground, and laying two poles across in front and rear of the forks and covered them with bark—by this they expected to hold four hundred acres of land," as one official surveyor, John Adlum, observed (Kent and Deardorff 1960, 288).

This growing evidence of the coming wave of American settlement made the Seneca uneasy, and this was coupled to their unhappiness with the outcome of the agreement they had made with Pennsylvania surrendering the Erie Triangle in 1789. In negotiating that sale, the Seneca had expressed a wish to retain lands east of Chautauqua Lake and Conewango Creek. Pennsylvania agreed, and the treaty allowed them to retain the lands from Chautauqua Lake and Conewango Creek *east* to the border between New York and Pennsylvania, under the assumption that the New York–Pennsylvania border actually fell to the east of those bodies of water. The eventual survey of the New York–Pennsylvania border in 1787 by Andrew Porter and Andrew Ellicott, with John Adlum in their employ (Kent and Deardorff 1960, 302), revealed that it lay to the *west* of the Chautauqua region, hence Pennsylvania had no authority to guarantee the lands for Seneca use (Kent 1974, 219).

General Israel Chapin served as the United States Indian agent to the Six Nations, handling the day-to-day diplomacy with the Seneca and other Iroquois. He often made the long journey from Canandaigua to Buffalo Creek to meet with the Six Nations and hear their demands. Cornplanter refused to come to a council held at Buffalo in October 1793, sending Chapin a string of wampum to inform him that to come would be "not without great inconvenience" (Jennings et al. 1984, reel 42: 1793 11 Dec). In January 1794, Farmer's Brother and Red Jacket requested that Cornplanter join them in meeting with Chapin, but again the Allegany chief begged off. Cornplanter dictated a letter to Chapin explaining "the sickness that we got at the Sundusky is very bad among us, so that we are not well, and not able to step forward this time." He requested a gift of fourteen for Guyasuta, who was also not well—"He is alive & that is all." Cornplanter then asked after his eldest son, Henry ("whether he is alive or not"), who was attending school in Philadelphia (Jennings et al. 1984, reel 42: 1794 1 Feb). Although Cornplanter did become ill after the tense Ohio councils of the summer of 1793, it is tempting to see Cornplanter's excuses for not attending these councils as also motivated by an unwillingness to submit to possible censure and verbal or even physical abuse for his role in previous negotiations with the Americans from the Senecas and others at Buffalo Creek (see Mohawk 2000, 59, 63n).

A council was held at Buffalo Creek on 21 April 1794 between the Six Nations and both British and American delegations. John Butler represented the Crown, and General Israel Chapin the Americans. Butler presented a speech of Lord Dorchester, Governor of Canada, that had been made to Mohawks and others outside Montreal. Chapin viewed the speech as "inflamatory" in that it raised the probability of a war between Britain and the United States. Brant spoke for the Six Nations, calling for a negotiated peace between the United States and all the Indian nations. When it came Chapin's turn, he attempted to clear away the "black clouds" raised by Dorchester's address, but he passed over the validity of earlier land surrenders (Jennings et al. 1984, reel 43: 1794 29 April).

When Cornplanter finally appeared, he was actively courted by Butler. Prior to presenting Dorchester's speech, Butler told the council: "Brothers . . . I particularly congratulate you on the recovery of our esteemed Captn. Brant and the Corn Planter." Butler had hoped to introduce Cornplanter and other chiefs to Lieutenant Governor John Simcoe, but Simcoe did not return to the Niagara region from Detroit before Cornplanter had to return home, a week after the council first convened (Cruikshank 1923–31, 2:218).

In the spring of 1794, Pennsylvania was anxious to occupy the Erie Triangle and establish its port on the Great Lakes. This was opposed by the Seneca and others of the Six Nations as well as by the British. The Seneca felt that an American base there would sever communications between them and the Ohio nations; the British saw a fortification on the southern shore of Lake Erie as a direct threat to Canada. Cornplanter was reported to have communicated by letter to the commander of Fort Franklin in May 1794 that the Indians and the British would oppose any party attempting to build a road to Presqu'Isle (present-day Erie; *ASP: IA,* 1:505).

The murder of a "friendly Indian" by a young man named Robertson in the vicinity of Fort Franklin on 1 May 1794 made tensions worse. Rumors about what Cornplanter and his Senecas might do spread through frontier communities in western Pennsylvania. The killing of two white men near Fort Franklin on 5 June fanned fears on the Pennsylvania frontier. Matters were made worse on 11 June in Pittsburgh, when Broken Twig, an old Seneca who had frequent dealings with the settlers, conveyed the message that "Cornplanter had been bought by the British" and that the British had supplied Cornplanter's village with canoes so that his men might descend the Allegheny to attack western Pennsylvania (*ASP: IA,* 1:509). People at Pittsburgh thought that Senecas might have killed the two white men, but in fact the deed was done by hostile Ohio Indians. It was five Senecas, with five white men from Fort Franklin, sent out by post commander Lieutenant John Polhemus to search for the men when they had been reported missing, who found them "shot, scalped, and tomahawked" (*ASP: IA,* 1:511).

In a letter dated 7 June to Secretary of War Henry Knox, Chapin speculated about why Cornplanter, "whose steadiness & fidelity has been until lately unshaken," was now taking a hostile stance toward Americians. He noted that Cornplanter had "lately returned from Niagara loaded with presents" from the British. On learning of the murder of a Delaware at Venango (Fort Franklin), Cornplanter had sent runners to convene a council at that place. Chapin viewed the real cause of Cornplanter's hostile posture toward the Americans, however, to be the sale of the Erie Triangle, made "by the Corn-planter & a small party without the consent of the nation." There had been no division of the payment received for the sale. Corn-planter was attempting to divert attention away from his earlier ac-tions by focusing attention on grievances against the Americans (Jennings et al. 1984, reel 43: 1794 7 June).

The Seneca chiefs continued their diplomatic activity, sending for Cornplanter. On 15 June, the chief's nephew, Governor Black-snake, arrived at Fort Franklin, explaining that Cornplanter had gone to a council at Buffalo, but had sent the chiefs a message. He blamed "bad men" for "the account given of their going to take up the hatchet." Unconvinced, Pennsylvania Captain Denny repeated the allegation that Cornplanter was ready to attack to his superi-ors—"Some of the nation say the English have bought O'Beal" (*ASP: IA*, 1:514).

When Superintendent Israel Chapin again came to Buffalo, in June 1794, Cornplanter spoke for the warriors, pointedly stating that it was their duty to find room for their children. He asserted that it was not fear of death that had led the Six Nations to seek peace, and that if "these difficulties are not removed, the conse-quences will be bad" (Campisi and Starna 1995, 478). Cornplanter stated that they had been informed that Big Tree had been killed by the American Army while on a friendly visit. He blamed the death of "one of our Nephews of the Delaware Nation" on the Pennsyl-vanians advancing to establish Presqu'Isle (Cruikshank 1923–31, 2:272–73). He asked Chapin and William Johnston, an interpreter for the British Indian Department, to go to Presqu'Isle to remove those who, in the view of the Six Nations, trespassed on their lands. Criticized for having signed away Seneca lands over the previous decade, Cornplanter had finally moved from his conciliatory posi-tion to one of militant defiance toward the Americans.

Although he lacked power to remove trespassers, Chapin agreed to go to Presqu'Isle, and his party included four chiefs and ten war-riors in addition to the British interpreter and his servant. Corn-planter met with them as they were traveling along the Erie shore, at Cattaraugus Creek. He feared another of his men had been murdered by American settlers, but begged off accompanying the delegation to Presqu'Isle (Fenton 1998, 650–51). Chapin warned those settling in western Pennsylvania that they risked provoking a war with the Seneca and the other Six Nations; more important, he wrote to his superior, Secretary Knox, urging the negotiation of a new treaty with the Six Nations.

The federal government had already embarked on a military campaign against the Ohio Indians. President Washington and Secretary Knox did not want to do anything that might draw the Seneca into the conflict. They were able to persuade Pennsylvania Governor Thomas Mifflin to rein in Captain Ebenezer Denny and his Pennsylvania militia, who had been advancing to occupy Presqu'Isle. The militia remained for the summer at Fort Le Boeuf (present-day Waterford, Pennsylvania; Kent 1974, 225–26).

Israel Chapin returned from Le Boeuf to Buffalo, where he met with Cornplanter and others in council on 4 July. The message Chapin brought back was an assertion of Pennsylvania's view of land transactions since the end of the Revolutionary War. Cornplanter replied that "the greater part they told us is not true." He went on to say: "There is but one word that was said at Le Boeuf that makes me glad, which was that they had given me land, but to compleat my wishes, I desire that the whole Six Nations might have land also" (Jennings et al. 1984, reel 43: 1794 4 July).

Chapin's actions and advice did not go unnoticed. On 25 July 1794, Secretary Knox wrote to his Indian superintendent praising him for having "endeavored to the utmost of your power to avert the storm" and informing him that he approved of Chapin's proposal for a council to settle outstanding issues between the Six Nations and the United States. Knox desired that the two sides meet at Canandaigua in September and indicated that Postmaster General Timothy Pickering would serve as commissioner to negotiate an agreement. To get the preliminaries started, Knox sent Chapin fifteen hundred dollars and five thousand wampum beads (Jennings et al. 1984, reel 43: 1794 25 July).

Timothy Pickering

Knox assigned the task of negotiating with the Six Nations to Timothy Pickering, who had served in the Continental Army as adjutant general and quartermaster general during the Revolution. In Washington's administration, he served as postmaster general and later succeeded Knox as secretary of war. While postmaster general, he was often sent to negotiate with the Indians of the Six Nations, many of whom he seems to have admired and liked. Indeed, he wrote that anyone dealing with them "must want sensibility, if he did not sympathize with them, on their recital of the injuries they have experienced from white men" (quoted in Densmore 1999, 33). When Knox changed the agenda of a council in 1792 from the economic goals that Pickering had assured the Indians was its purpose, Pickering was livid. He complained to President Washington, "Indians have been so often deceived by white people that *White Man* is, among them, but another name for *Liar*." He did not want to be placed in that category (Campisi and Starna 1995, 474). "Pickering was willing to negotiate with the Indians using the traditional forms of Indian diplomacy. Red Jacket, at Tioga Point in November 1790, and again at Painted Post in July 1791, was his teacher" (Densmore 1999, 35).[1]

Whereas the Indians consistently urged that treaties be negotiated at Buffalo, the Americans just as consistently demanded that locales be found that were farther removed from the influence of the British posts of Fort Niagara and Fort Erie. Because both supplies to feed those attending the council and gifts to pay those signing had to be transported to the treaty site, locations closer to their centers of population were far less troublesome and expensive for the Americans. Pickering proposed to meet in the autumn of 1794 at the old Seneca village of Canandaigua, now a center of

1. Although Cornplanter did not attend the council at Painted Post with Pickering, he and New Arrow, along with six other Cattaraugus and Allegany Seneca chiefs, signed a letter addressed to Pickering and the chiefs of the Five Nations at that meeting (see Congdon 1967, 47–49).

trade on the border between Indian and American settlements. The experienced Indian superintendent Israel Chapin also lived in Canandaigua.

John Adlum's Survey and Negotiations at Burnt House

It was not just the lands at Presqu'Isle that were attractive to the Pennsylvanians. The experienced Pennsylvania surveyor John Adlum was employed to survey lands near the upper Allegheny in the vicinity of Cornplanter's village, Burnt House. Traveling upriver from Pittsburgh, he had reached Fort Franklin in late July. Earlier surveys had led him to know well many of the Senecas in the region, and he knew some of the hunting party of twenty men who had been summoned to return to their home villages. Adlum joined their fleet of canoes traveling up river to Burnt House. The Seneca chief Halftown served as "commodore" (Adlum's term) of the seven canoes carrying Adlum and some forty men, women, and children (Kent and Deardorff 1960, 294–96).

Adlum's arrival provided Cornplanter and Halftown the opportunity to put on a show. Cornplanter had assembled all the males from Burnt House and the second Seneca town (the late New Arrow's village) nine miles up river. Adlum notes that "they were formed in a single line the men about six feet apart and dressed in all their finery and painted as if for war" (Kent and Deardorff 1960, 301). Adlum states they marked the left of their line (the upriver end) with "a colours," although he does not describe the flag in any detail. Adlum was told to stand in the first canoe while the remaining canoes followed in pairs. On Cornplanter's command, the line of warriors fired a salute to the approaching flotilla, and Adlum returned the compliment by firing the two pistols he carried in his belt, while Halftown's men fired their muskets. The smoke and the stench of gunpowder must have been impressive indeed. Adlum was met by the prominent men in the community, who shook his hand (they knew him well from his earlier surveying of the Pennsylvania–New York line and the western boundary of the Phelps and

Gorham purchase) and took him to the Council House.[2] There he was given a seat, with Cornplanter on his right and Black Chief on his left.

Adlum was to do more than survey lands that had been purchased from the Seneca. He carried a letter from Secretary Knox inviting Cornplanter and his following to meet at Canandaigua with Postmaster General Pickering in the fall, a letter from Governor Mifflin inviting the chiefs to Philadelphia in the winter, and credentials from Pennsylvania indicating his duties to hear their grievances (Kent and Deardorff 1960, 302).

Cornplanter brought out a calumet, which the Seneca had adopted from their neighbors to the west and south (see Fenton 1953), lit it, and, after taking a few puffs, passed it to Aldum who did the same and passed it to his left, the pipe going clockwise around the house.[3] Cornplanter rose and welcomed Adlum, who rose in turn and presented Cornplanter with Knox's letter. Cornplanter asked Aldum to read it. When the initial paragraph was interpreted, it was greeted "with an univer[sal] roar, *vulgarly called farting*" from

2. At the time of contact with Europeans, the Iroquoians resided in large, multifamily bark houses known as "longhouses." The chief's longhouse was used for religious and political functions and was larger than the number of its residents strictly required. By the time of the American Revolution, however, the residence pattern had changed, and nuclear families or minimally extended families lived in much smaller houses, usually log cabins, although sometimes also bark or wood frame houses. Because there was still need for a structure in which the community could hold religious and political events, each village had a large, rectangular building with two doors and benches around the walls, which was known as the "Council House" or the "Longhouse."

3. Fenton (1998, 653) says the ceremonial pipe went counterclockwise around the circle, which is what one would expect among the Iroquois where the living perform counterclockwise, whereas the dead perform rituals and dance clockwise. However, Adlum in his memoir clearly says the pipe was passed to the left, or clockwise. In the text here, I follow Adlum's memory, although I feel that Fenton's deep knowledge of Iroquois culture correctly led him to reject Adlum's assertion.

the young men and boys seated on the beams of the crowded Council House. The women were upset by this action of their brothers and sons, but Adlum responded with wit doubtlessly appreciated by the Seneca audience. He said the young men must have expended all their good powder and ball in firing their salute upon his arrival and that this more recent salute indicated "that their ammunition must be very bad and fired out of very dirty guns" (Kent and Deardorff 1960, 304–5). Adlum gave the young men half a keg of powder so they might amuse themselves while he conferred with the chiefs. Now free to speak without interruption, he went on to present the chiefs with a map indicating the region in which he wished to conduct his survey. Following their usual practice, the Seneca response was that they would consider the matter and reply in the morning.

The next morning, after some preliminary sparring about the roles of the British, the Americans, and the participants in the so-called Whiskey Rebellion, the Seneca chiefs took up the issue foremost on their minds—whether lands ceded at Fort Stanwix, in the treaty where Cornplanter had played a leading role, might revert in the eyes of the United States to Seneca hands. In his reply, Adlum blustered about the might of the United States and the inconstancy of British support. Moreover, he alluded to his own long friendly dealings with the Senecas on the Allegheny, and his observation of their increasing prosperity as they pursued their lives in peace. Adlum later wrote "that they must not suppose that I had any idea of intimidating them, . . . I knew there was not one man present who would shrink from death." However successful they might be in war at the outset, he argued, in the end, war would be disastrous for the Seneca Nation. For support, he put particular reliance on the women, especially the Wolf Clan matron identified by Donald Kent and Merle Deardorff as Guyasuta's sister and also the wife of the Black Chief, who Adlum states was a daughter of Sir William Johnson. As he left the Council House, these two women and others shook Adlum's hand and indicated their desire for peace (Kent and Deardorff 1960, 305–12; Fenton 1998, 653–54).

The Senecas debated the rest of the day and the next morning until noon. At about three, a horn was blown to summon Adlum and the others to hear the decision reached. After the preliminary ceremonies involving prayers and tobacco, Cornplanter rose to reply to Adlum's speech of the previous day. He recalled the negotiations at Fort Stanwix in which the Americans had asserted the King had given the thirteen fires (the United States) possession of the lands of the Indians. Since the King had not bought the land, Cornplanter reasoned, he must have stolen it, and the Iroquois had been taught by the missionary Samuel Kirkland that the one who accepts stolen property is as bad as the one who steals it. Because of the power of the Americans, though, the Indians had yielded vast lands at Fort Stanwix. Now all they asked for was a small portion of the lands back. Adlum's map was laid out and an arrow was placed on it, marking a line from present-day Warren, Pennsylvania, to Meadville on French Creek. Cornplanter said the Indians demanded lands north of that line, and informed Adlum he was free to survey lands south of the line. Cornplanter closed with an allusion to the two great defeats American forces had suffered in Ohio (Kent and Deardorff 1960, 313–16).

Adlum replied by minimizing the defeats and by contrasting General Saint Clair's army with the current force under General Wayne. He pointed out the extra cost he would incur if he failed to complete his assigned survey and had to return next year. He indicated his desire to have three chiefs and nine warriors protect him and his men. These would be paid with "a suitable present of Amunition &c. And to the Woemen I would give a present of flour, clothing and blankets &c." He asked for eighty days to complete the survey. He then left the Seneca chiefs to their deliberations (Kent and Deardorff 1960, 316–19).

When he was called back, he was told he could have the men he asked for but must complete his work in forty days. Halftown declined to accompany Adlum on the survey, but both Sken-de-sho-wa (Swimming Fish) and Tiawanias (Broken Twig) were willing, as was an old friend of Adlum's, whose name he writes as

"Co,ne-wan-yen-dau." Adlum asked for more time and disingenuously suggested that his surveys of lands over which the Seneca were trying to reassert a claim would have no impact upon that claim. The Seneca chiefs agreed he could survey lands south of a line running directly westward from Cornplanter's village (Burnt House) to French Creek, that is, some fifty thousand acres more than if the line had run from Warren to Meadville (Kent and Deardorff 1960, 320–22).

Adlum and his party returned to Fort Franklin on 5 August. He made two more trips to Cornplanter's village that year. On 17 August, Cornplanter invited Adlum to accompany him to Buffalo Creek, where he was to receive the American reply to Seneca demands for the return of lands. Arriving at Burnt House on 23 August, Adlum obtained permission to survey lands anywhere within Pennsylvania for an additional twenty days and returned to Fort Franklin on 31 August. He went again to Burnt House, possibly in mid-September, to discuss the presence of Timothy Pickering at Canandaigua. Although Adlum may have confounded these two journeys when he later set down his memoirs, his writing nonetheless reveals the divisions within Cornplanter's following with respect to policy toward the Americans (Kent and Deardorff 1960, 437–38).

Adlum reports finding Cornplanter, not at Burnt House, but rather at an upper town. The day after Adlum arrived, Cornplanter's Senecas welcomed a group of nineteen warriors from the Six Nations in Canada with a noisy salute. The warriors were led by Duquania, described by Adlum as "a very muscular man." Joseph Brant had sent the men to Cornplanter to keep watch on the Americans. Duquania reported that they had been informed by Alexander McKee of the British Indian Department that war between Britain and the United States was likely (Kent and Deardorff 1960, 444–45).

Desiring to discover the number of warriors who might follow Cornplanter to war, Adlum bought a hog and invited all the men to a feast. He asked that someone notch a stick with one notch for each man coming to his feast. Thus he determined there were approximately 170 warriors in the two towns, plus the 19 men from Canada under Duquania. While the food for Adlum's feast was cooking, the Seneca men danced the Eagle Dance (see Fenton 1953) and the War Dance, striking the war post and reciting past deeds. At the end of the dancing, Cornplanter struck the war post and gave a lengthy speech detailing his people's dealings with Adlum. He assured the surveyor that no harm would be done to him while he was in their towns, but warned him that if the Americans did not return their lands, war would follow. Cornplanter presented him with a pair of moccasins "handsomely ornamented with porcupine quills of various colours." Adlum then took the chief's tomahawk, struck the war post, and declared war would bring destruction to the Indians. This concluded the feast (Kent and Deardorff 1960, 447–53).

When Adlum and the others were summoned to the Council House by the sounding of a horn the next morning, he found that a number of young men had assembled "all painted, and clothed with all the insignia of war." These were Duquania and his eighteen men and another thirty-seven led by Cornplanter's son-in-law, Captain Crow, and Cornplanter's nephew, Governor Blacksnake. The young men were being sent toward the American Army, to hunt peacefully but to be ready to fall upon the Americans if Cornplanter sent them word of the outbreak of war. In the meantime, Cornplanter and others, including the lineage matrons, were going to Buffalo Creek, where policy toward the Americans would be decided by the "assembled chiefs, warriors, and the great Woemen." Cornplanter then turned to a runner who was to carry a message ahead of them to Buffalo, saying that they should meet with Pickering only if he would be returning lands to them and that they should only meet with Pickering in Buffalo (Kent and Deardorff 1960, 454–57).

Addressing the group, Adlum again stated that Pickering would not come to Buffalo, and that a war might lead to all Indians being driven west of the Great Lakes. When he asked them not to kill women and children if they went to war, "every man present, *simuntaneously* rose on his feet, and fixed their eyes on me with a mixture of Sterness & resentment" (Kent and Deardorff 1960, 458). Cornplanter asked Adlum whether an insult was intended, and Adlum replied in the negative. Cornplanter then launched into a long speech on Indian-white relations, arguing that books written by whites charged Indians with crimes they did not commit and ignored atrocities committed by whites. "Does your books tell you of indians legs being skin[n]ed and tanned? Does your books tell you of parts of indians being skinned, and those skins being dressed and made razor strops of? I know that all these things were done by the whites and I heard them boast of it" (Kent and Deardorff 1960, 459). Adlum left to return to Fort Franklin the next day.

The Council at Buffalo

John Deckhart was a nephew of Guyasuta, thus perhaps also a parallel cousin of Cornplanter. His mother was known to Adlum as "Mrs. Chit-ti-aw-dunk," a lineage matron of the Wolf Clan. Deckhart was going to Buffalo to be installed as a chief; Adlum recruited him as an "observer" (although "spy" would perhaps be a better term). Deckhart was given a horse, saddle, and bridle as well as a new suit of clothes including a hat; with him, Adlum sent William Saltsman, a white who had lived among the Indians as a captive during the Revolution. When the two arrived at Buffalo, the council was into its second or third day of deliberations. The women had decided against war, and Iroquois custom required the approval of the women to initiate hostilities. Cornplanter made a vigorous speech urging that this custom be abandoned, and warned the council chiefs that, if they journeyed to see Pickering, they would end up accepting the terms dictated by him. Deckhart's mother, Mrs. Chitty-aw-dunk, spoke in reply, stating the Creator had given the women this power to prevent foolish wars, and if the warriors followed Cornplanter to war without the approval of the women, the Creator would punish them. But, as she spoke, the council heard the three whoops that announced the approach of a messenger bearing news, and adjourned to give him time to prepare his speech.

The council chiefs received a detailed account of the defeat of the Ohio Indians by General Wayne at Fallen Timbers. But the more significance news concerned the behavior of the British military. The battle took place near Fort Miami, the post Britain had established at the Maumee Rapids. As the Indians were retreating before Wayne's troops, some thought they would find shelter within the British fort. Instead, the fort's commander locked the gates, and two Indians who had sought and were denied refuge were cut down by Wayne's cavalry. By the next morning, several Indians who had participated in the battle arrived in Buffalo and confirmed the messenger's report. It was clear that British support for Indian hostilities against the Americans was unreliable. The decision was made to go to Canandaigua and meet with the American commissioner Timothy Pickering (Kent and Deardorff 1960, 465–67). William Fenton has interpreted these events as a major defeat for Cornplanter: "The matrons had taken the measure of the most famous war chief of the Senecas. He never recovered from this humiliation" (Fenton 1998, 659).

The Canandaigua Treaty

Cornplanter returned to the Allegheny to gather more of his followers to attend the treaty session with Timothy Pickering at Canandaigua, a Seneca village burned by Sullivan's forces in 1779 (Cook 1887, 58, 74, 160, 174) that was now an American town of forty houses. A visiting Quaker admired the houses "several of which are built in a style of elegance which we could hardly have expected in this remote country, that particularly which belongs to Thomas Morris . . . would make a . . . respectable appearance on the Banks of our Schuylkil" (Fenton 1965, 291–92). Robert Morris's son, Thomas, was looking after his father's interests, which favored the return of lands to the Seneca from the United States. Having purchased the Massachusetts preemption right to buy the lands of the Six Nations in New York, the elder Morris would have the sole right to purchase any portion of the Seneca lands for resale to other parties at great profit. Accompanied by Cornplanter's eldest son, Henry O'Bail, Pickering arrived in Canandaigua on 19 September, having taken nine days to travel from Philadelphia; he would lodge in the Morris house for the duration of the treaty negotiations. That same day, two runners arrived from Buffalo, calling on Pickering to come to the council fire established there. When Pickering refused, the runners produced strings of white wampum to attest to the willingness of the Six Nations to come to Canandaigua. Pickering sent the runners back to Buffalo with his invitation (Fenton 1998, 662–63).

Farmer's Brother arrived with some 472 Senecas on 14 October, whereupon he and his followers were greeted with salutes fired by warriors among the 150 Oneidas who had been at Canandaigua nearly three weeks, salutes they readily returned (Fenton 1965, 289, 301). Two days later, Cornplanter arrived with some 400 Senecas (Fenton 1965, 302). David Bacon, one of four Quaker observers attending the council to see that the Indians were treated fairly, observed Cornplanter's men salute the American commissioner with three musket volleys, but expressed pessimism about upcoming negotiations over a "Council Fire which I fear will not Burn So Bright as I could wish" (Jennings et al. 1984, reel 43: 1794 15 Sept.–21 Nov.).

The nearly fifteen hundred Indians attending the council built themselves a village of some 300 houses in one or two days. The Quaker observer David Bacon noted "it is Admirable to see how soon those People and Build a Town So as to live in Comfortably in there way." When the Quakers visited the camp on 30 October, they "found the women at worke at Several Branches of Business Some making Mogasons others Belts & Shifts &c Baskets & Cooking Venson Plenty" (Jennings et al. 1984, reel 43: 1794 15 Sept.–21 Nov.). Another Quaker also marveled at this abundance of venison. He reported that at least one hundred deer had been killed by Indian hunters within a radius of ten miles from the camp (Fenton 1965, 317). In Cornplanter's camp, the Quakers encountered a woman whose age they estimated as at least one hundred, named Graneywagus, who had walked from her home a hundred miles distant to attend the council (Jennings et al. 1984, reel 43: 1794 15 Sept.–21 Nov.).

On 17 October, Cornplanter, Farmer's Brother, Red Jacket, Little Beard, and others came for a private meeting with the Quaker delegates, who were concerned about a tract of land in Virginia that had been settled by Quakers without compensation to the aboriginal owners. The chiefs informed the Quakers that the lands in question were part of the hunting territory of the Susquehannocks, and Cornplanter pointed to several who were descendants of that now-dispersed nation (Fenton 1965, 302–3; 1998, 671; Savery 2000, 269).

The first day of the council was taken up by the Condolence Ritual of the Iroquois Confederacy, as the two sides installed chiefs in place of those who had recently died. Then, on 20 October, Pickering rose to take the hatchet from the head of a slain nephew of the Six Nations, a Delaware murdered by an American settler during the past summer. Pickering presented the council with fifteen strings of black wampum to collect the man's bones and bury them where they would not disturb the negotiations (Fenton 1965, 303). The path of peace between the United States and the Six Nations was to be kept open by the American government "as long as the sun shone," a phrase the Seneca still recall (Fenton 1998, 672). To accompany his speech, Pickering presented strings of wampum worth about one hundred dollars (Savery 2000, 270). Farmer's Brother informed Pickering that the Six Nations would reply the next day.

Fish Carrier, the Cayuga chief, spoke for the Six Nations when the council met again, accepting Pickering's message of condolence for the death of the Delaware. Indicating his willingness to listen to their grievances, Pickering introduced the Quakers (Fenton 1998, 673), at which point the session was interrupted by the sudden appearance of Jemima Wilkinson, "dress'd in a compleat Clergyman's Surplice of black Silk." Wilkinson had founded her "New Jerusalem" some twenty miles from Canandaigua, claiming "it was the Lord who spoke by her" and that "she thought it her duty not to be a Man pleaser, therefore was she persecuted." Wilkinson and three of her followers fell to their knees for a long prayer. She then rose and preached to the council until night fell, both prayer and sermon being interpreted to the Indians present (Fenton 1965, 293–95, 304–5, 337).

Pickering spent the next two days, 22 and 23 October, negotiating with some of the chiefs in private councils, which he felt was more effective than discourse in public council. On the first day, both Cornplanter and Red Jacket spoke, recounting how the Indians had allowed the whites to settle on lands and how they had seen the whites greatly expand in numbers. They complained about the behavior of the American commissioners at the Fort Stanwix negotiations after the recent war and asked that land surrendered there be returned. The journals of the Quakers, who were present on the second day, provide us with an indication of issues discussed. The first issue was the death of an elderly Oneida. It was concluded that this death would not, as was customary, lead to a pause in the council's deliberations. Then three Seneca matrons approached Pickering and asked whether they, too, might speak, a white woman having addressed the council two days earlier. Pickering said he regretted the intrusion of the ill-informed white woman, but that he would hear what the Seneca women had to say. Red Jacket spoke for them, observing "they had understood that the White Woman had told the Indians to repent & turn from their evil Deeds & they now had to say the same to the White people to repent & turn from our evil Deeds." Their major concern, though, was that they "found themselves much distressed by being hemmed in," that they supported the call by the men for the return of lands ceded at Fort Stanwix. Pickering summarized the addresses of the previous day and admitted the haughty treatment given the Six Nations at Fort Stanwix was unjustified. He asked how much land the Six Nations claimed to the west. Cornplanter replied that, after a war with the "Lake Indians," it was agreed that Seneca hunting territory extended to a line drawn from Lake Erie to the point where the Muskingum River joins the Ohio. Pickering noted that the United

States had already purchased much of this land from the Wyandot and the Delaware and lamented the difficulties caused by several nations claiming the same territory. The private council adjourned, but the death of a second elderly Oneida meant the next day was spent conducting the funeral service for the two (Fenton 1965, 305–8, 323).

When the public council resumed on 25 October, it spent that day and the next discussing the arrival of William Johnston (or, as his surname is often spelled, "Johnson"), an interpreter in the British Indian service at Fort Niagara. Cornplanter expressed amazement that Pickering would not let Johnston attend the council now that Britain and the United States were at peace. Surely, the Americans and the British could sit at the same council fire. Pickering, however, was under strict instructions not to negotiate if British agents were present; what is more, he was still smarting from the treatment he and his fellow commissioners had received the previous year as they passed through British posts in an attempt to deal with the Ohio Indians. He ordered Johnston back to Niagara, threatening to cover the council fire if the British officer remained. Cornplanter sent a message with him to Joseph Brant. After welcoming Brant's safe arrival at Niagara, Cornplanter assured his "Elder Brother" (like Cornplanter, Brant was born into the Wolf Clan) that the Six Nations delegation would not betray earlier agreements with the "Lake Indians." Because Johnston had been forced to listen to a litany of complaints about British actions—"difficulties"—when Pickering denied him a place at the council fire, Cornplanter explained that "Mr. Johnston will be able to inform you what these difficulties are, and that his stomach was overcharged with them." Cornplanter further assured Brant he would notify him when the council ended and all the chiefs returned to Buffalo Creek (Cruikshank 1923–31, 3:154). Israel Chapin, who had attended the public council meetings, also sent a letter with Johnston to Brant, thanking the Mohawk chief for extending condolences upon the death of Chapin's wife and noting that the expulsion of the British interpreter from the negotiations at Canandaigua was "not for any unfavorable regard to the Gentleman" (Jennings et al. 1984, reel 43: 1794 26 Oct).

At the conclusion of five hours of tense council negotiations, Pickering hosted a candlelit dinner for fifteen chiefs (including Cornplanter) and the Quakers. The chiefs manifested a "high turn for wit and humor," as interpreted to the gathering by Horatio Jones, with Red Jacket exhibiting "the most conspicuous talent that way" (Savery 2000, 274).

Because the Americans believed that it was "the Cornplanter on whom seems to rest the principal weight of the Business" of the Seneca, Timothy Pickering invited the Seneca Chief Warrior to Thomas Morris's house for a private conference on 27 October, there being no public council that day. Pickering is reported to have told Cornplanter the details of the American offer to presented in public council the following day (Fenton 1965, 312).

Both Pickering and the Quakers overestimated Cornplanter's political power, however (see Mohawk 2000, 59). When the public council reconvened on 28 October, several chiefs spoke out, expressing their anger at the private meeting between Cornplanter and Pickering.[4] The chastised Cornplanter pouted, refusing to attend the council that day and threatening to leave the proceedings. Pickering publicly stated he needed to meet with Cornplanter because of his prominent role and understanding to the negotiations at Fort Stanwix and Fort Harmar. Pickering then announced his proposal to remove the rust from the chain that bound the Six Nations to the Fifteen Fires—the number of states in the United States at that time (Fenton 1965, 313).

Pickering's principal offer was to return to the Six Nations lands within the bounds of New York, from Buffalo Creek westward to the Erie Triangle. He refused, however, to return any lands in Pennsylvania or a four-mile-wide strip of land in New York running

4. While resident on the Allegany Reservation some thirty years ago, I found the members of the Seneca Nation convinced that their political leaders met in secret and concluded deals that were advantageous to the leadership rather than the nation as a whole.

along the eastern side of the Niagara River between Lake Ontario and Lake Erie. He promised to increase the annual payment to the Six Nations from $1,500 to $4,500, declaring he had $10,000 worth of goods to distribute at the conclusion of the treaty. The council adjourned so that the Indians could consider the offer (Jennings et al. 1984, reel 43: 1794 15 Sept.–21 Nov.; Fenton 1965, 314–16).

When the council fire was rekindled on Sunday, 2 November, Pickering was told that, because the Indians needed to use the land to exploit their fishery in Lake Erie, ceding the four-mile-wide Niagara corridor was not acceptable, even though it had been agreed to long ago with Sir William Johnson. After discussing the matter further, Red Jacket announced in council that the Indians would be willing to allow a road parallel to the Niagara river rather than ceding the four-mile-wide strip. This left only minor details to be settled (Jennings et al. 1984, reel 43: 15 Sept.–21 Nov.).

Cornplanter was still smarting from the criticism that came down on his head after his private meetings with Pickering. On Sunday, 9 November, he spoke in council saying that in the past the United States had deceived the warriors and that now the Americans might be deceiving the civil chiefs. Therefore, he concluded, the warriors would not sign this treaty, but would abide by it as long as the chiefs did (Savery 2000, 288). Pickering said that this was not acceptable and demanded the treaty be signed by both chiefs and warriors or there would be no agreement at all. Only if the warriors signed the treaty would the Chain of Friendship remain bright between the Six Nations and the United States. Faced with this ultimatum, Cornplanter was among those who signed the Canandaigua Treaty, on 11 November 1794 (Jennings et al. 1984, reel 43: 15 Sept.–21 Nov.).

The treaty preserved American ownership of the four-mile-wide strip from Lake Ontario to Fort Schlosser, which had long before been ceded in a treaty negotiated by Sir William Johnson after the war usually known as "Pontiac's Rebellion"; it allowed the Americans to build a road from the southern end of those lands to

Buffalo Creek, but recognized the remainder of lands within New York west of the lands purchased by Oliver Phelps as the property of the Seneca Nation. "Now, the United States acknowledge all the land within the aforementioned boundaries, to be the property of the Seneka nation; and the United States will never claim the same, nor disturb the Seneka nation, nor any of the Six Nations, or [any] of their Indian friends residing thereon and united with them, in the free use and enjoyment thereof: but it shall remain theirs, until they choose to sell the same to the people of the United States, who have the right of purchase" (Kappler 1904–41, 2:35).[5]

The order of the twenty-seven Seneca signatories is significant, reflecting hereditary ranking and political power. First came two chiefs from Buffalo Creek, Farmer's Brother of the Heron Clan and Red Jacket of the Wolf Clan (the pairing of chiefs from opposite moieties is a ruling principle of Seneca political organization—see Abler 2004).[6] They were followed by confederacy chiefs Handsome Lake, who held a Turtle Clan title, and Sha?takeonye:s of the Snipe Clan. Four Senecas having hereditary positions with a seat at the national council fire, but not on the Iroquois Confederacy Council, signed next. After them came the two hereditary war chiefs of the Confederacy—Sonehso:wa:? and Then:won:ya?s (Awlbreaker or Chainbreaker), as well as Big Kettle, who was a hereditary war chief of the Seneca. Last to sign in this first column was Cornplanter, whose mark Pickering designated as that of "Active Head Warrior," a status Fenton feels was achieved rather than hereditary. Fenton sees Cornplanter paired with another signatory, Little Billy (also known as "Green Grasshopper"). Sometime after 1794, Cornplanter's elder half brother and nephew would hold the confederacy titles of those who signed above him on the Canandaigua treaty,

5. The United States broke the first Canandaigua treaty in the 1950s when it seized Seneca Nation lands on the Allegany Reservation for the Allegheny River Reservoir (see Bilharz 1998).

6. The Seneca clans were grouped into two moieties. One consisted of the Wolf, Bear, Turtle, and Beaver clans. The second consisted of the Deer, Snipe, Hawk, and Heron clans.

Handsome Lake and Then:won:ya?s (see A. Wallace 1970, 358; Abler 1989, 20–21). Signing as witness "Henry Abeele" was Cornplanter's eldest son, Henry O'Bail, who had learned to read and write in school in Philadelphia[7]

Many read the Canandaigua treaty proceedings as a victory for Pickering and Red Jacket and a defeat for Cornplanter. Christopher Densmore characterizes the treaty as "the joint product of Pickering and Red Jacket" (Densmore 1999, 44). Fenton observes that the treaty talks left Cornplanter "at a point where the earth was narrow" and made Red Jacket the Seneca Nation's "dominant figure" (Fenton 1998, 699, 704). The Americans certainly no longer viewed the Chief Warrior as a champion of their interests and policy among the Seneca. Pickering promised Knox that, on his return to Philadelphia, he would reveal "the true character of that Chief" (Fenton 1998, 706). That said, Cornplanter's reputation appears not to have been as tarnished as these comments might suggest: he was given the written copy of the treaty to bring back to Buffalo Creek (Cruikshank 1923–31, 3:217–18). The proceedings clearly seem to have fed the rising influence of Red Jacket both in his home community of Buffalo Creek and among the Seneca. Pickering was especially proud of the agreement reached, writing to Joseph Brant on 20 November that a chief characterized the agreement as "a great light to us" and that he himself felt it signaled "a new era" in American Indian affairs (Jennings et al. 1984, reel 43: 1794 20 Nov). His task was not completed with the signing of the Canandaigua

7. William N. Fenton has spent a half century considering the Iroquois Condolence Ritual with its ordered list of confederacy chiefs, which opened councils. His discussion (Fenton 1998, 701–3) of the order in which the Iroquois signed the Canandaigua treaty and of Pickering's notes on them is particularly insightful. The 59 Indian signatories to the treaty are grouped in five columns. For his part, Charles Kappler (1904–41, 2:37) ignores the fact that these columns should be read from right to left, not from left to right, as he does in his printed version of the treaty, beginning with the first name in the leftmost column. Hence the thirteen most important Seneca signatories appear at the end of Kappler's listing.

treaty of 11 November 1794; he was obliged to negotiate a second treaty, with the Oneida, Tuscarora, and Stockbridge, signed 2 December 1794, before he could return home. Within two weeks of his return to Philadelphia, he received his reward—replacing Knox as secretary of war in Washington's cabinet (Phillips 1966, 200; Clarfield 1980, 152).

The Sale of Seneca Lands at Big Tree

As noted above, Robert Morris had come to hold the Massachusetts preemption right to the Seneca lands. Phelps and Gorham had anticipated paying Massachusetts for the preemption right in weakened Massachusetts dollars; when, however, those dollars rose in value, Phelps and Gorham returned to Massachusetts the preemption right to lands to the west of those they had purchased in 1788 at Buffalo Creek. Morris paid a large sum of money—variously reported as $225,000 (currency unspecified) and 100,000 pounds in Massachusetts currency—in a complicated transaction to acquire the Massachusetts preemption right to New York lands west of the Phelps and Gorham purchase (Abler and Tooker 1978, 508–9; Wilkinson 1953, 258; Sumner 1891, 2:256–58).

Robert Morris has been characterized as "the country's foremost speculator in lands during the 1790's" and that he "had pyramided, on credit and borrowed funds, his landed property into millions of acres" (Wilkinson 1953, 258). Although a review of the complexities of Morris's dealings, even limited to lands in New York State, is beyond the scope of this study (see Sumner 1891, 2:251–61), in 1792, Morris sold almost the entirety of the lands west of the Phelps and Gorham purchase to a Dutch consortium known as the "Holland Land Company," with Morris bearing the responsibility of extinguishing the Seneca titles to those lands. Morris did not include in this sale a strip of lands approximately twelve miles wide from the Pennsylvania border to Lake Ontario amounting to some 500,000 acres and known as the "Morris Reserve." To profit from these transactions, Morris had to extinguish the title in these lands that the Canandaigua treaty of 1794 guaranteed to the Seneca Nation.

From his base at Canandaigua, Robert's son, Thomas, took up the task of pursuing his father's interests. The elder Morris asked his son to discreetly encourage the Seneca leadership to look favorably upon the sale of lands. So that he might discuss the issue with them directly, he had his son to ask Cornplanter, Red Jacket, and Farmer's Brother to Philadelphia to meet with him. Thomas Morris gave Cornplanter $140 in travel money in February 1797 but, for reasons unknown, could not persuade or arrange for Red Jacket and Farmer's Brother to make the journey (Wilkinson 1953, 261–62).

Captain Israel Chapin, who had replaced his deceased father as Indian superintendent to the Six Nations, wrote Secretary of War James McHenry that Cornplanter and Joseph Brant left Canandaigua for Philadelphia on the morning of 6 February 1797. Brant was seeking an annuity for those of the Six Nations who had left their homes in New York State to settle on the Grand River in Upper Canada. Brant and Captain John Deserontyon on behalf of the Mohawk eventually signed a treaty on 29 March 1797 at Albany, with Isaac Smith representing the United States and three commissioners representing New York. The treaty relinquished Mohawk claims to lands in New York for $1,000 plus $600 to pay the expenses of Brant and Deserontyon. Cornplanter also signed the treaty as a witness (Kappler 1904–41, 2:50–51).

Chapin declined to comment on why Cornplanter was traveling to Philadelphia, but cautioned his superior that "it may not be improper to acquaint you that they have not gone forward by any direction [of] my own, but by an invitation of Mr T. Morris who lives in this country who has provided for the expenditures." According to Chapin, some Senecas had told him Cornplanter was to receive an indemnity to be paid to the family of one of his followers murdered near Venango (Franklin, Pennsylvania) two years earlier (Jennings et al. 1984, reel 44: 1797 6 Feb).

Robert Morris worked to convince Cornplanter of the wisdom

of a land sale, and reported in a letter to his son, dated 6 March 1797, that he had succeeded: Cornplanter was of the opinion that money from land sales should be invested to provide an annual income. This led Robert Morris to declare "before we part I hope to fix him my friend" (Wilkinson 1953, 262).

While in Philadelphia, Cornplanter also addressed President Washington, who was completing his second and final term in office. A fragment of the speech of 28 February 1797 survives. After indicating his pleasure in making "my last address to you as the great Chief of the fifteen fires," Cornplanter spoke of the decline in hunting success because of non-Indian settlement. he asked Washington, "if we should dispose of part of our Country and put our money with yours in that strong place, will it be safe? Will it yield to our children the same advantages after our heads are laid down as it will at present produces to us?" (Jennings et al. 1984, reel 44: 1797 28 Feb). Secretary McHenry told Cornplanter that, if the Seneca wished to part with a portion their lands, they should so inform the commanding officer at Fort Niagara (Jennings et al. 1984, reel 44: 1797 3 July).

Robert Morris could not leave Philadelphia to negotiate any land sale as "he was then a prisoner in his own house, 'The Hills' " having "to remain behind locked doors to escape the summonses sworn out by his angry creditors" (Wilkinson 1953, 265). On 1 August 1797, he wrote a letter granting power of attorney to his son, Thomas, and Charles Williamson to purchase the lands. He instructed them not "to starve the Cause or to be niggardly, at the same time it is natural to desire a consistent Oeconomy to be observed both as to the Expence of the Treaty and the price to be paid for the Lands." Even if they were able to purchase the entire tract, they were authorized to spend only $75,000, giving the Seneca an annual annuity in the neighborhood of $4,000.[8] In addition, per-

---

8. The values of state currencies fluctuated widely over this period, but it is noteworthy that Morris paid far more to Massachusetts for the preemption right to buy the land than he had expected and than he would finally pay to the Indians who actually owned the acreage being purchased.

sonal annuities of $20 to $60, totaling from $250 to $300, could be granted to influential chiefs. Such chiefs could also be promised a direct payment on the successful conclusion of the treaty, the elder Morris suggesting payment of "500 or 600, or if necessary 1,000 Dollars to the Chiefs" (Jennings et al. 1984, reel 44: 1797 1 Aug).

By 20 August, some 1,200 Senecas and others had gathered on the western boundary of the Phelps and Gorham purchase, at the village known as "Geneseo" or "Big Tree" (after the late Seneca chief who had made his home there), to hear of the offer for their lands from Robert Morris. The council was delayed by the late arrival of those representing the diverse interests in Indian lands and Indian affairs. As noted above, Thomas Morris and Charles Williamson represented the interests of Robert Morris, who held the preemption right to the lands. Representing the United States government was Colonel Jeremiah Wadsworth, appointed as a commissioner to oversee the conduct of the council. As superintendent for the Six Nations, Captain Israel Chapin was present and used the occasion to distribute the annuity goods due the Seneca. Observing the land transaction as commissioner from Massachusetts was Congressman and General William Shepard. A New York banker, William Bayard, looked after the interests of the Holland Land Company, which had already paid Robert Morris a substantial sum of money for the Seneca lands (Wilkinson 1953, 266).

Again in these treaty negotiations, the disagreement between the chiefs (sachems) and the warriors divided the Seneca. A brief discussion of English terms for Seneca political positions is in order here. Of Algonquian origin, "sachem" entered the English language in the early seventeenth century and soon came to mean "political leader among Native North Americans"[9] As used by those dealing

9. The *Oxford English Dictionary* notes that, as early as 1622, the term *sachem* appeared in print referring to a leader among the New England Algonquians (Simpson and Weiner 1989, 14:329–30). Lewis H. Morgan, however, in his classic 1851 Iroquois ethnography, muddied the issue by attempting to redefine *sachem* among the Iroquois by limiting it to individuals who held the fifty hereditary positions on the Iroquois Confederacy Council. Occasionally, writers since Morgan

with the Seneca in the late eighteenth and early nineteenth centuries, *sachem* appears to designate any of a group recognized as chiefs, who were central to decision making. A small number of these also held titles on the Iroquois Confederacy Council, but do not seem to have had any more influence on decisions than any other sachems, or chiefs. Occasionally, the general male population took part in decision making, when the council of chiefs faced a particularly contentious issue. The chiefs then would send to question to the warriors for their opinion. Similarly, the general female population, the "mothers of the nation," might be asked for an opinion on an issue. Both the warriors and the "mothers of the nation" also might independently express their views to the sachems if so inclined. It is clear that Cornplanter in the decades following the American Revolution was recognized as a Chief Warrior, which meant that he could speak for the warriors as distinct from the sachems, or chiefs. An underlying principle of Seneca political organization (and the Seneca here differ from the other members of the Iroquois Confederacy) is that political positions are to be filled in pairs by members of each moiety. Paired with Cornplanter in his position of Chief Warrior was Little Billy, also known as "Great Grasshopper" (Fenton 1998, 701–3).

The system was not without its intricacies, however, for Cornplanter and New Arrow were also seen to act as headmen of a geographical group of Senecas, those living along the Allegheny River. Thus Cornplanter is usually presented as both Chief Warrior and headman of the lower towns on the Allegheny River; New Arrow, as both sachem in the sense of the previous paragraph and headman of the upper towns on the Allegheny. It is not clear who replaced New Arrow upon his death sometime in 1793 or 1794.

Despite his position as Chief Warrior, Cornplanter played a public role even in the early days of negotiation at Big Tree, when affairs

---

have used *sachem* in this limited sense, leading to discussions and debate about such issues as to whether Red Jacket was "really" a "sachem" (see Densmore 1999, 7–8).

were dominated by the sachems or civil chiefs. When Thomas Morris arrived on the scene on 22 August, he apologized for the delay caused by the failure of the United States and Massachusetts commissioners to arrive. He promised to deal with the non-Indians who were attempting to disrupt the coming conference. It was Cornplanter who responded to Morris's message, indicating satisfaction on the part of the assembled Senecas (Jennings et al. 1984, reel 44: 1797 Aug.–Sept.).

Captain Israel Chapin took advantage of the interval to distribute the goods that were part of the annuity. On Sunday, 27 August, the Indians assembled to condole with Chapin on the death of his daughter.[10]

When the commissioners finally arrived and Morris had kindled the council fire on Monday afternoon, 28 August, it was Cornplanter who spoke for the Seneca, repeating the speech of invitation brought to the Seneca by Horatio Jones and Jasper Parrish.[11] As was customary, he returned the string of wampum that Jones and Parrish had brought with them to announce the date and place of a council. Morris then performed the Condolence Ritual necessary to open a conference. Both Commissioner Wadsworth and Commissioner Shepard addressed the assembled Senecas, emphasizing that, under the laws of the United States and Massachusetts, only Robert Morris had the right to make an offer to purchase their lands. Thomas Morris then read a speech prepared by his father: the Great Spirit (no mention was made of his creditors and their legal writs) had prevented him from appearing in person at the council. He praised the quality of the current leadership of the Seneca and suggested it would be better for these leaders to strike a

10. Unless another source is cited, the description of the events of the Treaty of Big Tree relies on the "Rough memoranda of the Treaty of Geneseo," the original in the O'Reilly Papers, The New-York Historical Society, available on microfilm in Jennings et al. 1984, reel 44: 1797 Aug.–Sept.

11. Both Jones and Parrish had been captured as boys and raised among the Seneca. Both frequently served as interpreters in issues involving the Seneca and the outside world (see Fenton 1998, 629; Harris 1903; Parrish 1903).

deal than to trust those who might succeed them. He implied that the President of the United States favored a treaty at this time and pointed to the presence of Commissioner Wadsworth at the council as proof of this. A string of wampum was laid on the table and the council fire covered for the day.

After the Senecas deliberated among themselves, Red Jacket presented the Seneca position to the reconvened council the following afternoon. He complained that Morris did not appear to have been candid with them but, rather, was holding something back. Morris expressed a willingness to lay everything before the council, but Red Jacket replied that, because the hour was late, the council fire should be covered and the matter taken up on the morrow.

Morris took the next day, 30 August, to lay his proposal before the chiefs and others. He argued that, because the game they hunted was disappearing from the lands he wished to purchase. the Seneca faced a poverty-stricken future. A greater income would come, he stated, if the lands were sold, the money invested in the Bank of the United States, and a yearly sum paid to the Seneca under the supervision of the President of the United States. He also promised that the Senecas could hunt and fish "forever" on the lands they sold. In the future, unwise chiefs might sell the lands in a way that was not in the general interest. He warned them that, if the lands were not sold now, his father would in future not be so generous in his offer, and would pay no more than Phelps did for the tract he purchased, but he did not specify the price his father was willing to pay.

The Senecas deliberated through the next day. On 1 September, a white man began selling whiskey, disrupting the proceedings until Farmer's Brother, on the advice of Thomas Morris, seized the barrel of spirits. Morris and Captain Chapin moved to prevent any further sales of alcohol to the Indians by whites in the vicinity.

On the afternoon of 2 September, the Indians were ready to reply. Farmer's Brother introduced Red Jacket, who stressed that owning their lands made the Seneca a significant people. Red

Jacket contrasted the Seneca's situation with that of the Oneida, who had sold their lands to New York and retained only small reservations.[12] Although the Seneca had been told that Morris was to offer a large sum of money, they had not been told how much, observed Red Jacket pointedly. In any case, they instructed Morris to keep his fists closed, for the Seneca had no intention of selling their lands.

Morris invited the "principal Sachims" to a private conference that evening. He told them that he could pay one hundred thousand dollars (twenty-five thousand dollars more than his father had suggested), which would yield an annuity of six thousand. The chiefs told him to make his offer in public council. This Morris did in a speech the following day. Red Jacket asked for the speech in writing.

Morris delivered a written version of the speech to the council on the afternoon of 4 September. Cornplanter spoke for the warriors, saying the chiefs had taken over the business of negotiations, although they had never addressed a proposal he had put forward some time ago at Buffalo Creek. Cornplanter announced his intentions of leaving the council for home the next day. Commissioner Wadsworth then rose and said that political divisions were a cause of difficulty among white people also, and he hoped the Seneca could unite. Farmer's Brother spoke for the chiefs. He thought it unseemly that the divisions among the Seneca had come out in public council. Cornplanter had proposed the trading of lands along Lake Ontario for lands near his village on the Pennsylvania border. The chiefs had been unable to answer Cornplanter because they did not know what Morris was going to propose. Farmer's Brother lectured Cornplanter that it was customary for the chiefs to reach a decision in council and then to present it to the warriors for approval. Wadsworth again addressed the council, stating he had no interest

12. Many of the Oneida land sales to New York were contrary to the Indian Nonintercourse Act of 1790, which required supervision and approval by the federal government of land acquisitions from Indians (see Locklear 1988).

in their lands, but was there on behalf of the President to assure that they were fairly dealt with. Nevertheless, being old and afflicted with gout, he desired them to unite and deal speedily with the matters of the council so that he might return home.

At some point during the negotiations—the manuscript notes of the treaty proceedings (Jennings et al. 1984, reel 44: 1797 Aug.–Sept.) are not clear about when—Young King appeared. Having inherited the title and position of Old Smoke, the famous leader of the eastern Senecas during the American Revolution, Young King had not participated in the first meetings of the council at Big Tree because he was distraught over the death of "his friend & Cousin." When he learned of the nature of the negotiations on the day after his friend's funeral, Young King is said to have spoken angrily about the prospect of selling Seneca lands, and several chiefs were ready to break off proceedings and follow him home. After two or three days of discussion, however, Morris and his friends were able to convince the reluctant chief to sell.

On 6 September, speaking as a Chief Warrior, Little Beard told the council that Seneca affairs should be handled by the chiefs in times of peace. Thus the fact that Cornplanter had sent him a wampum belt to enlist his aid was inappropriate. Little Beard returned the belt to Cornplanter.

Red Jacket then took center stage. The Senecas were willing to sell a piece of land six miles on a side, or 23,040 acres, and no more. Red Jacket said they wanted only one dollar an acre, but that Morris could easily sell the land at six dollars an acre. Red Jacket asked Morris for an answer the next day or, because Charles Williamson was also present for consultation, sooner. Morris rose and said there was no need for Williamson and him to consult on the matter. If Red Jacket had delivered the Senecas' final offer, it was not acceptable, so they might as well cover the council fire. "Red Jacket rose and in great passion said agreed let us cover the fire and furiously stretched his hand across the table let us shake hands and part friends and thus the business was considered as finally closed."

Thomas Morris seemed to have painted himself into a corner.

But the conflict between the peace chiefs and warriors that had been simmering among the Seneca since the close of the American Revolution presented him with a way out and a chance to revitalize his land deal. He would bypass the chiefs who had refused to sell him lands and directly approach the women of the Seneca Nation.

The next morning, 7 September, Morris sent the interpreters to gather "all the Chief Women" and bring them to Commissioner's Wadsworth's residence. There he told them that, though the sachems had covered the council fire, he was afraid the women were unaware of the offer that had been made to the sachems, and which would be of great benefit to themselves and their children. The annuity monies could be used to hire men to plow their fields and to buy clothing for their children. He suggested that the chiefs rejected this because they had continually been assured of payments when visiting seats of government on diplomatic missions. Although he would distribute the presents he had brought with him from Philadelphia, Morris told the women that the expenses of the council were such that he could not afford to give them the cattle as he had intended. He presented the women with a string of wampum, saying that "whenever hereafter they experienced the hardships of poverty to show it to their Chiefs and tell them with that Belt they had been offered Wealth which the Chiefs rejected." It is reported that the women "at once" announced they were in favor of the sale of their lands.

When the public council was reconvened that afternoon, the warriors took center stage to restore the good feeling that the exchange between Red Jacket and Morris had destroyed the previous day. Cornplanter rose first and said that the warriors desired "to smooth the business of yesterday" and introduced his cousin, that is, the Chief Warrior of the Bird Clan's moiety, whose position was paired with his own, Little Billy, also known as the "Great Grasshopper." Little Billy regretted that "too much warmth of expression was used by both parties yesterday" and he buried these comments. The warriors would take up the business that the chiefs had abandoned. Farmer's Brother then spoke on behalf of the chiefs, or sachems. He reported that when the nation was divided, the sachems by ancient custom could refer the matter to the warriors and head women. He expressed thanks that the conflict had been buried and that friendship prevailed. Both the United States and Massachusetts commissioners expressed satisfaction at this turn of events and wished for a speedy conclusion of business.

On 8 September, in inclement weather, both warriors and women conferred in small groups. A whiskey trader, Alexander Ewing, who attempted to tell the Indians they were being cheated in the negotiations was arrested and thrown in the jail in Canandaigua. This "gave alarm to intermeddlers."

When the council met again on 9 September, a Cayuga addressed the Senecas, speaking of the pain the split among the Seneca gave to the Tuscarora, Cayuga, and Oneida—the younger brothers' moiety of the Iroquois Confederacy. Little Billy then introduced Cornplanter, who later provided a written version of the speech he delivered.

Cornplanter noted that the sachems had covered the council fire but that Morris had asserted that it was not completely covered and that he had placed the business before the warriors and head women. He then chose to call attention to earlier promises made by the Americans. These included that "they would make our seats firm & permanent so that even if they are surrounded by white People, individuals should be undisturbed." Cornplanter had, he insisted, instructed his own people to look upon Washington as a father. Now he was sorry to learn that the United States had agreed to the sale of their lands, lands they had been told were for their children's children. On these lands lived not only the Seneca—"in every Town there is the bones of our ancestors which makes us very stingy of our lands"—but also other nations who had no longer had homes. In earlier negotiations, the sachems exhibited "pride & ambition," and Morris proved to be "proud & obstinate." In dealing with the warriors and the women, this pride had to be laid aside. If it was, the warriors were sure an agreement could be reached. Morris should consult his Bible to see whether it allowed him to impose or intrude on Indians.

Commissioner Wadsworth responded that the American government did recognize the lands as theirs and that the government would not take their lands from them. He assured the Seneca that he was there to see that no injustice would be perpetrated in the current negotiations.

For his part, Thomas Morris had hoped for a more explicit answer from the warriors and their women.[13] He conceded that nothing in the Bible approved of cheating Indians. Then, placing his hand upon the Bible, he declared his offer for their lands was "strictly honorable generous & calculated for your real benefit." The "generous" offer amounted to less than three cents an acre (Donaldson 1892, 27). Cornplanter promised a decision as soon as possible and asked whether the Senecas might borrow the large map of their country that Morris had brought to the council.

Illness prevented the U.S. commissioner from attending the council the following day, but he requested through the Massachusetts representative that the negotiations proceed. Little Billy introduced Cornplanter to speak to Morris's proposal.

Cornplanter suggested that the Great Spirit would be pleased that the Seneca Nation was not selling *all* the lands he had given them, but would be retaining reserves within the boundaries of those lands. The Seneca considered the price too low, but because they would be retaining lands they were willing to settle with Morris. Cornplanter anticipated that Morris would consider the lands proposed for Seneca use to be too large, but stated they needed the room to settle Indians who would in future be driven from their lands by whites. The Seneca were happy to sign, with the understanding that the lands they retained would be theirs forever. Mor-

13. Morris consistently uses a possessive pronoun when referring to Seneca women, as in "you & your women," whereas Cornplanter does not. I believe this may reflect that Cornplanter viewed the women as independent actors to a greater degree than did Morris.

ris replied that he needed to know the size of the reservations, but that because he had offered such a large sum for Seneca lands, the reservations should be small. Little Billy announced that each village should appoint representatives to set the boundaries for the lands to be reserved for their settlement.

The key to reaching an agreement appears to have been the private payments Morris made to political leaders among the Seneca. Even though Red Jacket had opposed the treaty as official spokesman for the Seneca chiefs, he was brought into Morris's camp with a cash payment of $600. Cornplanter was paid $300 cash, and an additional $1,000 was distributed to other individuals who agreed to favor the land sale. In addition, $24,000 was invested in United States government stock to provide personal annuities for key individuals. Cornplanter headed this list, with an annuity of $250; he insisted the stock be registered in his name (Wilkinson 1953, 274–75). Red Jacket, Farmer's Brother, Young King, and Little Billy received an annuity of $100 each; Pollard received an annuity of $50, and Little Billy's mother one of $10.

The next several days were spent in tense negotiations to determine the size of the reservations. Thomas Morris and his surveyor, Joseph Ellicott, met privately with delegations from each village. The delegation from Buffalo Creek, led by Red Jacket, and that from Cattaraugus demanded the most land. The Cattaraugus delegates demanded a reservation of over 1,000 square miles; in the end, they agreed to one of 42 square miles. The Buffalo Creek and Tonawanda delegations demanded over 1,400 square miles; together, they were reserved 200 square miles. When the boundaries of these two were established, Buffalo Creek (130 square miles) was the largest Seneca reservation, followed by Tonawanda (70 square miles). The other seven reservations established in the Treaty of Big Tree, signed 16 September 1797, were Allegany (42 square miles), Gardeau (28 square miles), Caneadea (16 square miles), Canawaugus (2 square miles), Big Tree (2 square miles), Little Beard's Town (2 square miles), and Squawky Hill (2 square miles). The last six reservations were all located on the Genesee River (Hill 1930, 351).

In addition, the Seneca reserved a strip of land one mile wide along the Niagara River, suggesting the importance of fishing in that river to the economy of the Seneca Nation (see Kappler 1904–41, 2:1028).

Not mentioned in the Treaty of Big Tree is the Oil Spring Reservation, one square mile in size, whose naturally upwelling petroleum, used for medicinal purposes, was much valued by the Seneca (A. Wallace 1970, 182). Cornplanter's half brother, Handsome Lake, noticed this omission and called it to the attention of Thomas Morris, who gave him a document asserting that Oil Spring was not part of the lands sold under the Treaty of Big Tree. The Seneca had to sue to confirm their ownership of this reservation, successfully doing so in 1856. Important in the suit was the testimony of Cornplanter's nephew, Governor Blacksnake, then over a century old. Blacksnake produced the original map of the Big Tree purchase, which included Oil Spring among the Seneca reservations (Donaldson 1892, 28).

The Tuscarora Reservation, within the bounds of the Holland Land Company purchase, also went unmentioned in the Treaty of Big Tree. After recognizing the grant of a square mile near Lewiston, New York, made to the Tuscarora by the Seneca in 1780, the company allowed the Tuscarora an additional two square miles. To these lands would be added 4,329 acres purchased by the Tuscarora in 1804 from the Holland Land Company with the proceeds of the sale of their ancestral lands in North Carolina. Less the 550 acres taken by the New York (State) Power Authority in the 1950s, they constitute the current Tuscarora Reservation (Donaldson 1892, 31; Hauptman 1986, 151).

Of the ten reservations established in the text or original map of the Treaty of Big Tree, only the Allegany, Cattaraugus, and Tonawanda Reservations remain in Seneca hands. The boundaries of all three of these have been modified by subsequent transactions (see Abler and Tooker 1978). The role played by Cornplanter in some of these transactions will be discussed in chapters 7 and 8. The Allegany Reservation is the most significant to Cornplanter's story, for it is there that his followers and descendants came to reside. When the Treaty of Big Tree was negotiated, and for some time thereafter, the vast majority of Senecas living along the Allegheny resided downriver from the Allegany Reservation in the village of Burnt House on Cornplanter's personal land grant in Pennsylvania. There, in 1799, events took place that would dominate the politics among the Allegany Senecas for two decades, and which continue to have an impact in Iroquois communities two centuries later.

7

Handsome Lake's Revelation

The Village of Burnt House

The Treaty of Big Tree had secured a number of reservations for the Senecas, including the forty-two-square-mile Allegany Reservation on the Allegheny River, immediately above Cornplanter's personal land grant in Pennsylvania. Joseph Ellicott surveyed the lands within the Holland Land Company Purchase surrendered in that treaty, but he was slow to survey the southern portion of the purchase, which in his opinion was far less attractive for settlement (Rothenberg 1976, 101). Although the size of the reservation was stipulated in the treaty negotiations, the boundaries were not. It was in the Holland Land Company's interest to keep the amount of land desirable to future non-Indian purchasers to a minimum. For his part, Cornplanter put pressure on Ellicott to confine the reservation to the agriculturally productive bottomlands along the Allegheny and its tributaries. Quakers present among the Senecas at the Cornplanter Grant urged that the reservation be no more than a half mile wide. By doubling that width, Ellicott ensured that more than 80 percent of the reservation would consist of mountains, unsuitable for agriculture (Rothenberg 1976, 89–90). Ellicott brought Cornplanter on board by adding two square miles to the forty allocated for the reservation; with gifts, he convinced the Buffalo Creek chief Farmer's Brother to support his proposed boundaries.

Although there were two Seneca settlements on the Allegany

Reservation in the fall of 1798, when Ellicott completed his survey, most of the Senecas in the region lived in the village of Burnt House on Cornplanter's grant, downriver from the reservation. A population of four hundred resided in some forty houses[1] on the meadow adjacent to the entrance of Cornplanter Run. Almost all were log structures with steeply pitched gable roofs of elm or hemlock bark. Although not longhouses (most were about 15 feet square), they do seem to have housed minimal extended families. Cornplanter's own dwelling was the most substantial, consisting of two houses joined by a covered porch. The larger house was some 15 by 30 feet; the smaller, some 15 by 20 feet. The doors to each house opened onto a connecting 10-foot-long covered porch. Cornplanter lived in one house with his wife, five daughters, and a mentally disabled son. It is likely that more than one of the daughters were married and that their husbands and children also lived there. Cornplanter's half brother, Handsome Lake, lived in the second house with two daughters, one married with children and a second who may have had a husband and children (A. Wallace 1970, 188–89; Rothenberg 1974, 158).

Religious and political events took place in Cornplanter's house, which served as a council house and may have been on a town square or plaza. The plaza contained a carved effigy of Tarachiawagon, the good twin of the Iroquoian creation myth (Deardorff 1951, 85; A. Wallace 1970, 192; on the Iroquoian creation myth, see Fenton 1962; Abler 1987c).

Surrounding the cluster of forty houses, some three hundred acres of farmland had been fenced with split rails to keep out deer that might ravage the crops. Because only sixty acres were under cultivation, however, Diane Rothenberg (1974, 159) suggests that fields outside the settlement, perhaps on islands in the Allegheny River, were also farmed to feed the village. There was little in the

1. Anthony Wallace (1970, 187) gives the population of Burnt House as "about four hundred persons" but this may be a high estimate. The census of Senecas entitled to annuity payments in 1800 reported the number of the Allegany Senecas to be 360 (Jennings et al. 1984, reel 44: 1800 26 Mar [II]).

way of livestock—three horses, fourteen head of cattle, a pair of oxen, and twelve hogs (A. Wallace 1970, 191).

Anthony Wallace (1970, 184) rather melodramatically describes Seneca villages of the time as "slums in the wilderness." To be sure, just two decades earlier, most of the Seneca homes and agricultural assets had been destroyed by the Sullivan and Broadhead expeditions, and the Seneca were hampered in their recovery by the uncertainty of their relations with the governments of the United States, New York, and Pennsylvania. Moreover, Burnt House was partially occupied by residents recently removed from New Arrow's town farther upriver. Flooding had destroyed much of their corn crop in 1797, so they had joined their kinsmen downriver (A. Wallace 1970, 221–22). However, the fields were reported as highly productive in 1798, keeping the women busy that autumn storing the harvest. That winter, the men went out for the traditional hunt; the better hunters were said to have taken nearly one hundred deer and perhaps even more. In many cases, because food was in abundance, a deer was taken for its hide, and the meat left in the woods for scavengers (Rothenberg 1976, 165; A. Wallace 1970, 228).

Accommodation and Divisions

Cornplanter and a Changing Culture

Well aware of the changing world of the post-Revolutionary Allegheny Valley, Cornplanter acted to create ways for his Senecas to cope with that world. Recognizing the need for members of his community to learn English, he had written the Society of Friends (Quakers) in February 1791 asking that they educate his eldest son, a second Seneca boy, and the son of interpreter Joseph Nicholson. A committee of Friends approved his request three months later (Cornplanter 1936). He wrote again in 1795, asking after his son and saying that "as soon as he is Learned enough I want him at Home [to] Manage My Business for Me" (Cornplanter 1890). Among those who signed the 1797 Treaty of Big Tree as witnesses and interpreters was Henry O'Bail. Cornplanter's son is the only

Seneca to sign his name ("Henry Abeel"), rather than affix an "X" (Kappler 1904–41, 2:1030). Recognizing, as well, the need the need to create sources of revenue in the evolving economy of American settlement, Cornplanter established the first sawmill in the region (Rothenberg 1974, 154).[2] Located at the junction of Saw Mill Creek and the Allegheny River, the sawmill was built by James Morrison in 1795 (Congdon 1967, 36–37). That summer, Cornplanter sold the output of his mill to the U.S. Army at Pittsburgh, writing Major Isaac Craig that he had set up the mill "in order to support my family by it. More so, because I am geting old and not able to hunt" (Sipe 1926, 465). To allow his Senecas to follow a lifestyle more akin to that of their non-Indian neighbors, Cornplanter enlisted Philadelphia Quakers as instructors in economic tasks.

The Society of Friends

Cornplanter's approach to the Quakers was well in keeping with the late-eighteenth-century liberal attitude among the white population that the Indians should be "civilized," that is, turned into small-scale family farmers. Robert Berkhofer (1965, 108) has noted how "annuity allocation, missionary example, and the government agent's harangue attempted to change aboriginal society in the direction of middle class White agrarian society." This agrarian ideal persisted through the history of Indian-white relations in America, even though most who espoused it lacked the skills or inclination to handle a plow or look after draft animals. The Quakers of late-

---

2. Cornplanter sometimes used income from his sawmill for national purposes. When a Seneca and an Onondaga were imprisoned in Pittsburgh for the murder of a white man, Cornplanter obtained their freedom by negotiating a loan of two hundred dollars, which seems to have been paid the victim's family. He attempted to obtain the money from the national annuity due the Seneca, but when the government did not respond, and his loan came due, he kept his lender at bay by paying him fifty dollars, which came from selling lumber from Cornplanter's sawmill. In a letter to Indian Agent Chapin, however, he pursued reimbursement from the annuity fund (Jennings et al. 1984, reel 44: 1798 16 June).

eighteenth-century Philadelphia and Pennsylvania, for example, were a merchant class, not an agrarian class (see Rothenberg 1974, 114–16). That the Iroquois and other eastern nations were already farmers went unnoticed. That their farming was primarily a female task, albeit after men had expended considerable sweat and toil in clearing the fields, led non-Indian observers to dismiss it and relegate the Seneca and other Native peoples to the status of "hunter states" (see A. Wallace 1993, 43–44, 114–16). Contrary to the usual picture of Seneca subsistence, however, farmwork by the males appears to have gone beyond clearing the fields, both at this time and well before. Indeed, there is significant evidence that men assisted their sisters and wives in that task after the fields had been cleared.[3]

The Philadelphia Yearly Meeting of Friends elected to send a mission to the Seneca, not to convert the Indians to their brand of Christianity, for that was not part of the Quaker creed, but rather to set up a demonstration farm that would encourage males and females among the Seneca to play their "proper" roles (in the view of European traditions) in agricultural production. Which is to say, women were to leave the fields and be completely replaced by men. They had considered several locales for this attempt, even briefly setting up residence among the Oneida, but they decided to focus their efforts on the Senecas along the Allegheny River. This was in part because they knew and liked Cornplanter. They also approved of the isolation of the upper Allegheny. They viewed the Senecas residing there as "an excellent experimental community, least subject, as the Quakers saw it, to the pernicious influence of white settlers" (Rothenberg 1974, 130).

Thus, on 17 May 1798, five Quaker men arrived at Burnt House. The two elder Quakers, John Pierce and Joshua Sharpless, were there to lay groundwork for the enterprise. The three young men—Henry Simmons, Halliday Jackson, and Joel Swayne—had volunteered to undertake the mission itself. The next day, with

---

3. Cornplanter working in his field is a key episode in the story of the vision experience of his half brother, Handsome Lake, which will be outlined below.

Henry O'Bail acting as interpreter, the Quakers stated their business (on Seneca-Quaker councils, see Bauman 1972). Cornplanter replied the next day, generally approving what they proposed to do, but noting divisions within the community and that "some others will not mind what you say" (A. Wallace 1970, 223). Because the Quakers intended eventually to bring their project to a close and turn over all improvements to the Seneca Nation, they decided to build their establishment on the Allegany Reservation rather than on the Cornplanter Grant. They purchased a log cabin for twenty dollars from a Seneca woman and her daughter on the site of New Arrow's Town. Because the Quakers' tools and seed had not arrived from Pittsburgh, the Senecas gave them seed and lent them farm implements (Rothenberg 1974, 163). In addition to instructing Seneca males in the arts of agriculture, the Quakers promised cash bonuses to Seneca men who raised specified amounts of wheat, rye, corn (at half the rate for wheat or rye), potatoes, and hay, and to Seneca women who wove cloth of linen or wool from their own flax or sheep. To receive the bonus, the claimant needed also to have been sober for six months (A. Wallace 1970, 225).

Pierce and Sharpless left on 7 June, leaving the younger men to work the demonstration farm. That summer, Simmons, Jackson, and Swayne attempted to show the Seneca men the benefits of plow farming. The following winter, Simmons attempted to teach school at Burnt House, with twenty children in irregular attendance (A. Wallace 1970, 227). His attempt was well enough received that, in March 1799, the villagers of Burnt House agreed to build a schoolhouse over the summer, about one half mile from Cornplanter's home (A. Wallace 1970, 235).

Social Conflict

Support for Cornplanter's policy of accommodation to white ways was not universal among the Burnt House villagers. In mid-February 1799, some were frightened by the dream a girl at Buffalo Creek reported having: she dreamed that all whites (including the Quakers) had the Devil in them and that Indians should not learn to read and write. Cornplanter denounced such dreams in a public council, saying no one should give credence to them (A. Wallace 1970, 230–31). He told Quaker Henry Simmons that he "had got very tir'd of hearing so much noise about Dreams" (Swatzler 2000, 259). Simmons saw the influence of Farmer's Brother and other Buffalo Creek chiefs behind the anti-Quaker sentiments.

Not long afterward, as Simmons attempted to teach school in Cornplanter's house, his class was disrupted by preparations for a "Dance & Frolick," as others set about cooking two large kettles of food. Excited about the dance, his students disappeared. Simmons went into the woods and cut down trees to relieve his frustration. He returned to find men dancing to the sound of turtle shell rattles in the chief's house (which often served as the venue for councils and religious ceremonies), with Cornplanter, his son Henry O'Bail, and many other relatives in the smaller house next door. Simmons confronted Cornplanter with the charge that such dances were the work of the Devil (Swatzler 2000, 260).

When Simmons arrived the next day to teach, he found a council convened in Cornplanter's house. He was called in and told by Cornplanter that, despite divisions, the assembled Senecas had decided "to quit such Dancing Frolicks for some of them thought it must be wicked, because they had Learned it of white people" (Swatzler 2000, 261), although they would continue to observe their two great religious festivals.

Not all dreams were condemned. As Simmons recalled with approval, a young man reported another dream before the council: he dreamed he was mortally wounded and journeyed to a place where he observed men being punished for having consumed alcohol, chasing women, and beating their wives, descriptions that would later be repeated in the visions reported by Cornplanter's half brother, Handsome Lake (Swatzler 2000, 262–63).

Cornplanter continued to express his support of the Quakers and their goals, although he admitted that "some of his People did not see & think as he did" (Swatzler 2000, 262). Indeed, some of the Burnt House villagers believed the true motivation of the

Quakers was their desire to gain title to Seneca lands (Rothenberg 1976, 165).

Alcohol consumption was both symptom and cause of social conflict in the Burnt House community. In mid–May 1799, Handsome Lake returned from Pittsburgh with a large group of Senecas. Having sold the deerskins obtained in the successful winter hunt, they had purchased a large quantity of rum or whiskey with the proceeds. The party they had begun on the journey home continued for a long time in the village of Burnt House itself. Fearful of the drunken revelers (such events had been marked by fights and even by deaths in the past), sober villagers fled to campsites in the bush. It is likely that Cornplanter did not participate in the spree; throughout his life, he enjoyed a reputation for sober behavior. Handsome Lake, however, seems to have imbibed with considerable enthusiasm. At the conclusion of the affair, a chastened community held a council with the Quakers. Cornplanter announced that the people were determined to have no whiskey brought among them in the future, with two young men being appointed to enforce this (A. Wallace 1970, 234–35; Swatzler 2000, 264–65).

Perhaps the most telling symptom of social conflict, however, were the accusations of witchcraft that sprang up in growing numbers. Four months after the death of one of Cornplanter's daughters, rumor had it that a newborn in his family, possibly a grandchild of the Chief Warrior, had been cursed by the same witch, a woman with a bad reputation. Cornplanter told three men to execute the woman.[4] On 13 June 1799, she was stabbed to death while working

4. Halliday Jackson (see A. Wallace 1952, 145–46) states that the woman was executed by Cornplanter's "sons," an allegation accepted by Merle Deardorff and George Snyderman (1956, 591) and by Anthony Wallace (1970, 236). Jackson did not reside at the Cornplanter settlement at the time, however; he was at the Quaker farmstead several miles upriver. Contrary to Jackson's assertion, a Quaker living on the Cornplanter Grant, Henry Simmons, identifies the executioners as simply "3 of his [Cornplanter's] men" (Swatzler 2000, 266). Given that Simmons was living in the village, I think it likely that it was not Cornplanter's sons who carried out the execution.

in one of the village's cornfields (A. Wallace 1970, 235; Swatzler 2000, 266).

Handsome Lake's Vision

Handsome Lake had never fully recovered from the mid-May bout of drunkenness that had marked the return of the traders from Pittsburgh. He lay bedridden in his portion of Cornplanter's house. Psychological anthropologist Anthony Wallace is convinced the chief was "suffering from the classic Iroquois bereavement syndrome [combining] depression, bitterness, and suspicion" (A. Wallace 1970, 240). Handsome Lake was so weak that, when he came to the door of his cabin and collapsed, his daughter was convinced he was dead. She sent her husband for Handsome Lake's nephew, Governor Blacksnake, and brother, Cornplanter. In one version of the story, Cornplanter was planting seeds in a field on an island in the Allegheny River when he heard the news but refused to come until he had covered the seeds (A. Parker 1913, 23). In another version, Cornplanter was supervising the construction of his new house near the schoolhouse the Quakers Simmons and Swayne were building (Deardorff 1951, 90; A. Wallace 1970, 240). All accounts agree, however, that it was Handsome Lake's nephew, Governor Blacksnake, who reached Handsome Lake and his daughter first, who determined that his uncle was still alive, and who remained at his side until the sick man revived.

Handsome Lake told those gathered around him that he had been visited by three angels, Indian men dressed in traditional fashion, their faces painted red. Each carried a berry bush and fed the berries to Handsome Lake as a cure. He must, they told him, convey his message to the people at the Strawberry Festival. This ceremony, with its songs, dances, prayers, and communal consumption of strawberry juice, and which was to be celebrated next on 16 June, must continue as part of the ceremonial cycle. He must tell the people of four evils that made the Creator unhappy: the consumption of alcohol, the practice of witchcraft, the use of love medicine, and the use of medicines to cause abortions and sterility.

Those who committed such evils must repent and confess. The angels warned him that another witch, a male, was living at Burnt House. They promised Handsome Lake that he would be visited by a fourth angel at some point in the future (A. Wallace 1970, 241; A. Parker 1913, 25–26).

When it came time for the Strawberry Festival, Handsome Lake was too weak to convey his message to those assembled. In his place, Cornplanter reported what Handsome Lake had been told, becoming the first of a long list of speakers who, from generation to generation, have recited the teachings of Handsome Lake at gatherings to celebrate events and rituals in the Iroquois ceremonial cycle (A. Wallace 1970, 242; see A. Parker 1913, 19; Deardorff 1951, 99; Shimony 1961, 192).

While recovering, Handsome Lake fell into a second trance on 8 August 1799. His experiences in this trance "would become the core of the new religion's theology" (A. Wallace 1970, 243). Led by the fourth angel on what has been called his "sky journey," Handsome Lake encountered many persons and things. The road he followed had a fork in it, with a wide road to hell and a narrow one to heaven. He observed Senecas suffering torments in hell for sins committed in their lives. (Prior to Handsome Lake's experiences and teachings, the idea of eternal punishment for sinful behavior had not been part of Seneca religion.) Following the narrow road to heaven, Handsome Lake encountered Cornplanter's daughter, who had been dead for seven months, and who told him how unhappy she was that her brothers, particularly Henry, refused to follow the wishes of their father. Henry's Philadelphia education had made him contemptuous of traditional Seneca practices and religion; in this, he had taken the wrong path. On the way home, after waking from his trance, Handsome Lake was again visited by the fourth angel, who said he must tell the people to conduct a white dog sacrifice.[5]

5. The Iroquois sacrificed a white dog as an offering to the Creator at their Midwinter Ceremony, although the practice ceased in the nineteenth century (see Tooker 1965; 1970).

Once more, Handsome Lake left it to Cornplanter to convey these experiences to the people of the village. A council met in the morning to hear the words of Handsome Lake spoken by his half brother. That afternoon, a white dog was sacrificed (A. Wallace 1970, 242–47).

According to one story in oral tradition among Christian Senecas in the 1940s, the prophet Handsome Lake developed the content of his message from knowledge of the Bible obtained from either Henry O'Bail or a white man living in the region (Deardorff 1951, 87–88). According to a variant of this story, told me in 1965 by an elderly Seneca man who claimed to have known a woman who had observed Handsome Lake in a trance when she was a girl, and who was himself a Presbyterian, Handsome Lake had been tutored by a young Seneca who had obtained an education and a black book in Philadelphia. Although these stories doubtlessly developed much later, in the nineteenth century, after Protestant missionaries had attracted a substantial following among the Seneca, no one can deny close parallels between Christian ideas and the religious code that developed from Handsome Lake's visions.

Handsome Lake and Witchcraft

Much has been made of Handsome Lake's attacks on witchcraft and witches. One case involved Cornplanter's daughter, known to us only as "Jiiwi." Of the many Munsees (a division of the Algonquian-speaking Delaware) residing among the Senecas at Cattaraugus, a number led by Chief Silver Heels and with Cornplanter's permission hunted in the vicinity of Burnt House in the winter of 1799–1800. It was not unusual at that time for young Seneca women to sleep with visiting dignitaries, and Jiiwi had done so with the Munsee chief. The following summer, after the Munsees returned to their homes at Cattaraugus, she bore his child. In the fall, she experienced a long, lingering illness. When Cornplanter asked his half brother to determine the cause, Handsome Lake was at first reluctant. Finally, he performed the necessary rituals and discovered that the girl was being bewitched by the Munsees, including their chief. It is an anthropological truism that witches are found to be more numerous in distant groups than at home, and the Seneca stereotype of their Munsee neighbors included the assertion that they practiced witchcraft.[6] The Munsees were told to remove their spells, whereupon one of them came to Burnt House and attempted to cure the sick woman. When she did not respond to his treatment, the Munsee was held hostage with the understanding that, if Jiiwi died, he would be executed as a witch. This would then mean war between the Munsee and the Seneca. The tension lasted through the winter and spring, but fortunately, even though Jiiwi continued to suffer from her illness, she did not die. The situation reached a climax in a June 1801 council at Buffalo Creek. Handsome Lake used the council to attack witches among both the Munsee and the Seneca. Whiskey and witchcraft were, in his view, at the root of all the social conflict that racked Seneca communities. Convinced, however, that the Munsee witches had repented, Cornplanter announced to the council that they were free to come and go in peace (A. Wallace 1970, 254–61).[7]

It may have been at this council that a widely reported incident revealed the political rivalry between the famous Seneca orator Red Jacket and the half brothers Handsome Lake and Cornplanter (A. Wallace 1970, 260). The incident was first reported in 1811 by DeWitt Clinton (1812), whose report was, in effect, repeated by William Stone (1841, 166–69) and by Arthur Parker (1919, 325). In Clinton's account, Handsome Lake charged Red Jacket with

6. While resident on the Allegany Reservation in 1966, I was told that there were no longer any witches on Allegany, but that there were several on the Six Nations Reserve in Canada. Because witchcraft had nothing to do with the subject of my research, I did not pursue the matter. It may be significant that among the population of the Six Nations Reserve are a number of Delawares. In 1970, 255 of the nearly 9,000 band members of the Six Nations Reserve—that is, members of the group legally recognized in Canada as the Six Nations Band— were identified as "Delaware" (Weaver 1978, 527).

7. There appear to be a large number of quite diverse variants of this Seneca oral tradition, as well as a Delaware version recorded on the Six Nations Reserve in Ontario (Fenton 1946, 52–55; Speck 1945).

witchcraft, only to have Red Jacket successfully defend himself and stave off execution with a three-hour speech. The thrust of his defense, according to Anthony Wallace, was that Handsome Lake was using "his visions and his charges of witchcraft for the purpose of restoring the fallen fortunes of his discredited [half] brother Cornplanter" (A. Wallace 1970, 260). Christopher Densmore recognizes that there certainly was rivalry between Red Jacket and Handsome Lake and that Red Jacket viewed the prophet as simply a political tool of Cornplanter, who, in Red Jacket's view, used the words of Handsome Lake to enhance his own influence among the Seneca. Nevertheless, Densmore (1999, 57) expresses doubt that this "trial" ever occurred, pointing out that the earliest account of this incident is by Clinton, and that it is not clear where Clinton heard the story.

Hostility between Handsome Lake and Red Jacket may have influenced the prophet's naming Red Jacket as the chief who, in the land of the tormentor (hell), must continually move dirt in a wheelbarrow as punishment for his role in the sale of Seneca reservations (A. Parker 1913, 68). There is ambiguity on this point, however, for oral tradition has variants of Handsome Lake's words in which the guilty chief is not Red Jacket but Farmer's Brother (Morgan 1851, 230, 254–55; A. Parker 1913, 11–12). It is probably of significance that Handsome Lake's political allies were most numerous, and his influence strongest, on the Allegany Reservation and at Tonawanda, whereas his influence was weakest at Buffalo Creek. Both Red Jacket and Farmer's Brother were chiefs at Buffalo Creek.

Journey to Washington, D.C.

Opposition was beginning to surface to the political power that Cornplanter had been exercising. Handsome Lake told Thomas Jefferson that Cornplanter "is cried down by the Sachems of Buffalo Creek," a fact the American President would "very well know" (Jennings et al. 1984, reel 44: 1802 13–17 Mar). Even among the Allegany Senecas, Cornplanter had faded somewhat into the political background, overshadowed by his half brother. It was Handsome Lake who led yet another Seneca delegation to the seat of the federal government, now in the new capital city, Washington, D.C. The president, Thomas Jefferson, was also new, and although he had an intellectual interest in the native populations of North America, he lacked the firsthand experience in dealing with Iroquois diplomats that George Washington had gained on the frontier before the American Revolution.

Handsome Lake seems to have had two reasons for making the journey to the new capital. First, he had concerns about land issues: he wanted to express the unease felt by the Senecas of Allegany and Cattaruagus, who had lost the written descriptions of the boundaries of their lands. His second reason was religious: he wanted to convince the American President that he had been ordained as the fifth angel to lead the spiritual reformation of his own people and then "to direct the People on earth" (for his speech to Jefferson, see Jennings et al. 1984, reel 44: 1802 13–17 Mar; A. Wallace 1970, 268). He told Jefferson that only half of his spirit was on this earth; the other half resided with the Great Spirit "above." He spoke at length of the need for temperance.

Cornplanter had come along to mend political fences, and was helped by Handsome Lake in this task. "I very well know he has done his endeavour for the benefit of our Nation," Handsome Lake said of his half brother. "He is a sober man, and endeavours to make all our young men sober and good. The Sachems at Buffalo Creek are all drunken men & dislike him" (Jennings et al. 1984, reel 44: 1802 13–17 Mar). By strengthening his ties to the federal government, Cornplanter hoped to increase his power at home.

But the Chief Warrior also had hopes for personal gains from this trip. He was upset that he had not received title "for the exclusive use, benefit and comfort of myself" to lands "ten miles square," which he said had been promised by Thomas Morris during negotiations for the Treaty of Big Tree.[8] It has been suggested (A. Wallace

8. Anthony Wallace (1970, 267) feels that it was Handsome Lake who demanded this personal land grant. The demand for the land grant appears in a series of addresses by Handsome Lake, Cornplanter, and the Blue-eyed Chief

1970, 269) that this land claim was put forward not by Cornplanter but by Handsome Lake to secure the Oil Spring Reservation, near Cuba, New York, on the border between Cattaraugus and Allegany Counties. The Oil Spring Reservation was only a mile square, however, far smaller than the tract claimed in the address to the government in Washington (Donaldson 1892, 26; Hauptman 1999). Morerover, there was no question in 1802 as to the Seneca right to the reservation, which had been surveyed by Joseph Ellicott for the Holland Land Company. In 1858, Governor Blacksnake, nephew of Cornplanter and Handsome Lake, testified in court that he had seen the marks on trees, "the same as around the other reservations," made by Ellicott to mark the boundaries of the Oil Spring tract, and he produced a map given him by Ellicott in which Oil Spring and the other Seneca reservations were marked in red (Hauptman 1999, 70–71). Blacksnake also noted that the tract was not a personal grant to Cornplanter but rather "the Senecas all were to have it" (Congdon 1967, 201). It was not until decades later that non–Indian squatters challenged the Seneca Nation title to the square-mile reservation, forcing the Seneca Nation to go to court to evict them.

The 1802 Treaties

Handsome Lake and Cornplanter joined their fellow Seneca chiefs at Buffalo Creek to negotiate land issues in June of 1802. The Seneca had retained the so-called mile strip, from Stedman's Creek (or Stedman's farm) to Buffalo Creek along the Niagara River. Commissioners appointed by Governor Clinton of New York wanted to purchase this land, with the idea that the federal government would found a military establishment at Black Rock. Red Jacket welcomed the New York State delegation, but the council was dominated by Handsome Lake and Cornplanter. The assem-

---

(often simply identified as "Blue Eyes"). The documents are somewhat ambiguous as to which chief is making each speech. As I interpret them, however, it was Cornplanter who asked about the status of a personal land grant (see Jennings et al. 1984, reel 44: 1802 13–17 Mar).

bled Senecas delayed for several days meeting with the New York commissioners, while Handsome Lake preached his message to the chiefs in council. The commissioners were informed that this took precedence over any other matters before the council. Ultimately, the chiefs, Cornplanter among them, refused to sell to them (Jennings et al. 1984, reel 44: 1802 12 July). Both the Great Spirit, speaking through Handsome Lake in his visions, and President Jefferson on their recent trip to Washington had, Cornplanter said, instructed him not to sell any more land (Jennings et al. 1984, reel 44: 1802° 6 July).

The assembled chiefs did, however, sign two treaties on 30 June 1802. The more important of these, signed with Joseph Ellicott, representing the Holland Land Company, in the presence of John Tayler, who had been appointed U.S. commissioner by President Jefferson, redefined the boundaries of the Cattaraugus Reservation (Kappler 1904–41, 2:60–61). The second, again with Tayler representing the federal government, conveyed the title to the two square miles of Little Beard's Town on the Genesee to Oliver Phelps, Isaac Bronson, and Horatio Jones. The price paid for these 1,280 acres was twelve hundred dollars (Kappler 1904–41, 2:62).

The first treaty was signed by nineteen chiefs; the second by a dozen. It is significant that, despite the attempts by Buffalo Creek chiefs to undermine his authority, Cornplanter is the second chief to sign each of these. It is also significant that Handsome Lake appears as the first chief to sign each treaty; their nephew, later known as "Governor Blacksnake," appears fifth on each.

With the blessing of U.S. Commissioner Tayler, New York decided to ignore the objections of Cornplanter and Handsome Lake to land sales. In August, Governor George Clinton welcomed a delegation of chiefs from Buffalo Creek to Albany, with whom he planned to negotiate the sale of the lands along the Niagara River desired by New York. The Buffalo Creek delegation had a more pressing issue on their minds, however. They were concerned that a Seneca, Stiff-Armed George, charged with the murder of a Buffalo resident, was to be tried in a New York State court. Pointing to the failure of American authorities to punish those who had murdered Senecas in the past, Red Jacket told Clinton that only the federal government and not New York State had the right to deal with the Seneca on the issue (Jennings et al. 1984, reel 44: 1802 18–20 Aug; see also Densmore 1999, 60–63). In the end, Governor Clinton obtained his land sale, with Farmer's Brother and Red Jacket leading the list of six Seneca chiefs who signed the treaty on 20 August 1802 (for the text of the treaty, see Jennings et al. 1984, reel 46: 1818 10 Dec (V)).

Cornplanter expressed his displeasure over the sale in a communication to the president dated 19 January 1803. Jefferson replied that his commissioner had determined that the Seneca had freely entered into the sale of the lands to New York (Jennings et al. 1984, reel 44: [ca. 1803]).

Handsome Lake Moves to Coldspring

The political alliance between the prophet Handsome Lake and Cornplanter may have come unraveled at about this time, although contemporary evidence is not clear as to what was actually happening at Burnt House. What does seem clear is that the displeasure with Cornplanter as a political leader that was earlier reported at Buffalo Creek spread to those Senecas living along the Allegheny.

Native North American communities today, and long into the past, have been suspicious and critical of their political leaders. Indeed, they have often accused these leaders of lining their own pockets at the expense of the people. While engaged in research on the Allegany Reservation some years ago, I heard charges that some politicians had adopted non-Indian ways, with their greed for money and the material goods money can buy (see Abler 1973). It seems likely that Cornplanter also faced such charges, perhaps not without justification. All of which may explain the Iroquois proverb that a chief should have skin "seven thumbs thick" (A. Wallace 1970, 42, 76, 97).

Although it is clear that Cornplanter personally benefited from the treaty making and land sales to which he was party, it is hard to tell whether the personal land grants, annuities, and other benefits he accrued were solicited or unsolicited by the chief. They may simply have been expressions of gratitude on the part of negotiators in response to his role in the treaty or land sale councils. It is also possible, however, that they were demanded or given as bribes to ensure his cooperation. Gifts, including gifts to chiefs, had long been essential to diplomacy on the colonial frontier (see Jacobs 1950). Whereas an ethos of economic egalitarianism and kinship obligations often drained the personal wealth acquired by a chief in the course of his diplomacy in former days, by the end of the eighteenth century, these cultural leveling mechanisms were less powerful. Joseph Brant (see Kelsay 1984) is perhaps the most prominent example of an Iroquois chief of the era who used his political position to enhance his personal wealth and create a comfortable lifestyle, but it seems that Cornplanter and other chiefs had learned from their non-Indian neighbors how to do so as well.

Cornplanter's establishing a sawmill in 1795 to provide income for his family is clear evidence he had adopted entrepreneurial values from his contacts with the non-Indian world. In 1798, even before their first visit to the Allegany Senecas, the commandant of Fort Pitt had warned the Quakers of Cornplanter's appetite for private property (Deardorff and Snyderman 1956, 590). The chief was having a new house built for his use at the time Handsome Lake experienced his first vision in 1799. Cornplanter later came into conflict with Quakers for selling alcohol to local whites (Rothenberg 1976, 214). Clearly, Cornplanter's behavior left him open to criticism from his followers. Cornplanter's sister's husband, known as "Mush," in an 1806 meeting with a Quaker delegation was reported "Reflecting upon Cornplant for being too forward heretofore in their Councils" (Deardorff and Snyderman 1956, 603). His disaffected followers finally moved off Cornplanter's land grant and onto the Allegany Reservation.

It was the sawmill that led to Cornplanter's fall from formal political power. When fluctuating water levels in Saw Mill Creek repeatedly idled his sawmill, Cornplanter proposed to move it to a more favorable locale on the Allegany Reservation. Strenuously objecting, his followers met in council and passed his position as Chief Warrior to Wundungohte of Cattaraugus. A Quaker observer credits "Tekiando or the Indian called Blacksnake" as having "been very active in effecting the revolt from under Cornplanter's government" and stated Blacksnake acted as "privy counsellor" to Handsome Lake (Deardorff and Snyderman 1956, 593). According to a confusing and undated document among the papers of Erastus Granger, who became the federal agent to the New York Iroquois in 1803, Governor Blacksnake and a second Allegany chief complained that "Cornplanter . . . said he was the greatest man amongst the Indians. [He] is selling pine timber [to the whites and] taking all to himself" (Snyder 1978, 88).

Handsome Lake, Governor Blacksnake, and most of the Senecas who had been residing at Burnt House migrated to Coldspring on the Allegany Reservation, traveling on the road the Seneca had built, which stretched some twenty-two miles upriver from Burnt House. Between 1803 and 1806, the migrants built about one hundred houses (A. Wallace 1970, 287–88; Abrams 1976, 55; Congdon 1967, 88; Deardorff and Snyderman 1956, 593).

Among those who moved off the Cornplanter Grant was Cornplanter's eldest son, Henry. Halliday Jackson visited "Henery Abeal's farm" in September 1806, and stated that he "hath a neat little house built with a Pannel Door and Sash windows on a stately eminence at the head of a rich flat" (Snyderman 1957, 578).

The Quakers also decided to move upriver at this time, away from their demonstration farm at Old Town, New Arrow's old village, on the Allegany Reservation, and it is likely their move influenced at least some of the Senecas to follow them up the Allegheny. On 30 August 1803, both Cornplanter and Handsome Lake agreed in council that the Quakers should move their activities to land off the reservation. Within a month, the Friends had decided to resettle on 692 acres of land purchased from the Holland Land Company at Tunesassa, only three miles downriver from Handsome Lake's settlement at Coldspring. A sawmill and grist mill were built there in

1804; the school established soon after continued in operation until 1938 (Congdon 1967, 87–90; Deardorff and Snyderman 1956, 593).

The Quakers regretted Cornplanter's removal from office. One observed, "We find Cornplant Stil Continues to be Displaced from being head Chief which We apprehend is a great Loss to the Indians here as he appears to be much the wisest man amongst them" (Deardorff and Snyderman 1956, 603). Despite his lack of political status, when a Quaker delegation visited the Senecas at Coldspring in September 1806, Cornplanter was sent for. An observer reported he "Looked Like an old sage with some Long hairs of beard upon his Chin" (Deardorff and Snyderman 1956, 600). In an effort to put himself back in favor, "at the council he put on a good Deal of voluntary humility appeared in a mean Dress &c" (Deardorff and Snyderman 1956, 603).

When John Norton, the Scottish-Cherokee mixed blood who had been adopted by the Mohawks of the Six Nations Reserve, visited Burnt House in April 1809, he found that "there are now only a few houses remaining at this place, which belong to the Old Chief's near relations; one of which, a house of two stories high neatly built, and painted, the property of his son, a well behaved young man. His eldest son [Henry O'Bail] now resides at Teyoghneganogh [Coldspring]" (Klinck and Talman 1970, 11). Norton had earlier visited Coldspring, which he described as "the most flourishing village of any of the Five Nations" noting that its population, which exceeded five hundred, resided for the most part in log houses. There were a few more substantial dwellings, including one "neatly framed and painted; [which] has four well finished rooms, two up stairs and two down stairs, with a kitchen adjoining the lower story." Hogs, cattle, and horses were abundant, and the cornfields "extensive" (Klinck and Talman 1970, 10).

It is clear that criticisms of Cornplanter's role in land transactions had reached Norton on the Six Nations Reserve in Ontario. He found these rumors had painted an overly harsh view of Cornplanter's actions. "The Corn Planter has done better for his people than, from report, I thought he had; for although the Reserve which he has retained is narrow, yet they enjoy and are likely for many years, to enjoy, all the advantages of the adjacent Country." The narrow Allegany Reservation "takes in the most valuable kind of land, and that purchased by the people of the United States adjoining to it, being rough and broken, and not likely soon to receive inhabitants, forms the most valuable hunting ground of any possessed by the Five Nations" (Klinck and Talman 1970, 9, 11).

Visiting the Allegany Senecas in 1806, the Quaker John Philips noted that, of those unhappy with Cornplanter's removal from the position of Chief Warrior, "many . . . want him Replaced again" (Deardorff and Snyderman 1956, 603). Halliday Jackson, who traveled with Philips, later wrote that Cornplanter was restored to Chief Warrior in 1807 (Jackson 1830b, 53), an observation accepted by more recent scholars (Deardorff and Snyderman 1956, 594; A. Wallace 1970, 291). The Seneca grant of land to the Tuscarora Nation, dated 30 March 1808, included Cornplanter's mark; he signed third on the list of Seneca signatories (after Farmer's Brother and Red Jacket; Jennings et al. 1984, reel 45: 1808° 30 Mar). This would suggest he had resumed his familiar political position. John Norton reports that Cornplanter had "retired" as chief when he visited him in April 1809 (Klinck and Talman 1970, 9), but in September of that year, a Quaker delegation to Allegany listed Cornplanter, Handsome Lake, Governor Blacksnake, and Captain Strong as four chiefs of the Wolf Clan. Among the four Snipe Clan chiefs were Cornplanter's sons, Henry and Charles, and Mush, the husband of Cornplanter's sister, is one of two Turtle Clan chiefs (Allinson 1809, 1:39).

Handsome Lake Leaves Allegany

Cornplanter does seem to have been reinstated as Chief Warrior when Handsome Lake was forced to leave Allegany in the fall or early winter of 1809. Anthony Wallace suggests that two of Handsome Lake's policies eroded his support at Allegany: his persecution of witches and his campaign against the performance of the rituals of the medicine societies. With respect to the first, Handsome Lake seems to have ignored a principle that anthropologists have long recognized in witchcraft accusations, namely, that the persons usually accused of witchcraft are deviants without support in the community and without strong kinship ties. In his initial witchcraft accusations, Handsome Lake, like his half brother, Cornplanter, accused just such individuals. As he came to use charges of witchcraft as a tactic against any person who questioned his teachings, however, he also accused those who were not universally viewed as pariahs at Allegany. Kinsmen of such persons saw their executions as unjustified murders. Whereas the lethal effects of the epidemic swirling through the Allegany community at this time only heightened Handsome Lake's fear of witchcraft, many blamed these effects on Handsome Lake's teachings, which had suppressed the rituals of the medicine societies.

A critical event was the execution of a woman from Onondaga, found to be a witch by a council that met in Cornplanter's absence, shortly after four other women had been killed on Handsome Lake's orders or in the wake of his accusations. A mother and daughter from Cattaraugus had died from a whipping, and an old woman had been executed during a council held in 1807 when Handsome Lake stated she was a witch (A. Wallace 1970, 291–92). The fourth woman, a Tuscarora, had been executed with a blow to the head and her body thrown on a fire (Allinson 1809, 1:25). Oral tradition suggests the Onondaga woman was the mother of the wife of Peter Crouse, a relatively famous white captive living among the Seneca.[9] Although oral tradition also states she had fled Onondaga because she had been accused of witchcraft there, the Quakers were told that she, her husband, and a few other relatives had been sent to Coldspring to be tried by Handsome Lake. After Handsome Lake pronounced her guilty, Old Fatty, a Deer Clan chief, stated that if he were younger he would kill her immediately.

9. For a biography of Peter Crouse, see Joseph A. Francello's *The Seneca World of GA-NO-SEY-YEH* (1989); but see also George H. Abrams's review (1990).

Sunfish struck her down with his ax, and then he (or John Watt according to one account) slit her throat (Turner 1849, 509; Congdon 1967, 92–93; Allinson 1809, 1:26).

When Cornplanter learned what happened, he expressed his unhappiness at the execution of the accused witch. His words reflected a growing community dissatisfaction with Handsome Lake. The prophet recognized "the people reviled me" at Allegany and declared his intention to remove himself to Tonawanda. "In that place I had relatives and friends and thought that my bones might find a resting place there." Revealing that Tonawanda would be the second stage in his messianic career, his angel messengers "told me that my life journey would be in three stages and when I entered the third I would enter into eternity of the New World, the land of our Creator" (A. Parker 1913, 47).

Handsome Lake had not yet left Coldspring when a delegation of visiting Quakers arrived there in mid-September 1809. A member of this delegation, William Allinson, described the longhouse where political and religious events took place:

> the Council House . . . is nearby the Centre of the Town—about 40 feet in Length & 20 in breadth, hav^g a Door at each End and two Holes in the peak of the Roof to admit the ascending of the Smoke from Council Fires, which are built on the Ground about 12 feet from each Door. These fires are daily used by the Inhabitants for Cooking or other purposes, being a Kind of public Priveledge, the Open Doors admitting ready Ingress & Egress to them at pleasure. The Floor is laid by Nature, and on each side from one end to the other, is a Platform laid coverd with Boards, skins &c— about 6 feet in width & 16 Inches in height—over these, about the height of 5 feet are other Platforms, which serve to throw up Skins, Corn, or any Lumbering articles, and to the Rafters was suspended a quantity of old Corn, some of it near the openings in the Roof being as black as smoke could make it. (Allinson 1809, 2:41)

At the blowing of a trumpet, the council assembled. Many who attended were dressed for the occasion, with painted faces and fur and feather ornaments. The chiefs listed as present included Cornplanter, Handsome Lake, Governor Blacksnake, Johnson Silverheels, John Pierce, Young Fatty, Tockewassee, and Jacob Snow (Allinson 1809, 2:45). Allinson describes the appearance of Handsome Lake, who opened the council welcoming the delegation of Friends:

> Old Conundiu [Handsome Lake] had a Blaze of Vermillion from the corner of each Eye—his Ears were cut round in their manner & extended to the size of a considerable length, on each Ear were two silver Quills, one about 3½ & the other 2 Inches long—the Erect one having a Tuft of Red Feathers stuck in at the lower End—part of his Forehead & on his crown were also painted red & being nearly bald & a very grave contenance he lookd venerable. On his arms were wide silver Bracelets—his leggings were of Red Cloth and his Covering a Blanket over all which he threw off in Council & took up his long Pipe. (Allinson 1809, 2:43–44)

The Quakers spoke first, warning of the dangers of alcohol consumption, gambling, divorce, and the execution of witches. After the Allegany Senecas conferred among themselves, it was Cornplanter who replied on their behalf, and whom Allinson describes as having an "Expressive Countenance & penetrating Eyes," one of which was kept half shut (owing to the injury suffered many years earlier in a carriage accident while traveling to New York City; Allinson 1809, 2:45). Allinson found Cornplanter's reply, addressed both to the delegation of Friends and to the assembled Senecas, "methodical & sensible" (Allinson 1809, 2:46).[10]

10. A second copy of the Allinson journal in the hands of a private collector is somewhat more expansive with respect to Cornplanter's response. Among the items mentioned by Cornplanter in his reply was the issue of the execution of witches. He felt it difficult to determine the guilt of persons accused of witchcraft. Cornplanter also expressed his approval of the Quakers's work at Tunessasa. There was a further exchange. The Friends asked about retaining those lands which the Seneca still held. Cornplanter told them that, in a recent council at Buffalo Creek, some warriors had threatened to kill any chief who agreed to a land sale, an action

It was sometime after this council that Handsome Lake left Coldspring and the Allegany Reservation to reside at Tonawanda. Cornplanter had formed a political alliance with his elder half brother, serving as his spokesman in the initial stages of the preaching of the prophet's message. This served Cornplanter's purposes well, for he favored many of the reforms advocated by Handsome Lake, particularly the control of alcohol abuse. Handsome Lake amassed considerable political power himself, making him a rival to his half brother as leader of the Senecas residing along the Allegheny River. Each man, however, came to feel the community censure that a society with egalitarian values levels at political leaders who grasp too much power. Cornplanter responded by assuming a humble and meek demeanor; Handsome Lake responded with a campaign to rid the community of witches. When Cornplanter withdrew his support for his half brother on this issue, and when the people of Coldspring also expressed their displeasure, Handsome Lake decided to leave the community he had founded and journey to Tonawanda.

Cornplanter approved of. He asked if the Quakers also approved. They said they did not condone the taking of any life, but, to this, Cornplanter said he thought it would be better to execute a chief who had sold lands than someone accused of being a witch because the truth could be easily found in the first case, but not in the second.

8

The Final Decades

The War of 1812

As the American republic took an increasingly hostile stance toward Britain and its North American colonies, both sides were concerned about the response of the aboriginal peoples to any conflict that might break out, particularly in the region of the Great Lakes, which formed the northern border of the United States. Complicating the issue was the emergence in the Ohio country of a prophet among the Shawnee, Tenskwatawa, with his brother, Tecumseh, attempting to form a confederation of Indian nations along the entire western border of the United States. I am aware of no convincing evidence to suggest that Tecumseh made any attempt to draw the New York Senecas into his confederation.[1] This may be because they were no longer a frontier people, but were surrounded by non-Indian settlements; it may also be because of the role played by Cornplanter and

---

1. Anthony Wallace (1970, 294) asserts that the Iroquois in New York "had been repeatedly solicited" by members of Tecumseh's confederation to join them, but that they had refused, assuring their non-Indian neighbors of their peaceful intentions. In describing the defeat of the Shawnee and their allies at Tippecanoe, William Stone states that "numbers of the young Seneca warriors were engaged in this battle," but cites no sources to support this allegation (Stone 1841, 221). The primary and secondary sources I have surveyed concerning the Seneca at this time surprisingly make no reference to conflict in the west be-

other Senecas, who advocated peace with rather than resistance to the Americans, in the 1790s.

Although Shawnees and other Ohio Indians did attend a council at Buffalo Creek in August 1807, they appear to have been more interested in the message of Handsome Lake than in trying to bring the Iroquois into Tecumseh's confederation. They were not successful in attempting to persuade the Seneca prophet to come to Ohio with them (Sugden 1997, 159).

Caleb Atwater later claimed he had served as interpreter on a visit by Tecumseh, Tenskwatawa, and two Winnebagos to an Iroquois council at Onondaga in 1809. Other than Atwater's testimony, however, there is no record of this meeting. David Edmunds (1984, 218) dismisses the tale, pointing out that there is no evidence that Atwater could speak any Iroquois language, much less Shawnee or Winnebago. John Sugden (1997, 182) is equally dismissive of Atwater's language skills, adding that the council fire of the Iroquois Confederacy at that time was at Buffalo Creek, not at Onondaga. Although certain that Atwater was not at such a meeting, nor a member of any Tecumseh party, Sudgen does feel that Atwater may have heard of a journey by Tecumseh from Tecumseh's Winnebago associates, whom Atwater later met in Wisconsin.

John Norton reports that the New York Senecas were visited in what seems to be the winter or early spring of 1811 by a delegation of Mingoes (Iroquois people resident in the Ohio country) with a message that the Senecas should abandon their New York homes and move to Ohio. This message may have come from Tecumseh. The Senecas refused to leave a land where the "Bones [of their ancestors] lye buried" and to "undertake a long Journey in which many may leave their Bones on the Road" (Klinck and Talman 1970, 286).

---

tween Indians and Americans, although rising tensions in British-American relations figure large in council discussions, and American observers contrast the message of Handsome Lake, the "peace prophet," with that of Tenskwatawa, the "war prophet" (A. Wallace 1970, 294).

Of more concern to the Seneca than Tecumseh's attempts at confederation in the west was the growing tension between the United States and Britain and the fact that the border between New York and Canada divided the Iroquois. A generation had matured in communities whose politics were influenced by interaction with either American or British officials. Many of the Senecas hoped that, with the outbreak of war between Britain and the United States, they would be allowed to remain neutral.

The United States declared war on Britain on 19 June 1812. Earlier in June, "a Deputation of Younger Chiefs . . . living within the American Boundary" visited the Iroquois settled on the Grand River Tract in Upper Canada (southern part of present-day Ontario). Little Billy spoke for the delegation and delivered wampum calling for neutrality in the case of war between the United States and Britain. After two days of deliberation, the Grand River chiefs declared their continued alliance to their Father, the King, and their hope that warriors from the American reservations would refrain from joining "the Common Enemy of our race" (Klinck and Talman 1970, 289–92).

Delegates from the Seneca, Onondaga, Cayuga, Tuscarora, and Delaware on the New York side of the border met at Buffalo Creek with American agent Erastus Granger in early July. Granger presented an ambiguous message. On the one hand, he asked the assembled Indians to remain neutral; on the other, he told them that if 150 or 200 wished to volunteer, they would "receive the same pay and provisions which our soldiers receive." Red Jacket replied with a speech favoring neutrality and proposed that another delegation go to the Grand River Tract. Granger tried to discourage this, for each side tried to keep "its" Iroquois from conversing with the other's. When, however, some did cross the Niagara River at Lewiston, British General Isaac Brock gave permission for two to meet with the Mohawks, but these could not persuade them to be neutral (Jennings et al. 1984, reel 45: 1812 6 and 8 July).

One of the delegates may have been Cornplanter's fellow Wolf

Clan chief Captain Strong, who journeyed to the Grand River to meet with the Canadian Iroquois from the Grand River Tract in June 1812. He warned his brethren on the Grand River that the King "has a smooth mouth but will deceive you" and pointed out that "God knows Great Britain has once cheated us." The British Indian superintendent, Colonel William Claus, countered Strong's speech. He told the council, "The United States talks loud, brags, and has a great mouth." He indicated the Great Spirit would by unhappy if the union with the King were broken. A Mohawk spokesman argued, "If you listen to the United States you will be destroyed and made slaves like the Negroes." He continued, "But I am a Mohawk. I will paint my face and be a man and fight Yankees as long as I live." Strong attempted to deliver a wampum belt, but the Mohawks would not accept it (Jennings et al. 1984, reel 45: 1812 June).

The split among the New York State Iroquois was manifested in two councils convened in September 1812. At Buffalo Creek, the sentiment was mostly pro-American because the village lay across the river from Canada and faced the prospect of a British invasion from a British force, including allies from the Grand River Tract. It was also at Buffalo Creek that the New York Iroquois had rekindled the council fire of the Iroquois Confederacy following the destruction of so many Iroquois communities during the American Revolution. Addressing the American agent at a council held at Buffalo Creek on 8 September 1812, Little Billy blamed the Iroquois in Canada for forcing them to go to war. He lamented, "We went to Grand-River lately to keep peace but in vain." He noted the Seneca "find there is no path left for us but between us and the U States." Because of this, he pledged to "prepare to defend against the common Enemy" (Jennings et al. 1984, reel 45: 1812° 8 Sept). Those opposed to entering the war met at Onondaga (near Syracuse, New York) and wrote a letter, dated 29 September 1812, to American President James Madison. Although neither the Mohawk nor the Cayuga were present from the Iroquois Confederacy, the correspondents reported they had kindled their council fire at Onondaga, "the Ancient Council ground of the Six Confederate Nations." They expressed their wish to follow the advice of George Washington and "our good prophet of the Seneca Tribe who is now with us in this Council" and remain at peace. They objected to having been "invited to take up the Tomahawk" at a recent council at Buffalo Creek (Jennings et al. 1984, reel 45: 1812° 29 Sept). Although Handsome Lake was present at the Onondaga council, there is no record that Cornplanter was at either this council or the earlier one at Buffalo Creek.

There is another curious report suggesting strong pro-American sentiments among the Seneca. The *Buffalo Gazette* stated on 29 September that "about one hundred and forty warriors of the Seneca Nation of Indians from the Alleghany River arrived in town last week" and that "yesterday they performed a war dance in the streets of this village" (Ketchum 1864–65, 2:275). The newspaper clearly got at least some of its facts wrong: the small population settled at Allegany could not have sent so many warriors.

In the meantime, the warriors from the Grand River Tract were active on the side of the Crown. When American forces crossed the Niagara River at Queenston on 13 October 1812, British General Isaac Brock was killed early in the ensuing battle. Among the forces responding to the invasion was a contingent of approximately eighty men from the Six Nations, who, under John Norton, the adopted Mohawk of Scottish-Cherokee ancestry, attacked the flank of the American detachment that had seized the height above the village of Queenston. They played a key role in the eventual American defeat. This was not without cost; five Iroquois were killed, as many as nine wounded, and a chief taken prisoner (Benn 1998, 89–97).

The government in Washington wished clarification of the commitment of the New York Iroquois to the American war effort. On 4 November 1812, delegates from the Seneca, Cayuga, and Onondaga met at Buffalo Creek. "The object of the Indians was to show that the Great Council fire of the Six Nations was now established at the Buffalo Village." The message delivered to the American agents was mixed, however. After Farmer's Brother acknowledged the communication from Washington, Young King supported the pro-war faction of the Seneca and attacked the legitimacy of the September council at Onondaga, stating that the principal council fire was at Buffalo Creek. Little Billy then expressed some misgivings, which even the pro-war faction of the Seneca shared, noting that the Americans had made no arrangements for them should they be forced to flee their homes in the face of a British invasion. Red Jacket was even less enthusiastic about efforts to enlist the Seneca in the American cause, accusing agent Erastus Granger of having "shaken" their peace. The famous Seneca orator promised only that they would examine the papers Granger had presented to the council (Jennings et al. 1984, reel 45: 1812° 4 Nov [III]).

In an effort to gain the support of the Seneca chiefs, gifts were distributed to them in November 1812. Cornplanter received a present along with twenty others including Allegany chiefs Captain Strong (although it is possible he had moved to Cattaraugus by this time), Johnson Silverheels, and Governor Blacksnake. Cornplanter was also one of eleven who fixed their marks to a receipt to Jasper Parrish for a special grant of eight thousand dollars, which was paid in lieu of the failed annuity from the United States Bank (Snyder 1978, 74).

The American government itself was apparently divided about the need to recruit Indian allies: later in November, after thanking the Six Nations for their offer to help defend the United States, General Alexander Smyth said it was not necessary (Jennings et al. 1984, reel 45: 1812° 22 Nov). Moreover, as Smyth proclaimed to the local non-Indian population, he refused "to follow a disgraceful example by letting loose these barbarous warriors upon the inhabitants of Canada" (Stone 1841, 238).

In June 1813, the agent Erastus Granger sent word to Allegany that they should supply 40 or 50 warriors to be part of a force of 150 Iroquois to assist General Henry Dearborn at the recently captured Fort George (Niagara-on-the-Lake, Ontario). The men from Allegany had only reached the Cattaraugus Reservation when they were met by a runner bringing word from Jasper Parrish that they should turn back. In a letter to Granger dated 30 June 1813, they complained: "This is twice that we have been called from our business, and traveled near one hundred miles at our own expense, . . . and when we arrive here, directed to return home, without any explination on the business, or any reward for our troubles." They closed with the comment, "We feel ourselves ready to turn out and defend our country, but cannot be treated in this way, as your brothers." The letter was signed by Cornplanter's son Henry ("Henry O'Beal"), and bore the mark of Cornplanter's nephew, Governor Blacksnake, and those of Johnston Silverheels and Big John (Ketchum 1864–65, 2:428–29; Cruikshank n.d., 103, 167).

As British and American forces exchanged blows in forays across the Niagara River, the Senecas living at Buffalo were drawn into the war. It has been claimed that the British seizure of Grand Island, felt to be Seneca territory, led to the abandoning of neutrality by the New York State Senecas (Stone 1841, 235–36). It was in fact the British attempt to capture the American stores in the warehouses of Black Rock, on the border of the Buffalo Creek Reservation, that drew the Senecas into the conflict on the American side. The British attacked across the Niagara River in the early hours of 11 July 1813, setting fire to the barracks and blockhouse at Black Rock. Forewarned of the possibility of such an attack, Indian Agent Erastus Granger had forty Senecas under Farmer's Brother ready to respond at dawn on 11 July. En route to repel the British invaders, the Senecas encountered the American commander, General Peter B. Porter, who had organized his own counterattack. The joint American-Seneca force routed the British, who fled in boats back across the river. The British commander, Lieutenant-Colonel Cecil Bisshopp, died of wounds received in the action. Two Senecas were wounded, one of them Young King (Stone 1841, 242–47; Benn 1998, 128–29).

Britain's allies reacted to news of this battle. At a 12 August 1813 council with British Indian Department officials, the Mohawk Te Karihaga presented thirteen strings of wampum expressing the dismay of both his people and of the Shawnee to the west that his brothers at Buffalo Creek had raised their tomahawks against the British and had spilled British blood (Cruikshank 1905, 10–11).

On 25 July 1813, representatives of the Seneca Nation gathered at Buffalo Creek to discuss their commitment to the American cause. Farmer's Brother opened the proceedings and called on each Seneca community to present its stand on the issue of peace or war.

Red Jacket spoke for Buffalo and noted the entire population would respond to an alarm. He asked that their pay be distributed among the population as a whole. He offered 162 warriors from Buffalo.

A spokesman for the villagers of Cattaraugus noted they always defended their shore of Lake Erie and the American shipping thereon. With Halftown in command, he promised the Senecas and Delawares of Cattaraugus would turn out at least 21 men in time of danger, and possibly more.

Captain Shongo from the Caneadea Reservation on the Genesee said that eleven from their village had been at Buffalo for a month and would stay a month longer. John Sky from Tonawanda refused to promise a contribution but said he would return home and consult local chiefs.

It was Cornplanter who spoke for Allegany and who brought up more general issues. Pleading that his people had "a great deal of Work to do in our Village," he offered only seven men to the Seneca force. But he did promise more if the danger increased. Turning to Erastus Granger, he told him, "You must pay well open your purses. You must pay some down. Take care of your taverns and do not let them supply our Warriors with Liquor. We find some difficulty. If our men fall in the war there is no promise of compensation do your best on our behalf."

Red Jacket concluded, stating that the Seneca had not wanted to go to war, but the Americans had persuaded them—"you have beat us." He requested, "If any of our friends the Six Nations except the

Mohawks, should fall into your hands we hope you will treat them Well."[2] He noted the Senecas needed to be supplied with shirts and shoes (Jennings et al. 1984, reel 45: 1813° 25 July).

Less than a month later, on 17 August 1813, a number of Senecas took part in an American raid across the Niagara River, attacking a British-Indian encampment near Fort George (the fort at what is now Niagara-on-the-Lake, on the Canadian side of the border, which at this point in the war was in American hands). The American commander included in his list of principal Seneca chiefs Cornplanter's eldest son, Major Henry O'Bail, as well as two of Cornplanter's old traveling companions, his nephew, Governor Blacksnake, and Halftown (Cruikshank 1905, 30–31).[3] Accounts of the skirmish at Ball's farm agree that two of the New York Iroquois were killed, but that the Senecas and other Iroquois captured approximately a dozen Indians, two members of the British Indian Department, Captain Robert Livingston and Captain Jean-Baptiste de Lorimier, and as many as four British regulars (see Cruikshank 1905, 27–28, 30–31, 37, 42–43; Leighton 1988). A source from the British side says seven Delawares and three Nipissings were captured, and five Ojibwas, a dragoon, and a member of the Glengarry regiment killed (Cruikshank 1905, 32). John Norton from the Grand River Tract fought in this action and said that it was Mohawks from Kahnawake who had been taken in addition to the Delawares (Klinck and Talman 1970, 338). Fighting was renewed the next day and the *Buffalo Gazette* reported the total American

2. Arthur Parker (1926, 145) records that the enmity between the Seneca and the Mohawk generated by the War of 1812 was such that when Cornplanter's grandson Solomon O'Bail met Colonel W. S. Kerr, a Mohawk from the Six Nations Reserve, at the dedication of the Caneadea Council House in Letchworth Park in 1876, the two initially refused to shake hands.

3. William Stone and William Ketchum get the date of the skirmish wrong, placing it on 17 July and 27 August 1813, respectively; unlike Ketchum, Stone also gets Blacksnake's name wrong, listing him as "Black-Smoke" (Stone 1841, 249–50; Ketchum 1864–65, 2:375–76).

losses over the two days were four Indians and one volunteer killed (Cruikshank 1905, 60–61).

The New York Senecas found themselves in yet another skirmish at Ball's farm on 6 September 1813. The American force of riflemen and Iroquois was driven back by Iroquois from the Grand River Tract led by Colonel William Claus and Captain William Kerr (Cruikshank 1905, 110).

Sensing the Seneca and other Indian allies were wavering in their resolve, the new American commander, Major General James Wilkinson, sent a message to them in the name of the President on 10 September 1813. He called on them to demonstrate their patriotism and organize a corps from among themselves with a promise "the whole to be allowed the same pay, subsistence, and emoluments as are allowed to the regular troops of the army of the U.S." (Cruikshank 1905, 111–12).

The American government apparently did not deliver the promised pay, however. A month later, Red Jacket complained to Erastus Granger: "We have not received pay according to promise. We think you were not authorized to promise us. We think we are trifled with. We were promised that all horses and cattle should be free plunder. We took horses: we had to give them up. We have been deceived. We, the Senecas and Onondagas, gave up the property we took. . . . We want you to state this to the President" (Cruikshank 1907, 86). Red Jacket himself had been forced to give up a yoke of oxen he had captured in Canada (Snyder 1978, 70).

The enthusiasm of many Senecas to fight on the side of the United States declined after the Battle of Chippawa, on 5 July 1814. There were relatively large Native contingents on each side, and even though Indians did not play a major role in the outcome of this battle, they suffered heavy casualties in a bloody first phase of the fight. One division of the Americans had captured Fort Erie and a second, smaller body of troops, including the New York Indians, was moving northward. They established a camp on the Niagara River just south of Navy Island. The British moved south across the Chippawa River and their Indians, including both western Indians and men from the Six Nations, were sent into the wood on the western flank of both armies to survey the American strength. They routed an American picket. The American commander, Major General Jacob Brown, sent his Indians and Pennsylvania Volunteers under the overall command of Brigadier General Peter Porter to drive the British Indians from the forest. This they did, also driving the Canadians of the Second Lincoln Militia before them, but as they emerged from the northern edge of the forest, they found themselves facing a regular light infantry battalion commanded by Lieutenant Colonel Thomas Pearson. A volley from this unit caused Porter to order a retreat. The remainder of the battle was largely fought between regulars; the steadiness of the American regulars has attained legendary status (Barbuto 2000, 170–78).

Both armies suffered high casualties (Barbuto 2000, 182). Barbuto estimates that 25 percent of the Indians on the British side and 6 percent of the men commanded by General Porter (including the New York Iroquois) were killed or wounded. After the battle, it was reported by the Americans that 87 of the Iroquois and western Indians on the British side had been killed, and that New York Iroquois lost between 9 and 11, with 4 wounded and 10 missing (Benn 1998, 163; Babcock 1927, 155). Among the Seneca dead was the chief Twoguns (Graves 1994, 175).[4] Iroquois on both sides began to see the logic in a mutual withdrawal. Two Senecas from the American side (one of whom had lived on the Grand River just four years earlier) appeared in the camp of the British Indians with a Cayuga chief who had been captured at Chippawa. They proposed that both parties withdraw and leave the fight to the regular armies and the non-Indian militias. Even though John Norton argued against them, their proposal was well received among the Iroquois (Klinck and Talman 1970, 353–55). Although there was at times a token presence of Iroquois among both the British and American forces during the remainder of the war, never again did they oppose each

---

4. About 1820, Red Jacket married the widow of Twoguns (A. Parker 1952, 175).

other in the numbers present at Chippawa. American officials believed that Cornplanter, Red Jacket, and Blue Sky were prominent
in the peace movement among the American Iroquois (Densmore
1999, 87).

The Americans and British concluded a peace agreement in
Ghent, Belgium, on Christmas Eve 1814. The only mention of aboriginal allies in the Treaty of Ghent was a promise that neither side
would employ Indian warriors in a future war. Word of the treaty
reached New York on 11 February 1815; Canada learned of the
peace on 1 March (Stanley 1983, 392–94). The British finally informed their Indian allies that the war was over on 24 April 1815
(Jennings et al. 1984, 1815 24–27 Apr).

Support for the American cause from the New York reservations
had been extensive. E. A. Cruikshank (1898, 70) notes that, as late as
1862, there were still 415 New York Iroquois collecting pensions
for their service in the War of 1812. More than half of these lived at
Cattaraugus. Two lived on the Cornplanter Grant and another 83
made the Allegany Reservation their home. Although Cornplanter
did not play an active role in the fighting along the Niagara border
during the War of 1812,[5] his eldest son, Major Henry O'Bail, is
reported to have commanded the Allegany Senecas on campaign
(A. Parker 1952, 156). Cornplanter's nephew, Governor Blacksnake,
was also active, later telling historian Lyman Draper that he had
killed two British soldiers and a Delaware during this war (DM
4-S-81–82).

The Quakers lamented that "continual alarms" and "frequent
calls on them [the Senecas] to assist in the invasion of Canada" dis-

5. Charles Snyder (1978, 73) claims that Cornplanter received a U.S. commission as a colonel (along with Farmer's Brother) and was paid forty dollars per
month; he also lists Little Billy, Pollard, Red Jacket, and "Black Snake" as receiving U.S. commissions, although he does not provide the source for this information. Louise Babcock (1927, 107) claims that a "payroll" dated 12 July 1813 listed
Farmer's Brother as a captain, not a colonel, but with pay of forty dollars per
month; although her list of Senecas receiving commissions otherwise agrees with
Snyder's, she makes no mention of Cornplanter.

rupted the progress that they had fostered in Euro-American domestic skills among the Seneca population. In addition, "their war excursions had a demoralizing effect, by exposing them again to the use of intoxicating liquors, which gained an ascendency over some" (Jackson 1830b, 62).

Arriving at Allegany in the summer of 1814, the Quakers heard complaints that recruiting efforts for the American cause had disrupted economic progress. When Cornplanter did not attend the council called for them, the Quaker delegates journeyed to the Cornplanter Grant to visit him. Cornplanter complained of abuse of alcohol caused by the war and also of the social problems caused by divorce. The site of the old village of Burnt House was "entirely deserted, and so overgrown with young timber, as almost to conceal the place where it stood." The five or six families remaining on the grant were "mostly his [Cornplanter's] connexions" (Jackson 1830b, 63–64). A census taken in 1816 listed the population of the Cornplanter Grant as 45, and that of the Allegany Reservation as 445. The total Seneca population was 1,879 (Snyder 1978, 30).

The Death of Handsome Lake

In a story recounted by Merle Deardorff (1951, 97), Handsome Lake had been told by his messengers that "he must 'take four steps from Burnt House.' " Deardorff lists Coldspring, Cattaraugus, and Tonawanda as the first three steps. In 1815, Handsome Lake took the fourth step, journeying to the Onondaga Reservation, near Syracuse, New York,[6] although Anthony Wallace (1970, 318) feels the journeys to Tonawanda and Onondaga were simply part of the annual visits that Handsome Lake routinely made to preach in other Iroquois communities.

Oral tradition records two dreams Handsome Lake experienced

6. I assume that Deardorff heard the story of "four steps" from someone on the Allegany Reservation. In the version of Handsome Lake's message published by Arthur Parker, the prophet relates: "Then the messengers told me that my life journey would be in three stages and when I entered the third I would enter into the eternity of the New World, the land of our Creator" (A. Parker 1913, 47).

on the long walk from Tonawanda to Onondaga. In the first, he reported, "I seemed to see a pathway, a trail overgrown and covered with grass so that it appeared not to have been traveled in a long time." In his second dream, he said, "I heard in a dream a certain woman speaking but I am not able to say whether she was of Onondaga or of Tonawanda from whence we came" (A. Parker 1913, 78–79).

At the edge of the Onondaga Reservation, Handsome Lake and his followers paused to eat. As they were entering the settlement, Handsome Lake missed a favorite knife and went back, alone, to look for it. The messengers had warned Handsome Lake that he should never be alone (A. Parker 1913, 47). The prophet suddenly became severely ill, such that he made it back to the community only with great difficulty. Unable to attend the council, he was placed in cabin on a creek that feeds into Onondaga Creek. The Onondagas staged a lacrosse game in the hope of curing him, but Handsome Lake was so weak he could not watch the entire match. It was there that he died on 10 August 1815 (A. Parker 1913, 79–80). The Onondagas had sent word to Coldspring, asking that Henry O'Bail come, but Cornplanter's son did not reach Onondaga before his father's brother had died (A. Parker 1913, 80n; A. Wallace 1970, 319–20). Anthony Wallace (1970, 320) feels Handsome Lake's title and position on the Confederacy Council "probably" passed to John Snow. Indeed, the missionary Laura Wright told local historian Orsamus Marshall in 1876 that John Snow had been raised to hold the title "Handsome Lake" (Snyder 1978, 29). The best evidence, however, suggests that the title of Handsome Lake was held by Turtle Clan member George Lindsey of Buffalo Creek in 1838 (Abler 2004, table 1).

Land Sales

In the years before the War of 1812, pressure had begun to build on the New York Senecas to sell their remaining lands and remove to a new homeland in the west. A new group of land speculators had entered the scene. The Holland Land Company had sold its preemption right to Seneca lands to the Ogden Land Company on 12 September 1810 (Abrams 1976, 55). Even before they had formally acquired the preemption right, the Ogdens secured the services of Jasper Parrish and Horatio Jones, both of whom had been captives among the Seneca during the Revolutionary War and who frequently served as interpreters during councils and treaty negotiations. The pair were hired to convince the Senecas of the wisdom of leaving New York and settling in the west (Robert Troup to Jasper Parrish in Jennings et al. 1984, reel 45: 1810 24 Aug).[7]

The Ogden Land Company sent its agent, a Mr. Richardson, to Buffalo Creek, where he met in council with New York Seneca chiefs to negotiate a land sale in the spring of 1811. The council is poorly documented, save for a pamphlet that was published to document the oratorical skills of Red Jacket, but there seems to have been no U.S. commissioner present, as required by law. The Senecas refused to look for lands in the west, saying that "if we should sell our lands and move off into a distant country, towards the setting sun, we should be looked upon in the country to which we go as foreigners, and strangers, and be despised by the red as well as the white men" (Jackson 1830b, 59; Stone 1841, 200; see Densmore 1999, 72–73, 143–45).

The preemption right did not apply to the islands in the Niagara River, the most important of which being Grand Island. Both Little Billy and Cornplanter put forward the Seneca claim to these lands at a council attended by Jasper Parrish, Horatio Jones, and U.S. Indian Agent Erastus Granger at Buffalo Creek on 16 September 1810. Raising once more the issue of payment for the Phelps and

7. Parrish and Jones managed to keep their employment by land speculators secret and to maintain good relations with the New York Senecas to their own personal benefit. In 1811, Farmer's Brother requested that Jones and Parrish be given title to two square-mile tracts of Seneca lands on Lake Erie because "We still feel our hearts beat with affection for them" and because he wished to reward them for their services as interpreters (Jennings et al. 1984, reel 45: 1811 10 Aug). Arthur Parker (1926, 149–50) also records this gift and speech by Farmer's Brother, but says it dates from "the Genesee council of 1798."

Gorham purchase of 1788, Cornplanter claimed the Seneca had been promised one thousand dollars per annum but were receiving only half that amount. Although Phelps was now dead, Cornplanter still felt the Seneca should receive their due. He called on Parrish and Jones as well as Indian Agent Granger to assist in pursuing the claim (Jennings et al. 1984, reel 45: 1810 16 Sept [II]).

Eager to purchase the Niagara River islands, particularly Grand Island, as authorized by the New York State legislature, Governor Daniel D. Tompkins had written to Jasper Parrish in April 1811, hoping to arrange a council at Buffalo that June. In May, however, the Governor had been told that the Seneca were unwilling to sell (Jennings et al. 1984, reel 45: 1811 11 Apr; 1812 12 Feb).

At war's end in 1814, New York was free again to pursue its interest in the islands in the Niagara River. On 12 September 1815, without formal sanction from the federal government, New York signed a treaty with the Seneca Nation at Buffalo in which it claimed to have acquired these islands for a payment of one thousand dollars and an annuity of five hundred dollars. Although the treaty was signed by Red Jacket, Little Billy, Colonel Pollard, and other Buffalo chiefs, it was not signed by any chiefs from Allegany; indeed, there is no record they even attended the treaty council (see Jennings et al. 1984, reel 46: 1818 10 Dec [XV]).[8] As part of the treaty negotiations, the Seneca stipulated that Jasper Parrish receive from New York State title to Squaw Island in the Niagara River at the mouth of Scajaquada Creek for two dollars per acre (Jennings et al. 1984, reel 45: 1815 13 Sept).[9]

On 31 August 1826, a treaty signed at Buffalo Creek, though never ratified by the U.S. Senate, conveyed Seneca lands covering

8. The Seneca Nation and the Tonawanda Band of the Senecas recently put forward a claim to the Niagara River islands based on the failure of the federal government to play its legally required role in the treaty negotiations and of Congress to ratify this treaty (see Hauptman 2000). The judge in the case ruled that the Seneca had surrendered these lands in the Fort Stanwix Treaty of 1768 and that the Canandaigua Treaty of 1794 had not conveyed title back to them.

9. See note 7.

more than 130 square miles, by the Quakers' estimate, to the Ogden Land Company. The five remaining Seneca reservations on the Genesee River were all sold, as were portions of the Buffalo Creek, Cattaraugus, and Tonawanda Reservations. As a reward for signing, Cornplanter's nephew, Blacksnake, who had assumed a leading role in council, was given a lifetime annuity of eighty dollars. James Robinson, a spokesman for the Christians among the Allegany Senecas, who had initially opposed the treaty but eventually signed, received an annuity of fifty dollars (see Jennings et al. 1984, reel 46: 31 Aug (II); 1826 6 Sept).

Although Cornplanter would on occasion appear in councils, in the last fifteen or so years of his life, meetings of Seneca chiefs at Allegany were dominated by his nephew, Governor Blacksnake, who represented the followers of Handsome Lake, and James Robinson, who represented the other "party" of the Senecas, those who had converted to Christianity (Jennings et al. 1984, reel 46: 1822 17 Oct). In the fall of 1822, Blacksnake told the Quakers that it had been missionaries who had divided the Senecas and that he did not think it good to teach Seneca children to read and write. If, however, others chose to send their children to school, he promised not to interfere.

Blacksnake also feared that Robinson and like-minded chiefs favored leaving New York for lands in the west, such as those at Green Bay, Wisconsin. Blacksnake and Robinson traveled together to a council at Buffalo in 1824. En route, they discussed issues that divided them. Blacksnake offered to have all children attend school if Robinson's Christians would follow Quaker practices and give up hymn singing. Robinson said his people would do this if Blacksnake's followers would give up dancing. Even though hymns continued to be sung in Christian services and dancing remained central to the Seneca religious observances in the Longhouse, the dialogue reduced the gap between the two factions (Jennings et al. 1984, reel 46: 1824 19 Sept).

The general U.S. policy to move all Indians west of the Mississippi River (see A. Wallace 1993) well suited the Ogden Land

Daguerreotype of Governor Blacksnake (Donaldson 1892, facing p. 28). Courtesy of the Robarts Library, University of Toronto.

Company's plans to acquire Seneca territories. The Seneca mobilized in opposition to this threat. Cornplanter was among the fifty-one chiefs who signed a document pledging never to sell their lands in 1832. It is perhaps a sign of the aging chief's declining participation in political affairs that his name appears, not among the dozen on the first page of the pledge, but after those of John Pierce and Young King on the second page (Jennings et al. 1984, reel 47: 1832 3 Nov). There is no record that Cornplanter attended a council held at Buffalo Creek in July of 1833, where the Seneca made clear they were not interested in lands proposed for Iroquois settlement at Green Bay (Jennings et al. 1984, reel 47: 1833 31 July). His name does appear, however, and in first place, on the 1834 petition to the U.S. superintendent of Indian affairs indicating the Seneca Nation had no interest in lands west of the Mississippi (Jennings et al. 1984, reel 47: 1834 29 Sept).

Christianity and the Cornplanter Grant

Although the Quakers had been on the Cornplanter Grant or working nearby since 1798, their primary goal had been cultural and social change, not religious conversion. After the War of 1812, other Christian groups looked seriously at converting the residents of the Seneca reservations. Congregationalists of the Western Missionary Society of Pittsburgh expressed an interest in proselytizing among the Cornplanter Senecas as early as 1807; in the autumn of 1814, Reverend Thomas Hunt visited for a month to inquire about establishing a mission. Cornplanter is reported to have addressed a council at Coldspring in 1815, arguing that the Seneca should adopt Christianity (Alden 1827, 19). On the Cornplanter Grant, a layman, Samuel Oldham, took the duties of schoolteacher, and he, along with Reverend John Law, initiated a Congregationalist mission on Cornplanter Grant that year (Congdon 1967, 74; Deardorff 1941, 18; 1965).

Reverend Timothy Alden visited Oldham and the Cornplanter Grant in the summer of 1816. He addressed an afternoon gathering in the school house and reports it was attended by "tawny natives neatly clad, and in some instances, with a display of silver brooches, stars, hat-bands, and other ornaments, for which they have a great predilection" (Alden 1827, 13). Alden interpreted the lip movements of Cornplanter during the prayers as evidence of his devotion, although it appears Alden's entire address to the meeting was in English with no interpreter. Eleven Seneca boys aged 10 to 15 years were in attendance at the school (there were also about ten white children who attended). Seneca girls came on occasion, but Alden reported even less interest in obtaining an education for females than for males. He gave Cornplanter credit when some Senecas agreed to send their sons to the school (Alden 1827, 13–17).

In September 1817, Alden preached two sermons on the Cornplanter Grant, with Henry O'Bail interpreting. Cornplanter publically endorsed the missionary's message, and privately offered to accompany him on the visit Alden planned to make to Red Jacket in Buffalo, although Cornplanter thought Red Jacket was firmly entrenched in the religion of his ancestors. Alden (1827, 26–30) reported that thirteen Seneca boys and eight to ten white children were attending Oldham's school at Burnt House.

When Cornplanter turned away from accommodation with Christianity, however, missionaries were forced to leave his grant as early as 1817 or 1818, although they continued their work on the Allegany Reservation. The Congregationalists reestablished a missionary presence among the Cornplanter Senecas after the old chief's death and maintained the Cornplanter Mission Church until 1883, when they were replaced by the Presbyterians (Deardorff 1965).

Cornplanter's Vision

Cornplanter had long urged the Seneca to adopt large segments of Euro-American culture, and had even sent his son Henry to be educated in Philadelphia. In December 1816, he wrote the Quakers that he thought American law should be applied in Seneca communities (Jennings et al. 1984, reel 45: 1816 Dec). Although the Quakers opposed any Seneca land sale, they were pressing the Allegany Senecas to divide their reservation into individual allotments. In October 1817, Cornplanter told a Quaker visitor that, though he favored dividing the lands into individually owned plots, he thought social problems among the Seneca, notably family instability and disorder in government, would negate any good that might accrue from it (Jennings et al. 1984, reel 45: 1817 16 Oct). By 1819–20, however, Cornplanter had moved from accommodating to resisting white culture. At this time, the Ogden Land Company wanted the Senecas either to move west out of New York or to settle on the Allegany Reservation.

Cornplanter attended the council in Buffalo on or about 10 July 1819 where Red Jacket referred to Allegany as "a bed of rocks" and to the U.S. president as "disordered in his mind," having been confused by the missionaries and Quakers. Red Jacket said the Seneca were determined to exclude all whites from their lands. When afterward Pollard and some other chiefs apologized for Red Jacket's speech, J. L. Ogden noted that Cornplanter was not among them (Jennings et al. 1984, reel 46, 1819 10 July; see Hyde 1903, 266–67).

Cornplanter's shift to nativism is usually associated with a dramatic vision experience, which he later reported in a long speech that he asked to be translated and recorded in English (DM 16-F-227-227 [9]; see A. Wallace 1970, 327–29; 2002; Rothenberg 1986). Cornplanter had been brooding about the prideful policies he had followed in the past, the pressures he was currently experiencing with his fellow Senecas over whether to convert to Christianity and whether to sell their lands and move west, and the personal troubles that lay upon his aging shoulders. The newly established Warren County had threatened to tax his land grant, although he and others may have seen this as a more general threat to the Seneca population. He was faced with the burden of his mentally retarded son, known in documents only as "the Idiot," whose ultimate fate, if Cornplanter were to precede him in death, was deeply troubling to the Seneca chief.

In a series of dreams or visions late in 1819, the Creator came to Cornplanter to tell him of his sins—and those of the white people. Cornplanter had committed a sin by killing people during the American Revolution, but the British had committed an even greater sin when they surrendered lands, lands that were not theirs, south of Lake Ontario to the Americans. The Americans themselves "live on borrowed soil," the Creator told him. Cornplanter revealed this encounter with the Creator (in the English translation referred to as the "Savio[u]r," the "Great Spirit," and the "Lord") in a "talk" given on 13 or 14 February 1820 (DM 16-F-227-227[9]).

The Creator also demanded that Cornplanter renounce and destroy objects that gave him pride and set him apart from the general
community. These were linked to Cornplanter's ties to the white
world and his military career. He therefore set about destroying a
French flag that had been acquired by ancestors of his wife (Alden
1827, 23), his sword, a gold-laced military hat, his captain's commission, and a wampum belt that had also been owned by his wife, and
which had been given by whites to be "worn as a token of great
men or warriors." The flag was the first to be destroyed, but when
Cornplanter did so surreptitiously while burning brush, the Creator reproved him. This was not proper. Cornplanter must destroy
these symbols publicly.

Timothy Alden claimed the sword had been presented to Cornplanter by George Washington and the military hat was a gift from
Pennsylvania Governor Thomas Mifflin. He writes that even though
Cornplanter had acquired neither the flag nor the wampum belt,
they were nevertheless "trophies of valour," which had belonged to
ancestors of Cornplanter's wife (Alden 1827, 142).

The Creator told Cornplanter that destroying these symbols
would add ten years to his life. Expressing concern for the fate of his
mentally retarded son, Cornplanter asked that his son go with him
when leaving this world. The Creator told him this would be so. But
Cornplanter must not travel beyond Buffalo and, when visiting his
farm or traveling by canoe, he must take his son with him (DM 16-
F-227 [6]).

Cornplanter was told that observing the Sabbath, preaching, and
hymn singing were appropriate among non-Indians, but if Indians
were to abandon their old ways, it would lead only to confused
minds and perhaps even to suicide (DM 16-F-227 [7]).

Taxation, Cornplanter was told, was to support the white people, hence there was no need for Indians of the Six Nations to pay
taxes. Paying taxes, obeying the white man's law, waging the white
man's wars, and observing the Sabbath—all were inappropriate for
Indians (DM 16-F-227 [7]–227[8]).

Finally, Cornplanter was told that "free use of cows milk . . .

puts some people out of their senses" (DM 16-F-227 [8]). Although this has been cited as evidence that Cornplanter was "deranged" or suffering from a "psychosis," Diane Rothernberg (1986) has argued convincingly that drinking milk and lactose intolerance may indeed have been causing problems among the Seneca population. It is certainly possible that the severe stomach cramps from drinking milk that Cornplanter observed, cramps that provoked an increase in quarreling and fighting, may have led him to hear the Creator warn against drinking the beverage. Rothenberg (1986) notes that severe and chronic diarrhea from drinking cow's milk poses a threat to the very lives of younger members of a lactose-intolerant population.

It was probably at this time that Cornplanter passed his political position to a Seneca from Tonawanda, whose English name was "Canada," sending him his tomahawk as token. Later, Ely S. Parker obtained the tomahawk from Canada's widow for the New York State Museum. She told Parker that, though the head was the original, the handle had been replaced (E. Parker 1851). Ely Parker's great-nephew, Arthur C. Parker, rescued the tomahawk from the fire that destroyed a large portion of the collections of the New York State Museum on 29 March 1911 (Porter 2001, 76).

Writing in 1820, Buffalo Creek missionary Jabez Hyde lamented Cornplanter's turning away from Christianity. He reported that Cornplanter "for two years past has been at seasons in a state of derangement" and become a prophet. "He says that it has been revealed to him that God never designed the Christian religion or habits of white men for Indians." Because Cornplanter had "become broken down with age and affliction," however, he was unable to influence many with his anti-Christian stance (Hyde 1903, 270).

At this same time, Red Jacket was also advocating an antimissionary agenda. In a letter to Indian Agent Jasper Parrish dated 18 January 1821, dictated in the presence of several chiefs including both Cornplanter and Jemmy Johnson, and translated by Henry O'Bail (Jennings et al. 1984, reel 46, 1821 18 Jan), Red Jacket again urged that missionaries be removed from Indian lands.

Deardorff (1941, 13) reports that in the year in which Warren County was organized, 1819, the sheriff of the county came to the Cornplanter Grant to collect taxes on the land. This action may have inspired at least a portion of Cornplanter's vision. According to Deardorff, Cornplanter received the sheriff in his home, but also present were thirty armed followers. The sheriff did not pursue the issue of collecting taxes at that time. In another report of this encounter, or perhaps a later, similar one (Day 1843, 656; see also Snowden 1867, 69–70; Sipe 1926, 467–68), Cornplanter meets the sheriff and a small armed posse and threatens to call up a hundred armed warriors to oppose the collection of taxes.

Although Cornplanter was finally persuaded to provide a promissory note for the $43.79 in taxes, he appealed to the governor of Pennsylvania. On 2 April 1822, the Pennsylvania legislature passed a bill exempting the Cornplanter Grant from taxation as long as it remained in the hands of Cornplanter or his heirs. Commissioners were delegated to meet with Cornplanter. This meeting took place on 6 July 1822 in Warren, and Cornplanter responded with a speech, "a really good speech—the most eloquent that Warren County has ever heard, I am sure" (Deardorff 1941, 13), in which Cornplanter declared that the Creator had made whites and Indians to be separate. Cornplanter had been told that cattle and farms were for whites, deer and bear were for Indians. He had been told to abstain from alcohol, not to observe the Sabbath, and to refrain from lusting after women other than his wife. He asked that the contents of his speech be taken back to the governor of Pennsylvania (Day 1843, 656–57; Sipe 1926, 468–69).

The Removal of Red Jacket from Office

The Christian community grew more rapidly at Buffalo Creek than among other Seneca communities. Cornplanter's colleague and rival Red Jacket remained the most eloquent opponent of conversion. A large portion of those who converted to Christianity were recognized as chiefs, and these Christian chiefs, the majority from Buffalo Creek but including James Robinson from Allegany, met on 15 September 1827 and deposed Red Jacket as chief. Those chiefs who supported him met in council on 16 October and repudiated the action of the Christian faction.

Red Jacket decided to journey to Washington, D.C., to make his case there before the commissioner of Indian affairs, Thomas McKenney, and President John Quincy Adams. Accompanying Red Jacket on the trip was Cornplanter's son Henry and one other Seneca. It is likely that Henry O'Bail was along to serve as interpreter, a role he had many times earlier played for the old Seneca orator. In his meetings with President Adams on 24 March 1828, Red Jacket also complained about unjust land transactions. While they were in Washington, Red Jacket and Henry O'Bail had their portraits painted by Charles Bird King. Upon their return to Seneca country, Red Jacket was restored to his position as chief, only to die two years later (Deardorff 1994, 11–12; Stone 1841, 380–88; Densmore 1999, 107–13; Viola 1976).

Cornplanter's Last Years

As the years progressed, the non-Seneca population surrounding the Cornplanter Grant in Warren County, Pennsylvania, grew rapidly, more than doubling each decade. In 1800, it was a scant 230; by 1810, it had grown to 827; in 1820, it was 1,976; and by 1830, it had reached 4,706 (Day 1843, 647).

At nine in the morning of 13 May 1829 (or perhaps 1830), the first steamboat to ascend the Allegheny River reached the Cornplanter Grant, an event reported in the *Pittsburgh Gazette*. Cornplanter's house was said to be "a two story log house, in a state of decay, without furniture, except a few benches, and wooden bowls and spoons to eat out of." Invited to board, Cornplanter, his son Charles O'Bail, and a son-in-law did so. The newspaper estimated the population of the Cornplanter Grant at 50, living in eight to ten houses. The residents included Cornplanter's wife and her mother, whose age was estimated at 115. The health of both women was reported to be good (Jackson 1830b, 113–14).

Cornplanter had become something of a tourist attraction in

this remote part of Pennsylvania. When Thomas Struthers was visited by some men from Pittsburgh and Butler, Pennsylvania, he took them from his home in Warren to the Cornplanter Grant. The elderly chief extended his hospitality, having makeshift benches arranged in a square for his visitors while he took a seat in the center to answer their questions. By this time, Cornplanter had become completely blind in the eye injured on his journey to New York City in 1786. However, Struthers noted the brightness in the old man's remaining eye as he spoke. In a long speech that was interpreted for the visitors, Cornplanter complained of the loss of their lands, but praised George Washington. He showed the visitors three documents signed by the American president, which he kept wrapped in a linen cloth in a valise. He then fed his visitors a meal of dried venison and corn mush (Snowden 1867, 71–72).

In February 1833, the Protestant missionaries who had been working at Cattaraugus and at Buffalo Creek came to Allegany and held a council there. They were told by Cornplanter that, although he had tried Christianity, he would no longer tolerate it, and that Christianity should not be preached among the Allegany Senecas (Congdon 1967, 75).

The Quakers were back at the Cornplanter Grant in the fall of 1835. Three days of heavy rainfall commencing 18 October 1835 had flooded the settlement and left the population destitute. The Quakers provided a thousand dollars in relief (Miller 1958, 104).

Cornplanter's physical infirmities were catalogued in his final year. He was stooped with a sunken chest. He had no use of one hand, and, as already has been mentioned, had vision in but a single eye. The brow drooped over the socket of his blind eye. His ears had been slit as was the fashion in his youth, but one was torn "and hung down his neck like a useless rag." His hair, though full, was white (Day 1843, 657). It is not clear if he still wore the beard that had adorned his face perhaps a decade earlier.

Cornplanter died on 18 February 1836, followed by his widow three months later (S. P. Johnson in Snowden 1867, 11). A sister of Cornplanter, purported to be two years younger than her brother, lived another decade, dying on 28 December 1846 (*Mental Elevator,* 14:120). Cornplanter's nephew, Governor Blacksnake, died in 1859 (Abler 1989).

A non-Indian, Benjamin G. Williams (not the Seneca Benjamin Williams associated with Governor Blacksnake), claimed to have witnessed the burial of Cornplanter:

> I was there and saw him buried. They had just a rough box nailed together. Four men carried him to the grave a short distance from the house. They went ahead and the Indians came next, marching in Indian form, single file; then the squaws the same way. They went by a path back of his house in the woods. There they had a hole dug in which they placed him and covered him up. Not a word was said by any of them. They did not know what to do. They went back to the house as they came out in single file, and there they sat down, mute and no talking, all quiet, not the least mark left to tell where he was buried, only the fresh dirt that did not last long. (Williams 1883, 12)[10]

10. Totally lacking in structure and organization and containing much more fiction than fact, Williams's book (1883) must be approached with a great deal of skepticism and care. Williams makes little attempt to indicate the sources of the statements found in his book, which are sometimes presented in the first person without any quotation marks in contexts that strongly suggest they are the words of others and not those of Williams.

9

~~~~~~~

Cornplanter's Legacy

The Cornplanter Grant and Cornplanter's Heirs

Membership in the Seneca Nation, and hence the right to reside on the Allegany Reservation, passes matrilineally, that is, one is a member of the Seneca Nation if and only if one's mother is a member of the Seneca Nation. Thus, as enrolled members of the Seneca Nation, many of Cornplanter's descendants were able to take up residence at Allegany or on other Seneca Nation reservations.[1] The Cornplanter Grant continued to be occupied by a portion of his descendants, notably his own children and grandchildren rather than those related to him matrilineally (see appendix, prepared by the Cornplanter Family Historian Jack Ericson). Their rights to the grant land were formalized in 1871, when the Warren County Orphans Court and a act of the Pennsylvania legislature divided the grant into six parcels, each to be shared or further divided among the descendants of each of Cornplanter's three sons and three

1. As a result of a series of events beginning with the Buffalo Creek treaty of 1838, the Seneca Nation has split into the Seneca Nation of Indians, which controls the Allegany, Cattaraugus, and Oil Spring Reservations, and the Tonawanda Band of Seneca Indians, which controls the Tonawanda Reservation (Abler and Tooker 1978, 511–12). Enrolled members of the nation or band may own land and housing, respectively, on the Allegany, Cattaraugus, or Oil Spring Reservations or on the Tonawanda Reservation in New York State, which may only be sold or given to another enrolled member of that nation or band.

daughters (Indian Committee Records, box 6: 241). The sons were Henry O'Bail, Charles O'Bail, and William O'Bail; the daughters were Polly Logan, Esther Pierce, and Ja-wa-yuh. A total of twenty-three heirs are listed (Donaldson 1892, 30). Only Polly Logan still survived in 1871; she died on 7 December 1871, probably eighty-six years of age (Ericson 1996, 5). Historical records suggest that Cornplanter certainly had other children (for example, his mentally handicapped son, referred to as "the Idiot," who died in 1821), but these in all likelihood had no descendants when the grant was divided in 1871.

Although a lengthy history of the descendants of Cornplanter or of the grant on which so many of them lived is beyond the scope of this volume, it is certainly worth touching on some of the salient points. Despite Cornplanter's opposition to both Christianity and formal education late in his life, his descendants embraced both, at least to some degree.

In 1837, after Cornplanter had died, the Quakers tried again to establish a school on the grant, but it closed within a year. Two decades later, however, Cornplanter's grandson Marsh Pierce persuaded the Seneca Nation Council to appropriate two hundred dollars to construct a schoolhouse, and the Pennsylvania legislature voted an annual operating grant of one hundred dollars. The school opened in September 1857, with the class being taught by eighteen-year-old Juliet Tome, who stayed with Marsh Pierce's family (Miller 1958, 105).

In 1903, Pennsylvania replaced the old wooden schoolhouse with a brick structure at a cost of three thousand dollars. Transportation into the grant was such that the bricks for the school's construction had to be dragged across the frozen Allegheny River on sleds. This brick school continued in use for half a century, finally closing in 1953. Miss Lucia E. Browne taught the Cornplanter children for the last twenty-three years of the school's operation. Although at times she had as many as forty scholars, after the school closed, no children remained on the grant (Miller 1958, 106–7).

Christian missionaries who preached on the Allegany Reservation also attempted to convert the population of the Cornplanter Grant. Cornplanter's daughters Esther Pierce and Polly Logan both joined the Protestant (Congregationalist/Presbyterian) church of Reverend William Hall. When the grant was partitioned in 1871, some land was set aside for community use, and a church was built there in 1885, with a manse constructed behind it. The church was something of a success under Reverend Morton F. Trippe, who served from 1881 until his death in 1915 (Deardorff 1965, 262).

Mention has already been made of the monument erected by the State of Pennsylvania over Cornplanter's grave on the grant in 1866 (see chapter 1). Cornplanter's grandson Solomon O'Bail opened the dedication ceremonies, and the three surviving children of Cornplanter attended (Snowden 1867).

In 1866, the population of the grant was estimated to be eighty (Snowden 1867, 85). In 1890, the population was reported to be ninety-nine, eleven of whom were Onondagas and one of whom was non-Indian. They occupied twenty-seven houses, nine being log cabins and the remaining eighteen, wood frame houses. They owned 4 horses, 24 pigs, 204 chickens, and 22 head of cattle (Donaldson 1892, 6–7, 14–15). Cornplanter heir Roy Bennett told Merle Deardorff that, when he was growing up in the early twentieth century, as many as three hundred resided on the grant. He recalled Charlie Gordon's Cornplanter Silver Cornet Band giving concerts in front of the school (Deardorff 1965, 262). By 1933, the population had fallen to thirty (Skinner 1933, 3). The decline in population was doubtless related to the relative remoteness of the community and the poor condition of the road that led to it (Skinner 1933, 3; Fenton 1945a, 28–29). Ultimately, the population of the grant dwindled to seven in 1964, residing in four houses. Three other houses on the grant were only occasionally used (Abrams 1965, 61).

Largely cut off from the outside world, many of the grant residents continued to exploit the rich flora and fauna found in the forests and streams of the region. A number provided Merle Deardorff and William Fenton with a wealth of information documenting their use of the natural resources available in the early twentieth century (see, for example, Fenton and Deardorff 1943; Fenton 1942; 1945a; 1945b; 1945c; 1945d; 1946).

The Cornplanters and Kinzua

The construction of the Kinzua Dam in the 1960s inundated all but sixty-nine acres of the Cornplanter Grant under the waters of the Allegheny Reservoir (Bilharz 2000, 164). The reservoir also flooded much of the Allegany Reservation, home to many of the Cornplanter heirs. The project was first proposed in the 1920s, but the Depression and World War II intervened. It was revived and formally planned during the Eisenhower administration (see Hauptman 1986, 85–122; Bilharz 1998; 2000); the dam was constructed during the Kennedy and Johnson administrations. The lands it flooded had been guaranteed to the Seneca by the 1794 Treaty of Canandaigua, also called the "1794 Pickering treaty" (Abler and Tooker 1978, 508–9; Campisi 1988). In that solemn document, the Seneca were assured that

> all the land within the aforementioned boundaries, [will] be the property of the Seneka nation; and the United States will never claim the same, nor disturb the Seneka nation, nor any of the Six Nations, or of their Indian friends residing thereon and united with them, in the free use and enjoyment thereof: but it shall remain theirs, until they choose to sell the same to the people of the United States, who have the right to purchase. (Kappler 1904–41, 2:35)

Under American law, the Congress of the United States has the right to break treaties. The Seneca did not believe that Congress would be willing to break a treaty so long in force, yet it allocated a million dollars of the 1958 national budget for a feasibility study of the Kinzua Dam project (see Hauptman 1986, 105–22). The Seneca Nation raised the question whether, in doing this, Congress knew it was breaking the Canandaigua treaty. The Supreme Court ruled that the inclusion of the single line item in the 1958 budget constituted all that was required of Congress to signal its intent to break the 1794 Treaty of Canandaigua, then the oldest treaty still honored by the United States government (see Josephy 1968). Unwilling to antagonize the Democratic leadership of Pennsylvania, whose support had been critical in his narrow election victory, President John F. Kennedy chose to regard the construction of Kinzua Dam as a fait accompli.

The project was carried out by the U.S. Army Corps of Engineers. The "negotiations" between the corps and the Cornplanter heirs over the relocation of the cemetery from the grant reveal the arrogance of the officers in charge and their unwillingness to make any concessions to Cornplanter's descendants (see Josephy 1968, 108).

With respect to the cemetery, the Corps of Engineers had first indicated it would remove the remains to a site chosen by the Cornplanter heirs, but not to the small portion of the grant that remained outside the area taken for the Allegheny Reservoir. After deeming a second location proposed by the heirs unsuitable, the corps unilaterally decided to relocate the graves to the Riverview-Corydon Cemetery, which the Cornplanter heirs were forced to share with a relocated non-Indian cemetery. In protest, more than 150 heirs signed a petition against this move, but the corps won its case in court in March 1964 (Josephy 1968, 108–9).

Some Pennsylvania and Warren County politicians did not think the Cornplanter monument should be moved to the Riverview-Corydon Cemetery. Both the Warren County Planning Commission and the Warren County Historical Society favored a location more attractive to potential tourists. It was argued that the Pennsylvania Historical and Museum Commission should decide on "a suitable site" for the monument. With no Cornplanter heirs taking part, the commission decided in mid-September 1963 to maintain the association between the monument and the remains of Cornplanter and his descendants, but to do so at the Riverview-Corydon Cemetery (Bilharz 1995, 5–6).

A team from the State University of New York at Buffalo

(SUNY-Buffalo), under the supervision of Marian E. White and Dr. James E. Anderson, attempted to recover osteological and cultural data while the burials were being removed by a commercial contractor. George Abrams (1965, 60) reports the difficulty encountered by the lack of a formal government with authority over the grant and its affairs. In response to the threat of the Kinzua Dam, the Cornplanter Landowners Association had been formed to represent the individuals who held lands on the Cornplanter Grant. Abrams, himself a Cornplanter heir, reports the presence of three factions, "based on long-standing policy differences concerning Cornplanter affairs aggravated by personality conflicts and individual animosities" (Abrams 1965, 60). The anthropological team was eventually to obtain permission to observe and study the removal of about two-thirds of the 98 individuals whose burial sites were known and the remaining 263 graves, which held the remains of individuals whose identity had been lost. The commercial firm relocating the burials completed its work in just eight days, leaving the anthropological team little time to gather data (Abrams 1965, 65). Nonetheless, data were gathered from 110 of the graves (Sublett 1965, 89).

There was some question about whether the monument was in fact located over Cornplanter's grave. Benjamin Williams from nearby Warren, who is not the most reliable of sources, wrote that "when they came to raise the monument they did not know where the grave was. No one was there that could tell, so they had to guess the best they could" (Williams 1883, 12). According to Abrams (1965, 63), several Cornplanter heirs related that, before the monument was erected, the coffin was dug up and opened, and the body indeed identified as that of Cornplanter. Many other heirs, however, believed the body had been moved and buried in a secret location. Some thought it was on Cornplanter Peak to the east of the cemetery; others thought it was on the hill to the west (Abrams 1965, 71). Although the SUNY-Buffalo anthropologists were not allowed to observe the disinterment as closely as they desired, after examining the remains under the monument, physical anthropologist Audrey Sublet was able to conclude: "Osteologically, I found nothing which opposed the idea that this skeleton was Cornplanter himself" (Sublet 1965, 89; see also Abrams 1965, 71–72).

The monument was moved with the bones found under it to the Riverview-Corydon Cemetery. Approaching a century and a half in age, the marble monument had weathered badly. In Warren, Pennsylvania, the Chief Cornplanter Council of the Boy Scouts of America (the local scouts in Warren had taken this name in 1954) embraced the cause of replacing the old monument. A new version made in granite was erected and dedicated in October 1998 (Chief Cornplanter Council 2004; Hoover 2004, 63).

On the old Cornplanter Grant, what had started as a Lee family reunion in 1934 grew to become an annual picnic for the Cornplanter heirs. There was a hiatus after the grant was lost to the Allegheny River Reservoir because no suitable location was available. The last picnic was held on the grant on 3 August 1964 (Hoover 2004, 76). At the urging of Merrill Bowen, the heirs and the Seneca Nation combined resources to construct a gazebo behind the Haley Building in the Jimersontown relocation area on the Allegany Reservation. Although the event was discontinued for a few years, Seneca Nation Treasurer Cheryl Ray encouraged Harriet Pierce and Duce Bowen to revive the picnic. It continues to be held on the first Saturday in August and attracts more than one hundred heirs and attached family members (see Bilharz 1997).

Cornplanter's Place in Seneca History

As noted in chapter 7, there is an Iroquois proverb that the skin of a chief should be "seven thumbs thick" (A. Wallace 1970, 30–31). Certainly, Cornplanter endured criticism in his lifetime, and continues to receive the occasional negative evaluation of his role in Seneca history. As a graduate student, I heard a former president of the Seneca Nation dismiss his role: "Some say he was a great chief; I think he was just an appeaser!" In 1941, with the surrender of France to Hitler's Germany fresh in the news, Merle Deardorff observed, "he was in a way the Marshal Pétain of his day, and for nearly fifty years his town of Jennesadaga on the Cornplanter Grant was his Vichy, so to speak" (Deardorff 1941, 8). On the other hand, in the same paper, Deardorff (1941, 1) refers to Cornplanter as "one of the greatest of his race."

It is remarkable that the surviving historical record of the Chief Warrior is almost universal in the praise of Cornplanter and his abilities. I have not found a negative evaluation of Cornplanter in the writings of persons of such diverse backgrounds as General Anthony Wayne, missionary Samuel Kirkland, or the numerous Quakers with whom he had intimate contact. The only censure of his actions that appears in the historical record follows his vision and preaching of an anti-Christian stance in the 1820s, and even this censure suggests admiration for his abilities and behavior earlier in life.

A human side of Cornplanter seldom commented on is his devotion to his mentally challenged son. The vision alluded to above demonstrated his concern as a father for "The Idiot," as the son is universally identified in the historical documents.

Clearly, Cornplanter favorably impressed his non-Indian neighbors. This praise, of course, might be damning, for it may simply indicate that Cornplanter was a prominent Seneca willing to follow policies that were pleasing and beneficial to those non-Indian neighbors. Was this the case?

It is clear that during the most influential portion of his political career he took a decidedly pro-American stance. His motivations in so doing are, of course, open to a great deal of speculation. My own reading of the documents is that Cornplanter, perhaps better than many of his contemporaries among the Seneca, saw what was unfolding in the future. I do believe that Cornplanter was sincerely concerned about the survival of the Seneca Nation and the maintenance of its land base. He saw that continued conflict and the shedding of still more Seneca blood after their long and bloody participation in the American Revolutionary War would not assure the Seneca a land base close to the bones of their ancestors.

His perception of the future led Cornplanter to consider carefully his own future as well. Very early on, he anticipated that the traditional tribal economic base would be radically altered by the tide of American settlers and the cash economy they brought with them.

One indication of Cornplanter's perception of the future, all the more surprising because he never became familiar enough with the culture of the American invaders of the continent to acquire English, was the fact that he sent his eldest son, Henry O'Bail, off to school in Philadelphia. Cornplanter indicated this was so that his son could acquire the skills that would be necessary to manage his affairs and to look after him in his old age.

Another striking aspect of Cornplanter's perception of the future was described by General James Wilkinson, who referred to Cornplanter's "strong sense of private property" (Kent and Deardorff 1960, 270). Perhaps because he had little faith that his fellow chiefs would protect the remaining Seneca land base, Cornplanter never resided on a Seneca reservation; he lived the balance of his life after the American Revolution on his personal land grant, which could not be sold out from beneath him by the actions of a council of chiefs. Cornplanter took care that annuities promised him in treaty negotiations were in his own name. However avaricious Cornplanter may have been, he could not acquire as large a personal land base as he had hoped because of shady actions on the part of his even more avaricious neighbors, who swindled him (according to the murky historical record; see Deardorff 1941) out of several parcels of land. It is ironic that Oil City, which would have belonged to the Cornplanter heirs but for these questionable land transactions, has erected a life-sized statue of Cornplanter, sculpted by C. V. Curll, in a city park (Duce Bowen, personal communication, 18 May 2005).

A legacy of Cornplanter's acquisitiveness may be the highly negative stereotype carried by many contemporary Senecas of the behavior of politicians (see Wilson 1960; Abler 1969; Bilharz and Abler 1999). It is widely believed that Seneca Nation political officials loot the public treasury and use their office to enhance their personal wealth. Cornplanter certainly was not the only Seneca leader to have been given personal gifts and to have been provided with a personal annuities by federal and state officials seeking to secure favorable votes in councils. But it does seem that, among the Seneca leaders of his generation, Cornplanter received the gifts of greatest value.[2] It should also be noted that charges of mishandling community resources, of nepotism, and of graft and corruption leveled at leaders of reserve and reservation communities by those not holding political positions are pervasive across Canada and the United States. Thus the negative views held by the residents of the Allegany and Cattaraugus Reservations of the president and council of the Seneca Nation are certainly not unique, or even unusual.

While Cornplanter doubtlessly gained personally from the political role he played in the treaty-making era that followed the American Revolution, the question still remains whether his actions, rewarded by the federal and state officials with whom he was negotiating, were a betrayal of the Seneca people. I believe that the only reasonable conclusion is that they were not. The feasible options open to Cornplanter and his fellow leaders of the Seneca Nation were few. The Seneca had suffered extreme economic losses when most of their villages, crops, and orchards had been burnt to the ground by the armies of Sullivan and Broadhead. They had been formally abandoned by their British allies in the peace the Britain made with the American republic. The reluctance of the British to remove themselves from posts in the Ohio country gave hope to the Native peoples of that region that they could resist the Americans. Even the Senecas residing at Buffalo had continuing contact with the British at Niagara. By contrast, Cornplanter's people were far removed from potential British support. Pittsburgh, geographically the logical place for them to trade, was held by the Americans, not the British. From his home on the Allegheny River, Corn-

2. At the Treaty of Big Tree, Red Jacket received a cash grant of $600, twice the $300 that Cornplanter received, but because Cornplanter's annuity was more than twice Red Jacket's—$250 versus $100—in just two years, the total received by Cornplanter equaled that of Red Jacket (A. Wallace 1970, 183)

planter perceived the inability of their small and isolated population to resist the populous Americans to the east. Although it may in part have been bluster, the Americans time and again expressed their willingness to pursue a military solution to problems they encountered with the Seneca Nation. As Cornplanter himself stated, "you told us you could crush us to nothing" (*ASP: IA,* 1:140).

The peace policy of Cornplanter and other Seneca leaders gave the Americans neither cause nor excuse to use military force to crush the Senecas to nothing. Again and again, however, federal and state officials attempted to crush the Seneca Nation to nothing by force of diplomacy and law. The extinguishing of the Seneca's title to all lands in New York State was viewed by many, if not most, of the non-Indian residents of the state as desirable and indeed inevitable. Cornplanter and his fellow Seneca leaders resisted these efforts, although the pressure was so great they could not halt the steady erosion of the Seneca land base through Cornplanter's lifetime. Remarkably, they successfully resisted the complete surrender of that land base. Attempts to "crush us to nothing" have continued since Cornplanter's death, notably the failed attempt to remove all Senecas from New York in 1838, as well as the successful attempts both to buy up the Buffalo Creek Reservation in 1842 and to cover over Allegany lands (as well as the Cornplanter Grant) with the Allegheny River Reservoir in 1969. However, as the twenty-first century unfolds, the Allegany and Cattaraugus territories of the Seneca Nation (as well as the lands at Oil Spring) and the lands of the Tonawanda Band of the Seneca remain today as a real legacy to the hard-won diplomatic achievements of Cornplanter and his fellow Seneca leaders in the closing decades of the eighteenth century.

Appendix

References

Index

Cornplanter Genealogical Charts

Family history research for the heirs of Chief Cornplanter began in 1990, when the Cornplanter Descendants Association elected me as their family historian. Then, in August 1994, I edited and the association printed the first issue of the *Cornplanter Descendants Association Newsletter,* which was distributed to the heirs at the annual Cornplanter Picnic. Issues have appeared every year since 1994.

The newsletter was primarily a vehicle to present as complete family history charts as possible. Each issue focused on the descendants of one of Cornplanter's children. Photographs and historical articles were also included.

The charts presented here are a simplified version of what appears in the newsletters. These charts cover Cornplanter's children, grandchildren, and in some cases, great-grandchildren.

A word of caution: I must stress that these charts are based on my research. Although I have been dutiful in this research, the lack of nineteenth-century vital records among the Seneca has led to errors and omissions. The spellings of certain names are variants of those appearing in the text. Some of these charts are based on family oral histories, later corroborated by yearly annuity census rolls. Some information was collected by Philadelphia Yearly Meeting Quakers for the Warren County Orphans Court in 1871, when the Cornplanter Grant was partitioned among the heirs of Cornplanter. Please regard these charts as a work in progress.

Jack T. Ericson, *Curator Emeritus*
Special Collections, Daniel A. Reed Library
State University of New York at Fredonia

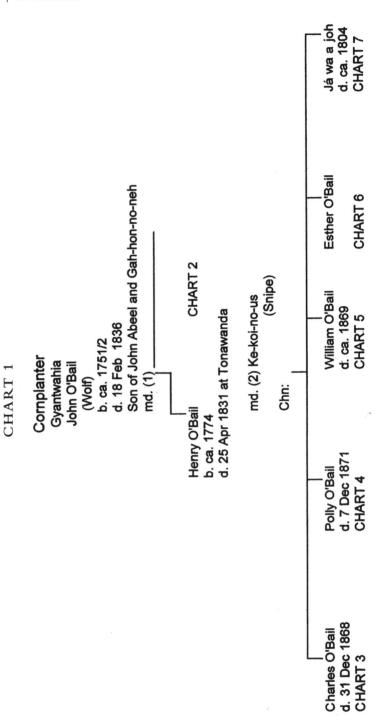

CHART 1

Cornplanter
Gyantwahia
John O'Bail
(Wolf)
b. ca. 1751/2
d. 18 Feb 1836
Son of John Abeel and Gah-hon-no-neh

md. (1)

Henry O'Bail
b. ca. 1774
d. 25 Apr 1831 at Tonawanda
CHART 2

md. (2) Ke-koi-no-us
(Snipe)

Chn:

Charles O'Bail
d. 31 Dec 1868
CHART 3

Polly O'Bail
d. 7 Dec 1871
CHART 4

William O'Bail
d. ca. 1869
CHART 5

Esther O'Bail
CHART 6

Já wa a joh
d. ca. 1804
CHART 7

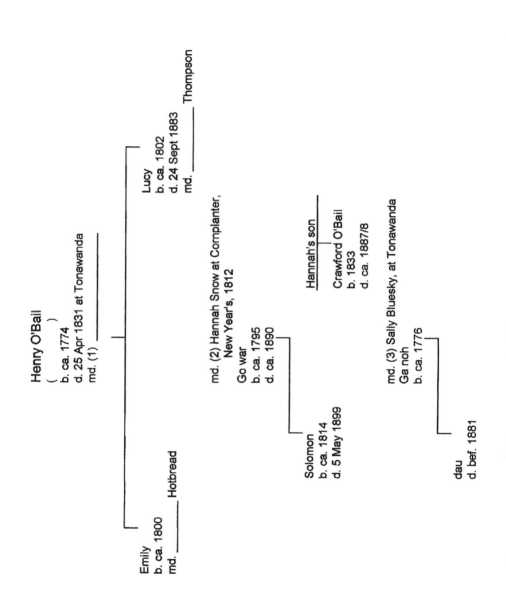

Henry O'Bail
( )
b. ca. 1774
d. 25 Apr 1831 at Tonawanda
md. (1) _____

Lucy
b. ca. 1802
d. 24 Sept 1883
md. _____ Thompson

Emily
b. ca. 1800
md. _____ Hotbread

md. (2) Hannah Snow at Cornplanter,
New Year's, 1812
Go war
b. ca. 1795
d. ca. 1890

Solomon
b. ca. 1814
d. 5 May 1899

Hannah's son

Crawford O'Bail
b. 1833
d. ca. 1887/8

md. (3) Sally Bluesky, at Tonawanda
Ga noh
b. ca. 1776

dau
d. bef. 1881

CHART 3

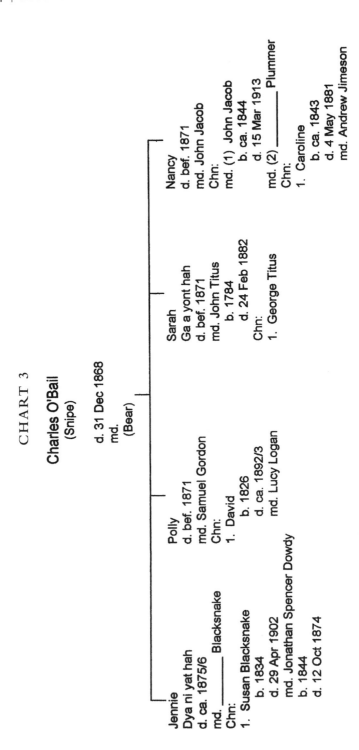

Charles O'Bail
(Snipe)
d. 31 Dec 1868
md.
(Bear)

Jennie
Dya ni yat hah
d. ca. 1875/6
md. _____ Blacksnake
Chn:
1. Susan Blacksnake
   b. 1834
   d. 29 Apr 1902
   md. Jonathan Spencer Dowdy
   b. 1844
   d. 12 Oct 1874

Polly
d. bef. 1871
md. Samuel Gordon
Chn:
1. David
   b. 1826
   d. ca. 1892/3
   md. Lucy Logan

Sarah
Ga a yont hah
d. bef. 1871
md. John Titus
   b. 1784
   d. 24 Feb 1882
Chn:
1. George Titus

Nancy
d. bef. 1871
md. John Jacob
Chn:
md. (1) John Jacob
         b. ca. 1844
         d. 15 Mar 1913
md. (2) _____ Plummer
Chn:
1. Caroline
   b. ca. 1843
   d. 4 May 1881
   md. Andrew Jimeson

Polly O'Bail
(Snipe)
d. 7 Dec 1871
md. John Logan
(Cayuga)
b. ca. 1744
d. 1844
Son of Capt. John and Vastina Logan

Ruth
b. 1821
d. 1911
md. John Jacobs
b. 1811
d. 1882
Chn:
1. Owen
   b. 1844
   d. 4 Oct 1938

Lucy
b. ca. 1823/4
d. ca. 1888/9
md. David Gordon
b. 1826
d. ca. 1892/3
Son of Polly and Samuel Gordon
Chn:
1. William
   b. ca. 1848
   d. 16 Mar 1884
2. Mary
   d. Sept 1871
3. Jane
4. Charles
   b. ca. 1855
   d. ca. 1936
5. Lucinda
   b. 1861

Mary
b. 1827
d. 1885
md. Chauncey Lee
d. bef. 1881
Chn:
1. Laura
   b. 1857
   d. 23 Jan 1914
2. George
   b. ca. 1861
3. Morris
   b. ca. 1864/5
   d. ca. 1910/1
4. Sarah
5. Joseph

Jesse
b. ca. 1833
d. 16 Feb 1916
md. (1) Sally Thompson
on 20 Jan 1867 at Cornplanter
md. (2) Susan Blacksnake Dowdy
b. 1834
d. 29 Apr 1902
Chn:
1. James
   b. 1866
   d. ca. 1896
2. Lucy
3. Wesley

Lyman
d. ca. 1873

CHART 5

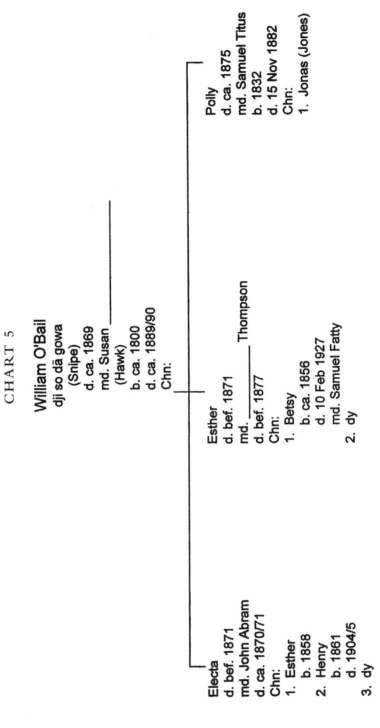

William O'Bail
dji so dā gowa
(Snipe)
d. ca. 1869
md. Susan
(Hawk)
b. ca. 1800
d. ca. 1889/90
Chn:

Electa
d. bef. 1871
md. John Abram
d. ca. 1870/71
Chn:
1. Esther
   b. 1858
2. Henry
   b. 1861
   d. 1904/5
3. dy

Esther
d. bef. 1871
md. _____ Thompson
d. bef. 1877
Chn:
1. Betsy
   b. ca. 1856
   d. 10 Feb 1927
   md. Samuel Fatty
2. dy

Polly
d. ca. 1875
md. Samuel Titus
b. 1832
d. 15 Nov 1882
Chn:
1. Jonas (Jones)

CHART 6

Esther O'Bail
(Snipe)
md. Moses Pierce

Susan
d. bef. 1848
md. James Pierce, Sr.
  b. 1806
  d. 5 Feb 1884
  S of Robert Pierce
Chn:
1. William Wallce
   b. 1834
2. Lucinda
   b. ca. 1835
3. James, Jr.
   b. ca. 1836/7
4. Elizabeth
   b. ca. 1837
5. John
   b. ca. 1839
6. Mary Ann
   b. ca. 1840
   d. 26 Jun 1866
7. Eleanor
   b. ca. 1842
   d. 19 May 1895

Marsh
b. 1821
d. 3 Nov 1897
md. Cassandra Silverheels
   (Beaver)
   b. 1833
   d. 20 Jan 1878
   dau of Oliver Silverheels
   and Sally Jemison
Chn:
1. Gibson
   b. 18 Sept 1856
   d. ca. 1938/39
   (Cassandra's son)
2. Oakley
   b. 27 Nov 1858
   d. 23 Sept 1926
3. Cordelia
   b. 25 Nov 1860
   d. 18 Apr 1878
4. Marsh, Jr.
   b. 1 Sept 1862
   d. 9 July 1882
5. Amos
   b. 7 Feb 1864
   d. 3 Feb 1944
6. Scomer
   b. 17 Feb 1866
   d. 18 Mar 1874
7. Topley
   b. 17 May 1870
   d. ca. 1939
8. Windsor Elijah
   b. 14 May 1872
   d. 23 May 1943
9. Augusta
   b. 10 Jun 1874
   d. 15 Apr 1882
10. Markes
    b. 28 Jul 1876
    d. 28 Sept 1876
11. John
    b. 6 Jan 1878
    d. 20 Jan 1878

dau
d. June 1848
md. Fisher Pierce

Jonathan
b. 1825
d. 7 Jul 1884
md. Hannah
   b. ca. 1830
   d. ca. 1910
Chn:
1. Irene (Phebe)
   b. 1843
   d. 6 Sept 1877
2. Lewis
   b. 1845
   d. 28 Sept 1883
3. Adam
   b. 1855
   d. ca. 1890/1
4. Ida
   b. 1864
   d. 23 June 1884
5. Gillett
   b. 1867
   d. ca. 1885/6
6. Carson
   b. 1870
   d. ca. 1883/4
7. Scott
   b. 1874
   d. 15 Dec 1877

CHART 7

Já wa a joh
d. ca. 1804
md.

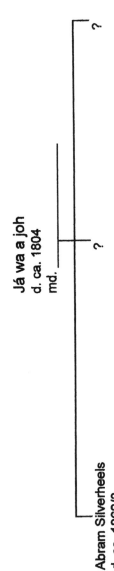

Abram Silverheels
d. ca. 1862/3
md.
Chn:
1. ?
2. ?
3. ?
4. **Hannah Silverheels**
   (Deer)
   b. ca. 1827
   d. 1894
   md. James Cooper
   b. 1827
   d. bef. 1888
   Chn:
   1. Mary, b. 1848
   2. Hiram, b. 1849
   3. Julia, b. 1852
   4. Mary, b. 1854
   5. Lewis, b. 1859
   6. James, b. 1862
   7. Phoebe, b. 1868
   8. Silas, b. 1872

References

Archival Sources

Allinson, William. 1809. William Allinson (1765?–1841), Journal of, describing visit to Indians of New York State in 1809. Quaker Collection. Haverford College.

ASP: IA (American State Papers: Indian Affairs). Washington, D.C.: Gales and Seaton, 1823–61.

Cruikshank, E. A., ed. n.d. *The Documentary History of the Campaign upon the Niagara Frontier in the Year 1813. Part II. (1813) June to August, 1813.* Welland, Ontario: Tribune for the Lundy's Lane Historical Society.

————. 1905. *The Documentary History of the Campaign upon the Niagara Frontier in the Year 1813. Part III (1813) August to October, 1813.* Welland, Ontario: Tribune Office for the Lundy's Lane Historical Society.

————. 1907. *The Documentary History of the Campaign upon the Niagara Frontier in the Year 1813. Part IV (1813) October to December, 1813, with Additional Documents, June to October, 1813.* Welland, Ontario: Tribune Office for the Lundy's Lane Historical Society.

————., ed. 1923–31. *The Correspondence of Lieut. Governor John Graves Simcoe: With Allied Documents Relating to his Administration of the Government of Upper Canada.* 5 vols. Toronto: Ontario Historical Society.

Day, Sherman. 1843. *Historical Collections of the State of Pennsylvania; Containing a Copious Selection of the Most Interesting Facts, Traditions, Biographical Sketches, Anecdotes, etc.* Philadelphia: George W. Gorton.

DM (Draper Manuscripts). State Historical Society of Wisconsin, Madison.

Indian Committee Records. Department of Records of Philadelphia Yearly Meeting of the Religious Society of Friends. Philadelphia.

Jennings, Francis, et al., eds. 1984. *Iroquois Indians: A Documentary History of the Six Nations and Their League*. Microfilm edition. 50 reels. Woodbridge, Conn.: Research Publications for the D'Arcy McNickle Center for the History of the American Indian and the Newberry Library.

Kappler, Charles J., comp. 1904–41. *Indian Affairs: Laws and Treaties*. 5 vols. Washington, D.C.: U.S. Government Printing Office.

Michigan Historical Collections. *Collections and Researches Made by the Pioneer and Historical Society of the State of Michigan*. Lansing: Robert Smith.

New York State Assembly. 1889. *Report of the Special Committee to Investigate the Indian Problem of the State of New York, Appointed by the Assembly of 1888*. Albany: Troy Press.

NYCD (New York Colonial Documents). *Documents Relative to the Colonial History of the State of New York*. Edited by Edmund B. O'Callaghan. 15 vols. Albany: Weed, Parsons, 1853–87.

NYSH (New York State Historian). 1929. *The Sullivan-Clinton Campaign in 1779: Chronology and Selected Documents*. Albany: State Univ. of New York.

PA (Pennsylvania Archives). Edited by Samuel Hazard. Philadelphia: J. Stevens, 1853–87.

PSWJ (The Papers of Sir William Johnson). Edited by James Sullivan, et al. Albany: State Univ. of New York, 1921–65.

Samuel Kirkland Papers. Special Collections. Dartmouth College Library. Hanover, New Hampshire.

All Other Sources

Abler, Thomas S. 1969. "Factional Dispute and Party Conflict in the Political System of the Seneca Nation (1845–95): An Ethnohistorical Analysis." Ph.D. diss., Univ. of Toronto.

Abler, Thomas S. 1973. "The Political Significance of Incongruent Boundaries: The Case of the Seneca Nation." *Man in the Northeast* 5:37–46.

———. 1979a. "Kaieñ?kwaahtoñ." In *Dictionary of Canadian Biography*, vol. 4:404–6. Toronto: Univ. of Toronto Press.

————. 1979b. "Kayahsota?." In *Dictionary of Canadian Biography,* vol. 4:408–10. Toronto: Univ. of Toronto Press.

————. 1987a. *The Iroquois.* Canada's Visual History 78. Ottawa: Canadian Museum of Civilization/National Film Board of Canada.

Abler, Thomas S. 1987b. "Governor Blacksnake as a Young Man? Speculation on the Identity of Trumbull's 'The Young Sachem.' " *Ethnohistory* 34:329–51.

————. 1987c. "Dendrogram and Celestial Tree: Numerical Taxonomy and the Iroquoian Creation Myth." *Canadian Journal of Native Studies* 7:195–221.

————. 1992. "Scalping, Torture, Cannibalism and Rape: An Ethnohistorical Analysis of Conflicting Cultural Values at War." *Anthropologica* 34:3–20.

————. 1999. *Hinterland Warriors and Military Dress: European Empires and Exotic Uniforms.* Oxford: Berg.

————. 2004. "Seneca Moieties and Hereditary Chieftainships: The Early-Nineteenth-Century Political Organization of an Iroquois Nation." *Ethnohistory* 51:459–88.

————, ed. 1989. *Chainbreaker: The Revolutionary War Memoirs of Governor Blacksnake as Told to Benjamin Williams.* Lincoln: Univ. of Nebraska Press.

————, and Elisabeth Tooker. 1978. "Seneca." In *Handbook of North American Indians.* Vol. 15, *Northeast,* edited by Bruce G. Trigger (vol. ed.) and William C. Sturtevant (gen. ed.), 505–17. Washington, D.C.: Smithsonian Institution.

Abrams, George H. 1965. "The Cornplanter Cemetery." *Pennsylvania Archaeologist* 35:59–73.

————. 1976. *The Seneca People.* Phoenix: Indian Tribal Series.

————. 1990. "The Seneca World of Ga-No-Say-Yeh." Review. *American Anthropologist* 92(4): 1041–42.

Alden, Timothy. 1827. *An Account of Sundry Missions Performed among the Senecas and Munsees in a Series of Letters.* New York: J. Seymour.

Babcock, Louis L. 1927. "The War of 1812 on the Niagara Frontier." *Buffalo Historical Society Publications* 29:1–248.

Barbuto, Richard V. 2000. *Niagara 1814: America Invades Canada.* Lawrence: Univ. Press of Kansas.

Bauman, Richard. 1972. "An Analysis of Quaker-Seneca Councils, 1798–1800." *Man in the Northeast* 3:36–48.

Beauchamp, William M. 1905. *A History of the New York Iroquois, Now Commonly Called the Six Nations.* Bulletin 78. Albany: New York State Museum.

Benn, Carl. 1998. *The Iroquois in the War of 1812.* Toronto: Univ. of Toronto Press.

Berkhofer, Robert F., Jr. 1965. "Faith and Factionalism among the Senecas: Theory and Ethnohistory." *Ethnohistory* 12:99–112.

Bilharz, Joy A. 1995. "Monumental Differences." *Cornplanter Descendants Association Newsletter* 1(2): 1–8.

———. 1997. "Please Pass the Baked Beans! A History of the Cornplanter Picnic." *Cornplanter Descendants Association Newsletter* 1(4): 1–2.

———. 1998. *The Allegany Senecas and the Kinzua Dam: Forced Relocation through Two Generations.* Lincoln: Univ. of Nebraska Press.

———. 2000. " 'Broken Promises Come High.' " In *Treaty of Canandaigua 1794: 200 Years of Treaty Relations between the Iroquois Confederacy and the United States,* edited by G. Peter Jemison and Anna M. Schein, 162–74. Santa Fe: Clear Light.

———, and Thomas S. Abler. 1999. "L'héritage de Kinzua: La reconquête du pouvoir chez les femmes sénécas" [Kinzua's Legacy: The Reempowerment of Seneca Nation Women]. *Recherches amérindiennes aux Québec* 29 (2): 51–62.

Boswell, James. 1776. "An Account of the Chief of the Mohock Indians, Who Lately Visited England (with an Exact Likeness)." *London Magazine* 45:339.

Buffalo Historical Society. 1885. *Red Jacket.* Buffalo Historical Society Transactions 3. Buffalo, N.Y.: Buffalo Historical Society.

Calloway, Colin G., ed. 1994. *Early American Indian Documents: Treaties and Laws, 1607–1789.* Vol. 18. *Revolution and Confederation.* Edited by Alden T. Vaughan (gen. ed.). Bethesda, Md.: Univ. Publications of America.

Campisi, Jack, and William A. Starna. 1995. "On the Road to Canandaigua: The Treaty of 1794." *American Indian Quarterly* 19:467–90.

Cartwright, Conway Edward. 1876. *Life and Letters of the Late Hon. Richard Cartwright.* Toronto: Belford Brothers.

Chadwick, Edward M. 1897. *The People of the Longhouse*. Toronto: Church of England.

Chafe, Wallace L. 1963. *Handbook of the Seneca Language*. Bulletin 388. Albany: New York State Museum and Science Service.

————. 1967. *Seneca Morphology and Dictionary*. Smithsonian Contributions to Anthropology 4. Washington, D.C.: Smithsonian Press.

Chief Cornplanter Council. 2004. *Chief Cornplanter Council's "Good Turn."* <http://users.penn.com/~cccbsa/council.html> Accessed 28 January 2004.

Clarfield, Gerard H. 1980. *Timothy Pickering and the American Republic*. Pittsburgh: Univ. of Pittsburgh Press.

Clinton, DeWitt. 1812. *Discourse Delivered before the New-York Historical Society, at their Anniversary Meeting, 6th December 1811*. New York: James Eastburn.

Coe, Stephen Howard. 1968. "Indian Affairs in Pennsylvania and New York 1783–1794." Ph.D. diss., American Univ., Washington, D.C.

Congdon, Charles E. 1967. *Allegany Oxbow: A History of Allegany State Park and the Allegany Reserve of the Seneca Nation*. Salamanca, N.Y.: Charles E. Congdon.

Cook, Frederick, ed. 1887. *Journals of the Military Expedition of Major General John Sullivan against the Six Nations of Indians in 1779*. Auburn, N.Y.: Knapp, Peck, and Thompson.

Cooper, Helen A. 1982. *John Trumbull: The Hand and Spirit of a Painter*. New Haven: Yale Univ. Art Gallery.

Cornplanter. 1890. "Letter of Cornplanter." *Pennsylvania Magazine of History and Biography* 14:320.

————. 1936. "Documents: Letter of Chief Cornplanter to the Children of the Friends of Onas." *Bulletin of the Friends' Historical Association* 25:86–7.

Cruikshank, E. A. 1898. "Blockade of Fort George, 1813." *Niagara Historical Society Publications* 3. Welland, Ontario: Welland Tribune Presses.

Dearborn, Henry A. S. 1904. "Journals of Henry A. S. Dearborn." *Buffalo Historical Society Publications* 7:33–225.

Deardorff, Merle H. 1941. "The Cornplanter Grant in Warren County." *The Western Pennsylvania Historical Magazine* 24 (1): 1–22.

Deardorff, Merle H. 1946. "Zeisberger's Allegheny River Indian Towns: 1767–1770." *Pennsylvania Archaeologist* 16 (1): 2–19.

———. 1951. "The Religion of Handsome Lake: Its Origin and Development." *Bureau of American Ethnology Bulletin* 149:79–101.

———. 1965. "Cornplanter Church and School." *Stepping Stones* 9 (1): 261–62.

———. 1994. "Henry Obail 1774–1832: 'The Young Cornplanter'." *Cornplanter Descendants Association Newsletter* 1 (1): 1–5, 8, 10–12. Reprinted from *Stepping Stones* 13 (3). 1970.

———, and George S. Snyderman, eds. 1956. "A Nineteenth-Century Journal of a Visit to the Indians of New York." *Proceedings of the American Philosophical Society* 100:582–612.

Deloria, Philip J. 1998. *Playing Indian*. New Haven: Yale Univ. Press.

Densmore, Christopher. 1999. *Red Jacket: Iroquois Diplomat and Orator.* Syracuse, N.Y.: Syracuse Univ. Press.

Deraunian-Stodola, Kathryn Zabelle, and James Arthur Levernier. 1993. *The Indian Captivity Narrative, 1550–1900.* New York: Twayne.

Donaldson, Thomas. 1892. *Extra Census Bulletin. Indians. The Six Nations of New York: Cayugas, Mohawks (Saint Regis), Oneidas, Onondagas, Senecas, Tuscaroras.* Washington, D.C.: United States Census Printing Office.

Downes, Randolph C. 1940. *Council Fires on the Upper Ohio: A Narrative of Indian Affairs in the Upper Ohio until 1795.* Pittsburgh: Univ. of Pittsburgh Press.

Drake, Samuel. 1832. *Indian Biography, Containing the Lives of More than Two Hundred Indian Chiefs: Also Such Others of that Race as Have Rendered their Names Conspicuous in the History of North America, from Its First Being Known to Europeans, to the Present Period.* Boston: Josiah Drake.

Edmunds, R. David. 1984. *Tecumseh and the Quest for Indian Leadership.* Boston: Little, Brown.

Einhorn, Arthur, and Thomas S. Abler. 1998. "Tattooed Bodies and Severed Auricles: Images of Native American Body Modification in the Art of Benjamin West." *American Indian Art Magazine* 23 (4): 42–53, 116–17.

Ericson, Jack. 1996. "Polly Logan's Will." *Cornplanter Descendants Association Newsletter* 1 (3): 5–10.

Fenton, William N. 1941. "Iroquois Suicide." *Bureau of American Ethnology Bulletin* 128:80–137.

————. 1942. "Fish Drives among the Cornplanter Seneca." *Pennsylvania Archaeologist* 12:48–52.

————. 1945a. "Place Names and Related Activities of the Cornplanter Senecas. I. State Line to Cornplanter Grant: Northern Approaches." *Pennsylvania Archaeologist* 15:25–29.

————. 1945b. "Place Names and Related Activities of the Cornplanter Senecas. 2. Cornplanter Grant: The Place Where Handsome Lake Rose to Preach." *Pennsylvania Archaeologist* 15:42–50.

————. 1945c. "Place Names and Related Activities of the Cornplanter Senecas. 3. Burnt-house at Cornplanter Grant." *Pennsylvania Archaeologist* 15:88–96.

————. 1945d. "Place Names and Related Activities of the Cornplanter Senecas. 4. Cornplanter Peak to Warren." *Pennsylvania Archaeologist* 15:108–18.

————. 1946. "Place Names and Related Activities of the Cornplanter Senecas. 5. The Path to Conewango." *Pennsylvania Archaeologist* 16: 42–57.

————. 1950. "The Roll Call of the Iroquois Chiefs: A Study of a Mnemonic Cane from the Six Nations Reserve." *Smithsonian Miscellaneous Collections* 111 (15): 1–73.

————. 1951. "Locality as a Basic Factor in the Development of Iroquois Social Structure." *Bureau of American Ethnology Bulletin* 149:35–54.

————. 1953. "The Iroquois Eagle Dance: An Offshoot of the Calumet Dance." *Bureau of American Ethnology Bulletin* 156.

————. 1962. "This Island, the World on the Turtle's Back." *Journal of American Folklore* 75:283–300.

————. 1986. "A Further Note on Iroquois Suicide." *Ethnohistory* 33:448–57.

————. 1998. *The Great Law and the Longhouse: A Political History of the Iroquois Confederacy.* Norman: Univ. of Oklahoma Press.

————. 2002. *The Little Water Medicine Society of the Senecas.* Norman: Univ. of Oklahoma Press.

————, ed. 1965. "The Journal of James Emlen Kept on a Trip to Canandaigua, New York; September 15 to October 30, 1794; To Attend the Treaty between the United States and the Six Nations." *Ethnohistory* 12:279–342.

————, and Merle H. Deardorff. 1943. "The Last Passenger Pigeon

Hunts of the Cornplanter Senecas." *Journal of the Washington Academy of Sciences* 33 (10): 289–315.

Francello, Joseph A. 1989. *The Seneca World of GA-NO-SEY-YEH.* New York: Peter Lang.

———. 1998. *Chief Cornplanter (Gy-ant-wa-kia) of the Senecas.* Allentown, Pa.: Glasco.

Fredrickson, N. Jaye, and Sandra Gibb. 1980. *The Covenant Chain: Indian Ceremonial and Trade Silver.* Ottawa: National Museums of Canada.

Froman, Frances, Alfred Keye, Lottie Keye, and Carrie Dyck. 2002. *English-Cayuga/Cayuga-English Dictionary.* Toronto: Univ. of Toronto Press.

Godcharles, Frederic A. 1935. "Chief Cornplanter." *Pennsylvania Archaeologist* 5:67–69.

Goddard, Ives. 1978a. "Eastern Algonquian languages." In *Handbook of North American Indians.* Vol. 15. *Northeast,* edited by Bruce G. Trigger (vol. ed.) and William C. Sturtevant (gen. ed.), 70–77. Washington, D.C.: Smithsonian Institution.

———. 1978b. "Central Algonquian languages." In *Handbook of North American Indians.* Vol. 15. *Northeast,* edited by Bruce G. Trigger (vol. ed.) and William C. Sturtevant (gen. ed.), 583–87. Washington, D.C.: Smithsonian Institution.

———. 1979. "Comparative Algonquian." In *The Languages of Native America: Historical and Comparative Assessment,* edited by Lyle Campbell and Marianne Mithun, 70–132. Austin: Univ. of Texas Press.

Graves, Donald E. 1994. *Red Coats and Grey Jackets: The Battle of Chippawa 5 July 1814.* Toronto: Dundurn Press.

Graymont, Barbara. 1972. *The Iroquois in the American Revolution.* Syracuse, N.Y.: Syracuse Univ. Press.

———. 1979. "Koñwatsiʔtsiaiéñni." In *Dictionary of Canadian Biography,* 4:416–19. Toronto: Univ. of Toronto Press.

———. 1983. "Atiatoharongwen." In *Dictionary of Canadian Biography,* 5:39–41. Toronto: Univ. of Toronto Press.

Green, Rayna. 1988. "The Indian in Popular American Culture." In *Handbook of North American Indians.* Vol. 4. *History of Indian-White Relations,* edited by Wilcomb E. Washburn (vol. ed.) and William C. Sturtevant (gen. ed.), 587–606. Washington, D.C.: Smithsonian Institution.

Guthman, William H. 1975. *March to Massacre: A History of the First*

Seven Years of the United States Army 1784–1791. New York: McGraw-Hill.

Haas, Marilyn L. 1994. *The Seneca and Tuscarora Indians: An Annotated Bibliography.* Native American Bibliography Series no. 17. Metuchen, N.J.: Scarecrow Press.

Hale, Horatio E. 1883. *The Iroquois Book of Rites.* Philadelphia: D. G. Brinton.

Hall, William. 1879. "Garyanwahgah, The Cornplanter." *Potter's American Monthly* 12 (85): 31–35.

Harris, George H. 1903. "Life of Horatio Jones." *Buffalo Historical Society Publications* 6:383–514.

Hauptman, Laurence M. 1986. *The Iroquois Struggle for Survival: World War II to Red Power.* Syracuse, N.Y.: Syracuse Univ. Press.

———. 1999. "Governor Blacksnake and the Seneca Indian Struggle to Save the Oil Spring Reservation." *Mid-America: An Historical Review* 81:51–73.

———. 2000. "Who Owns Grand Island (Erie County, New York)?" In *Treaty of Canandaigua 1794: 200 Years of Treaty Relations between the Iroquois Confederacy and the United States,* edited by G. Peter Jemison and Anna M. Schein, 127–47. Santa Fe: Clear Light.

Hill, Esther V. 1930. "The Iroquois Indians and their Lands since 1783." *New York State Historical Association Quarterly Journal* 11:335–53.

Hoover, William N. 2004. *Kinzua: From Cornplanter to the Corps.* New York: Universe.

Hough, Franklin B., ed. 1861. *Proceedings of the Commissioners of Indian Affairs Appointed by Law for the Extinguishment of Indian Titles in the State of New York.* Albany: Joel Munsell.

Hunt, George T. 1940. *Wars of the Iroquois: A Study in Intertribal Trade Relations.* Madison: Univ. of Wisconsin Press.

Hunter, William A. 1956. "Refugee Fox Settlements among the Senecas." *Ethnohistory* 3:11–20.

———. 1978. "History of the Ohio Valley." In *Handbook of North American Indians.* Vol. 15. *Northeast,* edited by Bruce G. Trigger (vol. ed.) and William C. Sturtevant (gen. ed.), 588–93. Washington, D.C.: Smithsonian Institution.

Hyde, Jabez B. 1903. "A Teacher among the Senecas. Historical and Personal Narrative of Jabez Backus Hyde, Who Came to the Buffalo

Creek Mission in 1811. Written in 1820." *Publications of the Buffalo Historical Society* 6:239–80.

Jackson, Halliday. 1830a. *Sketch of the Manners, Customs, Religion and Government of the Seneca Indians in 1800.* Philadelphia: Marcus T. C. Gould.

———. 1830b. *Civilization of the Indian Natives.* Philadelphia: Marcus T. C. Gould.

Jacobs, Wilbur R. 1950. *Diplomacy and Indian Gifts: Anglo-French Rivalry along the Ohio and Northwest Frontiers.* Stanford, Calif.: Stanford Univ. Press.

Jefferson, Thomas. 1955. *Notes on the State of Virginia,* edited by William Peden. Chapel Hill: Univ. of North Carolina Press. Originally published in 1784.

Jennings, Francis. 1984. *The Ambiguous Iroquois Empire: The Covenant Chain Confederation of Indian Tribes with English Colonies from Its Beginnings to the Lancaster Treaty of 1744.* New York: Norton.

Johnston, Charles M., ed. 1964. *The Valley of the Six Nations: A Collection of Documents on the Indian Lands of the Grand River.* Toronto: Champlain Society.

Johnston, Jean. 1971. "Ancestry and Descendants of Molly Brant." *Ontario History* 63:86–92.

Jones, Dorothy V. 1982. *License for Empire: Colonialism by Treaty in Early America.* Chicago: Univ. of Chicago Press.

Josephy, Alvin M., Jr. 1968. "Cornplanter, Can You Swim?" *American Heritage* 20(1): 4–9, 106–10.

Karklins, Karlis. 1992. *Trade Ornament Useage among the Native Peoples of Canada: A Source Book.* Ottawa: Parks Service, Environment Canada.

Kelsay, Isabel Thompson. 1984. *Joseph Brant, 1743–1807: Man of Two Worlds.* Syracuse, N.Y.: Syracuse Univ. Press.

Kent, Donald H. 1974. "Historical Report on Pennsylvania's Purchases from the Indians in 1784, 1785, and 1789 and on Indian Occupancy of the Areas Purchased." In *Iroquois Indians,* 1:29–303. New York: Garland.

———, and Merle H. Deardorff, eds. 1960. "John Adlum on the Allegheny: Memoirs for the Year 1794." *Pennsylvania Magazine of History and Biography* 84:265–324, 435–80.

Ketchum, William. 1864–65. *An Authentic and Comprehensive History of Buffalo*. 2 vols. Buffalo, N.Y.: Rockwell, Baker and Hill.

Klinck, Carl F., and James J. Talman, eds. 1970. *The Journal of Major John Norton 1816*. Toronto: Champlain Society.

Knopf, Richard C., ed. 1975. *Anthony Wayne: A Name in Arms . . . The Wayne-Knox-Pickering-McHenry Correspondence*. Westport, Conn.: Greenwood.

Landy, David. 1978. "Tuscarora among the Iroquois." In *Handbook of North American Indians*. Vol. 15. *Northeast,* edited by Bruce G. Trigger (vol. ed.) and William C. Sturtevant (gen. ed.), 518–24. Washington, D.C.: Smithsonian Institution.

Leighton, Douglas. 1988. "Lorimier, Jean-Baptiste de." In *Dictionary of Canadian Biography*. 7:516–17. Toronto: Univ. of Toronto Press.

Locklear, Arlinda F. 1988. "The Oneida Land Claims: A Legal Overview." In *Iroquois Land Claims,* edited by Christopher Vecsey and William A. Starna, 141–53. Syracuse, N.Y.: Syracuse Univ. Press.

Lossing, Benson John. 1872–73. *The Life and Times of Philip Schuyler*. New York: Sheldon.

Lounsbury, Floyd G. 1964. "The Structural Analysis of Kinship Semantics." In *Proceedings of the 9th International Congress of Linguists,* edited by Horace G. Lunt, 1073–93. The Hague: Mouton.

————. 1978. "Iroquoian Languages." In *Handbook of North American Indians*. Vol. 15. *Northeast,* edited by Bruce G. Trigger (vol. ed.) and William C. Sturtevant (gen. ed.), 334–43. Washington, D.C.: Smithsonian Institution.

Lowenthal, Larry, ed. 1983. *Days of Siege: A Journal of Siege of Fort Stanwix in 1777*. New York: Eastern Acorn Press.

Maracle, David R. 1990. *Iontewennaweienhstáhkwa': Mohawk Language Dictionary*. Belleville, Ontario: Mika.

McKenney, Thomas L., and James Hall. 1836–44. *The Indian Tribes of North America, with Biographical Sketches and Anecdotes of the Principal Chiefs*. 3 vols. Philadelphia: Edward C. Biddle. Reprint, Edinburgh: John Grant, 1933–34. Edited by Frederick W. Hodge.

McLoughlin, William G. 1986. *Cherokee Renascence in the New Republic*. Princeton, N.J.: Princeton Univ. Press.

Manley, Henry S. 1932. *The Treaty of Fort Stanwix: 1784*. Rome, N.Y.: Rome Sentinel.

Mental Elevator, 1846. 31 Dec., 14:120.

Miller, Ernest C. 1958. "Pennsylvania's Last Indian School." *Pennsylvania History* 25:99–108.

Mintz, Max M. 1999. *Seeds of Empire: The American Revolutionary Conquest of the Iroquois.* New York: New York Univ. Press.

Mithun, Marianne. 1979. "Iroquoian." In *The Languages of Native North America: Historical and Comparative Assessment,* edited by Lyle Campbell and Marianne Mithun, 133–212. Austin: Univ. of Texas Press.

Mohawk, John C. 2000. "The Canandaigua Treaty in Historical Perspective." In *Treaty of Canandaigua 1794: 200 Years of Treaty Relations between the Iroquois Confederacy and the United States,* edited by G. Peter Jemison and Anna M. Schein, 43–64. Santa Fe: Clear Light.

Morgan, Lewis H. 1851. *League of the Ho-dé-no-sau-nee or Iroquois.* Rochester, N.Y.: Sage.

———. 1871. *Systems of Consanguinity and Affinity in the Human Family.* Smithsonian Contributions to Knowledge 17. Washington, D.C.: Smithsonian Institution.

Namias, June. 1993. *White Captives: Gender and Ethnicity on the American Frontier.* Chapel Hill: Univ. of North Carolina Press.

Overton, Albert G. 1980. "Cornplanter Speaks to the Thirteen Fires." *Pennsylvania Heritage* 6 (2): 20–24.

Parker, Arthur C. 1910. *Iroquois Uses of Maize and Other Food Plants.* Bulletin 144: 5–113. Albany: New York State Museum.

———. 1913. *The Code of Handsome Lake.* Bulletin 163. Albany: New York State Museum.

———. 1916. *The Constitution of the Five Nations.* Bulletin 148: 7–158. Albany: New York State Museum.

———. 1919. *The Life of General Ely S. Parker: Last Grand Sachem of the Iroquois and General Grant's Military Secretary.* Buffalo Historical Society Publication 23. Buffalo: Buffalo Historical Society.

———. 1926. *An Analytical History of the Seneca Indians.* Researches and Transactions 6. Rochester, N.Y.: New York State Archeological Association (Lewis H. Morgan Chapter).

———. 1927. *Notes on the Ancestry of Cornplanter.* Researches and Transactions 5, no. 2. Canandaigua, N.Y.: New York State Archaeological Association (Lewis H. Morgan Chapter).

———. 1952. *Red Jacket: Last of the Seneca.* New York: McGraw-Hill. Reprint, Lincoln: Univ. of Nebraska Press, 1998.

Parker, Ely S. 1851. "The Cornplanter Tomahawk, in the State Collection." *Fourth Annual Report of the Regents of the University of the State of New York on the Condition of the State Cabinet of Natural History.* 99–101.

Parkman, Francis. 1889. *Montcalm and Wolfe.* Thirteenth Edition. 2 vols. Boston: Little, Brown.

Parrish, Jasper [?]. 1903. "The Story of Captain Jasper Parrish, Captive, Interpreter and United States Sub-Agent to the Six Nations Indians." *Buffalo Historical Society Publications* 6:527–38.

Peckham, Howard H. 1947. *Pontiac and the Indian Uprising.* Princeton, N.J.: Princeton Univ. Press.

Peterson, Harold L. 1971. *American Indian Tomahawks.* Revised edition. Contributions from the Museum of the American Indian, Heye Foundation 29. New York: Museum of the American Indian, Heye Foundation.

Phillips, Edward Hake. 1966. "Timothy Pickering at his Best: Indian Commissioner, 1790–1794." *Essex Institute Historical Collections* 102: 163–202.

Pilkington, Walter, ed. 1980. *The Journals of Samuel Kirkland: Eighteenth-century Missionary to the Iroquois, Government Agent, Father of Hamilton College.* Clinton, N.Y.: Hamilton College.

Porter, Joy. 2001. *To Be Indian: The Life of Iroquois-Seneca Arthur Caswell Parker.* Norman: Univ. of Oklahoma Press.

Reed, John Elmer. 1926. "Chief Cornplanter." *Erie County (Pennsylvania) Historical Society Publications* 1 (1): 5–27.

Richter, Daniel. 1987. "Ordeals of the Longhouse: The Five Nations in Early American History." In *Beyond the Covenant Chain: The Iroquois and their Neighbors in Indian North America, 1600–1800,* edited by Daniel K. Richter and James H. Merrell, 11–27. Syracuse, N.Y.: Syracuse Univ. Press.

———. 1999. "Onas, the Long Knife: Pennsylvanians and Indians, 1783–1794." In *Native Americans and the Early Republic,* edited by Frederick E. Hoxie, Ronald Hoffman, and Peter J. Albert, 125–61. Charlottesville: Univ. Press of Virginia.

Rothenberg, Diane. 1976. "Friends Like These: An Ethnohistorical

Analysis of the Interaction between Allegany Senecas and Quakers, 1798–1823." Ph.D. diss., City Univ. of New York.

———. 1986. "On the Insanity of Cornplanter." Paper presented to the Annual Meeting of the American Anthropological Association, December 1986. Philadelphia.

———. 1992. *The Mothers of the Nation and Other Essays.* Encinitas, Cal.: Ta'wil.

Savery, William. 2000. "The Savery Journal: The Canandaigua Treaty Excerpt." In *Treaty of Canandaigua 1794: 200 Years of Treaty Relations between the Iroquois Confederacy and the United States,* edited by G. Peter Jemison and Anna M. Schein, 260–94. Santa Fe: Clear Light. Originally published as *A Journal of the Life, Travels, and Religious Labors of William Savery,* 1837.

Seaver, James E. 1990. *A Narrative of the Life of Mrs. Mary Jemison,* edited by June Namias. Syracuse, N.Y.: Syracuse Univ. Press. Originally published in 1824.

———. 1992. *A Narrative of the Life of Mrs. Mary Jemison.* Edited by June Namias. Syracuse, N.Y.: Syracuse Univ. Press. Originally published in 1824.

Shimony, Annemarie A. 1961. *Conservatism among the Iroquois at the Six Nations Reserve.* Publications in Anthropology 65. New Haven: Yale Univ. Press. Reprint, Syracuse, N.Y.: Syracuse Univ. Press, 1994.

Siebeneck, Henry King. 1928. "Cornplanter." *Western Pennsylvania Historical Magazine* 11 (3): 180–93.

Simpson, J. A., and E. S. C. Weiner. 1989. *The Oxford English Dictionary.* 2nd edition. Oxford: Clarendon Press.

Sipe, C. Hale. 1926. *The Indian Chiefs of Pennsylvania or a Story of the Part Played by the American Indian in the History of Pennsylvania, Based Primarily on the Pennsylvania Archives and Colonial Records, and Built around the Outstanding Chiefs.* Butler, Pa.: Ziegler Printing.

Skinner, Dorothy P. 1933. "The Pennsylvania Seneca." *Pennsylvania Archaeologist* 3(5): 3–5.

Smith, Marc J. 1946. "Joseph Brant: Mohawk Statesman." Ph.D. diss., Univ. of Wisconsin, Madison.

Snowden, James Ross, 1867. *The Cornplanter Memorial: An Historical Sketch of Gy-ant-wa-chia*—*The Cornplanter, and the Six Nations of Indians.* Harrisburg: Singerly and Myers.

Snyder, Charles M., ed. 1978. *Red and White on the New York Frontier: A Struggle for Survival: Insights from the Papers of Erastus Granger, Indian Agent 1807–1819.* Harrison, N.Y.: Harbor Hill Books.

Snyderman, George S., ed. 1957. "Halliday Jackson's Journal of a Visit Paid to the Indians of New York (1806)." *Proceedings of the American Philosophical Society* 101:565–88.

Sosin, Jack M. 1965. "The Use of Indians in the War of the American Revolution: A Reassessment of Responsibility." *Canadian Historical Review* 46:101–21.

Stanley, George F. G. 1983. *The War of 1812: Land Operations.* Canadian War Museum Historical Publication no. 18. Toronto: Macmillan of Canada in collaboration with the National Museum of Man, National Museums of Canada.

Stone, William L. 1838. *Life of Joseph Brant—Thayendanegea.* 2 vols. New York: Blake, Dearborn.

———. 1841. *The Life and Times of Red–Jacket, or Sa-go-ye-wat-ha; Being the Sequel to the History of the Six Nations.* New York: Wiley and Putnam.

Sturtevant, William C. 1978. "Oklahoma Seneca-Cayuga." In *Handbook of North American Indians.* Vol. 15. *Northeast,* edited by Bruce G. Trigger (vol. ed.) and William C. Sturtevant (gen. ed.), 537–43. Washington, D.C.: Smithsonian Institution.

———. 1984. "A Structural Sketch of Iroquois Ritual." In *Extending the Rafters: Interdisciplinary Approaches to Iroquoian Studies,* edited by Michael K. Foster, Jack Campisi, and Marianne Mithun, 133–52. Albany: State Univ. of New York Press.

Sublett, Audrey J. 1965. "The Cornplanter Cemetery: Skeletal Analyses." *Pennsylvania Archaeologist* 35:74–92.

Sugden, John. 1997. *Tecumseh: A Life.* New York: Henry Holt.

Sumner, William Graham. 1891. *The Financier and the Finances of the American Revolution.* New York: Dodd, Mead. Reprint, New York: Augustus M. Kelly, 1968.

Swatzler, David. 2000. *A Friend among the Senecas: The Quaker Mission to Cornplanter's People.* Mechanicsburg, Pa.: Stackpole Books.

Swiggett, Howard. 1933. *War Out of Niagara: Walter Butler and the Tory Rangers.* New York: Columbia Univ. Press.

Sword, Wiley. 1985. *President Washington's Indian War: The Struggle for the Old Northwest 1790–1795.* Norman: Univ. of Oklahoma Press.

Tanner, Helen Hornbeck. 1978. "The Glaize in 1792: A Composite Indian Community." *Ethnohistory* 25:15–39.

———. 1987. *Atlas of Great Lakes Indian History.* Norman: Univ. of Oklahoma Press for the Newberry Library.

Thomas, Cyrus. 1907. "Cornplanter." *Handbook of Indians North of Mexico.* Frederick Webb Hodge, ed. *Bulletin of the Bureau of American Ethnology* 30 (1): 349–50.

Thatcher, B. B. 1836. *Indian Biography, or An Historical Account of Those Individuals Who Have Been Distinguished among North American Natives as Orators, Warriors, Statesmen, and Other Remarkable Characters.* 2 vols. New York: Harper.

Thwaites, Reuben Gold, and Louise Kellogg, eds. 1908. *The Revolution on the Upper Ohio, 1775–1777.* Madison: State Historical Society of Wisconsin.

Tome, Philip. 1854. *Pioneer Life; or, Thirty Years a Hunter being Scenes and Adventures in the Life of Philip Tome, Fifteen Years Interpreter for Cornplanter and Gov. Blacksnake, Chiefs on the Allegany River.* Buffalo: The Author. Reprint, New York: Arno Press, 1971.

Tooker, Elisabeth. 1965. "The Iroquois White Dog Sacrifice in the Latter Part of the Eighteenth Century." *Ethnohistory* 12:129–40.

———. 1970. *The Iroquois Ceremonial of Midwinter.* Syracuse, N.Y.: Syracuse Univ. Press.

———. 1978a. "The League of the Iroquois: Its History, Politics, and Ritual." In *Handbook of North American Indians.* Vol. 15. *Northeast,* edited by Bruce G. Trigger (vol. ed.) and William C. Sturtevant (gen. ed.), 418–41. Washington, D.C.: Smithsonian Institution.

———. 1978b. "Iroquois since 1820." In *Handbook of North American Indians.* Vol. 15. *Northeast,* edited by Bruce G. Trigger (vol. ed.) and William C. Sturtevant (gen. ed.), 449–65. Washington, D.C.: Smithsonian Institution.

Trelease, Allen W. 1960. *Indian Affairs in Colonial New York: The Seventeenth Century.* Ithaca, N.Y.: Cornell Univ. Press.

Turner, Orsamus. 1849. *Pioneer History of the Holland Purchase of Western New York*. Buffalo, N.Y.: Jewett, Thomas; Geo. H. Derby.

Vail, R. W. G. 1949. *The Voice of the Old Frontier*. Philadelphia: Univ. of Pennsylvania Press.

Viola, Herman J. 1976. *The Indian Legacy of Charles Bird King*. Washington, D.C.: Smithsonian Institution.

Wallace, Anthony F. C. 1970. *The Death and Rebirth of the Seneca*. New York: Knopf.

————. 1993. *The Long, Bitter Trail: Andrew Jackson and the Indians*. New York: Hill and Wang.

————. 2002. "Cornplanter's Talk." Paper presented to the Conference on Iroquois Reseach, 5 October 2002. Rensselaerville, New York.

————, ed. 1952. "Halliday Jackson's Journal to the Seneca Indians, 1798–1800." *Pennsylvania History* 49:117–47, 325–49.

Wallace, Paul A. W. 1946. *The White Roots of Peace*. Philadelphia: Univ. of Pennsylvania Press.

————. 1961. *Indians in Pennsylvania*. Harrisburg: Pennsylvania Historical and Museum Commission.

Walsh, Susan. 1992. " 'With Them Was my Home': Native American Autobiography and *A Narrative of the Life of Mrs. Mary Jemison*." *American Literature* 64:1–18.

Waugh, Frederick W. 1916. *Iroquis [sic] Foods and Food Preparation*. Geological Survey of Canada Memoir 86. Ottawa: Government Printing Bureau.

Weaver, Sally M. 1978. "Six Nations of the Grand River, Ontario." In *Handbook of North American Indians*. Vol. 15. *Northeast,* edited by Bruce G. Trigger (vol. ed.) and William C. Sturtevant (gen. ed.), 525–36. Washington, D.C.: Smithsonian Institution.

Wilkinson, Norman B. 1953. "Robert Morris and the Treaty of Big Tree." *Mississippi Valley Historical Review* 40:257–78.

Williams, B. G. 1883. *Life and Speeches of Cornplanter: Once Chief of the Seneca Nation of Indians*. Warren, Pa.: Warren Ledger.

Wilson, Edmund. 1960. *Apologies to the Iroquois*. New York: Farrar, Straus and Cudahy.

Windrow, Martin, and Gerry Embleton. 1973. *Military Dress of North America 1665–1970*. London: Ian Allan.

Wise, S. F. 1970. "The American Revolution and Indian History." In *Character and Circumstance: Essays in Honour of Donald Grant Creighton,* edited by John S. Moir, 182–200. Toronto: Macmillan.

Woodbury, Hanni, ed. 1992. *Concerning the League: The Iroquois League Tradition as Dictated in Onondaga by John Arthur Gibson.* Algonquian and Iroquoian Linguistics Memoir 9. Winnipeg: Univ. of Manitoba.

Index

Italic page number denotes illustration.

Other titles in The Iroquois and Their Neighbors